Death By Media

Such is the case of Wendy Bergen of Denver's KCNC, who exposed the story of vicious pit bull dogfights. When the truth emerged, the tapes, which supposedly had been sent to her anonymously, turned out to be dogfights staged for the television crews to record. She had, apparently, mailed the tapes to herself to make the story appear authentic. While the interests of animal rights activists may have been served, the media chose an untruthful method and the result was a hoax foisted on an unsuspecting public. Another station, KCCO-TV in Alexandria, Minnesota, showed scenes of teenagers downing beers at a party as part of a special report on underage drinking. They failed to tell the public the TV crew bought two cases of beer for the kids to drink and then filmed them while they consumed it.

Special interst groups often, use the media to disseminate their stories, which may or may not be true. When *NBC Nightly News* featured a story on the environmental dangers of logging in Idaho's Clearwater National Forest, Dick Jones, an experienced hydrologist in the forest, happened to watch the footage. He was shocked to see dead fish floating belly up in a stream. He knew logging did not cause that kind of devastation. As it turned out, the film was shot in a forest more than 400 miles away and sent to the station by an environmental group committed to ending the logging of ancient forest on public land.

As Pulitzer Prize-winning TV critic Howard Rosenberg points out, "When viewers become seduced by TV's aura of authenticity, the potential exists for distorted reality to become society's reality." The special interest groups have seized that knowledge and are using it today to force acceptance of their agendas. As intelligent citizens, we must be aware that this mutual co-dependency exists and carefully evaluate what we see and what we hear in order to sift out the grains of truth and discard the chaff of subterfuge.

Death By Media

by
Tony Vercillo

Commonwealth
Publications

A Commonwealth Publications Paperback
DEATH BY MEDIA

This edition published 1997
by Commonwealth Publications
9764 - 45th Avenue,
Edmonton, AB, CANADA T6E 5C5
All rights reserved
Copyright © 1997 by Tony Vercillo

ISBN: 1-55197-219-0

Printed in Canada

To the real unsung heroes; those few journalists and other mediamakers who report news and information with utmost integrity.

Acknowledgments:

There are so many people to thank. First, to my life–partner, best friend, and wonderful wife, Kim, for her never–ending encouragement and support. To my children, Anthony Jr., Darien Alyxandra, and Nicolas Ryan for providing such joy in my life. Thanks to Marilyn Martin for all the help with research and editing. Her values, morals, and deep belief system are unparalleled. Thanks to Dick and Kay Bathurst for all they have done to simplify and improve my life. Finally, let's not forget mom.

DON'T BELIEVE EVERYTHING YOU READ

You will find some of these headlines amusing. Some will not be so amusing, but all serve to illustrate the voice of the media is often that of the siren seeking to lure its listeners away from a safe passage through the events of the day.

REPORTS OF MY DEATH WERE GREATLY EXAGGERATED

MARK TWAIN

DEWEY ELECTED

IRAQ INVADES KUWAIT; STUDENTS MAY LOSE PARKING

MGM BOUNCES CHECKS, BUT SAYS FINANCES OK

HIGH CRIME AREAS SAID TO BE SAFER

BUSH GETS BRIEFING ON DROUGHT; SAYS RAIN NEEDED TO END IT

WALL STREET LAYS AN EGG

LIVING TOGETHER LINKED TO DIVORCE

SCIENTISTS NOTE PROGRESS IN HERPES BATTLE; EAR PLUGS RECOMMENDED

SOME PIECES OF ROCK HUDSON SOLD AT AUCTION

DROUGHT TURNS COYOTES TO WATERMELONS

32 IGNORANT ENOUGH TO SERVE ON NORTH JURY*

*My thanks to Jay Leno for having accumulated many of these headlines.

Contents

Introduction

Let's get something straight from the beginning. This book is not about abolishing the freedom of the press. I wholeheartedly support the first amendment. Neither is it an attack on the media in general, nor merely a conservative viewpoint on media bias. I wrote **Death By Media** to express my deeply rooted frustration over the abuse of this nation's freedom of the press.

In my travels, I have spoken to hundreds of people who feel the same way I do–something needs to be done about all the hype and the pressure to achieve high Neilson ratings and newspaper sales. Professors, family members, friends, associates, clients, students, and seatmates on flights across the country echo my sentiments. Something needs to be done. It is my sincere hope that one day the media will be viewed as a tool to communicate truth, justice, and unbiased information.

This series of essays on various aspects of media bias and media abuse serves as an effort to share my deep concerns with you. We will explore how the media distorts facts, how sensationalism and violence are used to generate an audience, and the effects of the control of the media by the liberal element in our society. In these essays, I will also share with you the uneasiness I feel for the future of the nation unless this malignant proliferation of the media bias and abuse is halted.

The intent of this book is to show how a certain few journalists abuse freedom of the press. This is an offensive against their methods; an offensive against their distortion of events to serve avowed purposes; and an offensive against their irresponsible attitudes and reporting techniques.

Is this abuse and distortion something that only a few people feel is occurring in the United States today? It appears not to be the case. In a recent poll of 1,703 adults surveyed nationwide, the *Los Angeles Times* found that only 17% felt that the media were doing "a very good job." This number is down from 30% in 1985.

Comments from those who felt the media were not doing a very good job in a survey conducted by *USA Today* ranged from "The media tend to be geared to the soap opera crowd," "It really depends on the reporter," "...there are some reporters and newscasters who fail to present every side of a story and often present only one point of view. Some also tend to shoot from the hip before investigating something thoroughly." to "Too often the media go after what will sell, reporting on the sensational approach rather than the news approach." The American public seems to have lost confidence in the integrity of the media.[1]

Conservative commentator Rush Limbaugh's book, *The Way Things Ought to Be*, had sales of over 2.5 million in the first few months after publication and conservative magazines are flourishing. The *American Spectator* has more than six times its circulation at the beginning of 1992. The *National Review* is experiencing its highest circulation in history.

In a recent issue, the *National Review* claims that mainstream journalists seek not to inform but to instruct, and states if newspapers hope to survive, "they should be less concerned with a liberal social agenda and more with the lives, hopes, and fears of their potential readers."[2]

In the July 20, 1992 issue of *Forbes Magazine*, Thomas Sowell stated that it often seems the only news that's fit to print is news that conforms to the media's liberal bias. The August 10, 1992 issue of *Jet* published the results of two national surveys that show many blacks feel the news media reflects the biases of society and that in their case, this bias reflects our society's bigotry. A study released in 1989 traced the decline of the traditional morally ethical world view from a position of influence in the news media to being replaced by a more liberal, cosmopolitan philosophical framework.[3]

USA Today reports a high percentage of journalists and reporters surveyed hold a liberal philosophy. Robert Lichter, co-director of the Washington, DC based *Center for Media & Public Affairs* questions whether mediamakers are projecting their own biases on news and entertainment when they produce images of America that differ sharply from the American reality.

Bruce Hershenson on KFI–AM radio in Los Angeles made an interesting observation. "The media uses psychological brainstorming and manipulation to fuel the liberal point of view. For example, the word defense-spending is the only governmental word that gets hyphenated. How come we don't hear about healthcare-spending. All the Liberal spending schemes are called "programs."[4]

Walter E. Williams, syndicated columnist and economics professor at George Mason University in an editorial expressing his concerns over the decline in moral values states, "There are good reasons why the elite and the liberal press attack what they derisively call the religious right and the 'Ozzie and Harriet' family. They attack religion for the identical reason the communists attack it. Religion is about moral absolutes."[5]

I don't know about you, but I think we could use a little more Ozzie and Harriet, and a lot less of Prince and Madonna.

In his book, *Media Circus: The Trouble with America's Newspapers,* Howard Kurtz accuses the industry of pursuing a mindless quest of sex and sensation, copping out on coverage of some of the great issues of our time, such as the savings and loan scandal and the Iran-Contra affair. He claims the press has lost touch with its leadership, sacrificing credibility for a misguided notion of what sells and abdicating its watchdog function while showcasing media manipulators.

John Koblyt, in an editorial titled "Forget the Ideology–Radio's a Business" stated, "Radio is a hard, cold, numbers-driven business. Nothing more. A talk host must draw a large audience, and that must be sold to advertisers to make the company money."[6] That type of criteria leads one to believe that mainline America is conservative.

Witness the ratings of the Rush Limbaugh show and that of ex-radio host Daryll Gates. Even controversial David Duke, whose conservative talk–show was blasted by Robert Namer, the owner of WASO-AM, as dull, was also praised by him as being good for the ratings and business.[7]

Even in trying to help those less fortunate, the press tends to "play God." They single out the person who will be the recipient of the public's largess while ignoring hundreds, or even thousands, of others who share the same fate.

The diversified point of view is rapidly disappearing from the American press by the consolidating of the media under a few mastheads. The merger of the *New York Times* and the *Boston Globe* sent up warning flags in many quarters, especially in light of the Associated Press news release that stated, "They hope to lure advertisers targeting customers across the Northeast on the theory that two prestigious newspapers can jointly attract more business than they could separately." Critics ask if another point of view was sacrificed on the altar of economics again? Associated Press also stated, "The deal continues a trend toward consolidation of media ownership, as other media, entertainment and communications companies are laying aside differences in a bid to revolutionize how people are informed and entertained."[8] The question remains, however. Will the *Globe* and *Times* merger ultimately result in only one point of view being represented?

SELECTIVE CENSORING

In a criticism of the industry, UC Irvine history professor John Wiener stated that publishers sometimes kill controversial books when they are pressured by the affected corporations. He cited the unflattering biographies of Walt Disney and John Lennon as cases in point. Singling out a major publisher as having more integrity than some of the others, he stated, "its not yet become part of the conglomerate."[9] I share this concern because even though I was convinced there was a need to have the viewpoint presented in **Death by Media** published, I was not sure I could find a publisher willing to do it.

Where you live may also make a big difference in the news you receive. The Sunday, April 18, 1993 editions of most major newspapers featured stories on both the Rodney King beating verdicts and the Waco compound stand–off. However, the *Seattle Times-Seattle Post-Intelligencer* did not deem either story newsworthy. Does that mean if you lived in Seattle, a major city of the Northwest, you do not know what is happening to the south and in the midwest? As Kevin (McCauley Caulkin)

in *Home Alone* so adeptly stated, "I don't think so."
Sometimes, you simply have to go to other sources
for your news.

On the other hand, you have others like Joann
Byrd, Washington Post ombudsman, who states
the pursuit of news should be what brings two sides
together on an issue, not what separates them. In
an address before the University of Hawaii's
Department of Journalism, she encouraged the
students not to report everything as a world divided. "We ought to make it hard for a conflict to
get on the agenda without the next item being attention to its repair."

In addition to the 5Ws and an H (WHO, WHAT,
WHERE, WHY, WHEN AND HOW), she adds an S
for Solution and a C for Common Ground. Newspapers should not tell people what to think, but
what to think about.[10]

What used to be entertainment and laughs is
being commandeered for delivering a message. Real-
life issues like gays, drugs, and condoms have invaded the comic strips. However, there are those
like Dik Browne, creator of Hagar the Horrible, who
says, "messages are for the Western Union. I'm more
interested in giving people a laugh and a smile."[11]

Another way in which the media disseminate
misinformation is in reporting political speeches.
Recently, historians criticized the politicians for
using weak historical reasoning, irresponsible use
of evidence, and dangerous analogizing. Specifically
cited were comparing allowing gays in the military
to the earlier racial integration of the armed forces;
is Saddam Hussein another Adolf Hitler? Did the
Persian Gulf War have the makings of another
Vietnam? Are the basic issues the same?

The historians claim that policy–makers have
misused history. If historians were allowed access

to press releases, they could scan them for historical accuracy, thereby strengthening the reasoning. By the same token, many feel that if the press generally had a better historical background, they could point out such errors when reporting.[12]

Even the position of an article may lend credence to its statements. A recent item placed in the midst of factual news articles stated that families stay together better in towns with Major League teams than they do in places rejected by the baseball owners. While written with tongue in cheek, the fact that it was placed among major news items may lead undiscerning readers to accept it as an actuality.[13]

Conclusions that are not documented bend the public's viewpoint in a certain direction. Undisciplined journalists can use the views to foist their own opinions on the public. A report of the poor turnout of parents for a tobacco education forum in a large Southern California city prompted a school district administrator to say, "The turnout confirms that the public doesn't view tobacco as the danger that it is." This was duly reported. However, the statement was not qualified in any way or identified as just an opinion. The truth might have been that there was another issue being debated that same evening, which the parents deemed more critical and turned out in droves for it.[14]

In a letter to the *Orange County Register,* two staff members of Rancho Santiago College protested the paper's coverage of a peaceful and legal demonstration protesting state funding cuts. Instead of being reported as a statement for quality education, it was headlined, "Protest blocks traffic." This, they complained, was not even an accurate appraisal of the situation. Police had not closed a major

street for an hour as the article stated. The only
section closed was the entrance to the college, and
the only time traffic was blocked was when some
protesters walked over to the traffic median and
back. In fact, campus security had helped the police keep the demonstration peaceful and legal.[15]
The letter writers demanded an explanation for the
coverage because the public deserves one.

The choice of words that are eye-catching
rather than completely accurate also contributes
to the bias presented by some mediamakers. "More
couples taking financial vows" as the headline for
an article that describes prenuptial agreements is
a benign example. [16]To most people signing a con-
tract does not have same meaning as taking a vow.
The headline, "'Generation X' Singing *Amour
Blues*,"[17] places a degrading label on those in their
twenties who, in many cases, are just finding their
places in society and becoming ready to assume
their responsibilities. Most people would rather be
something—even if it's not too flattering—than be
nothing.

The primary headline of an article about the
death of Pierre Beregovoy claimed "Ex-Premier of
France Kills Himself." The continuation headline
of the same article, "French Ex-Prime Minister of
France Apparent Suicide Victim," has a subtle but
distinct change in meaning.[18]The first is a statement of a fact. The second implies that this is
only what appeared to have happened. Which is
correct?

Recent articles about military base closures
across the nation frequently identify which papers
are in favor of these closures, and which papers
oppose them. The choice of words often betrays
this stand.

The main headline of an article about the

regional commission hearings regarding which bases should be closed was middle of the road: "Tactics to Fight Base Closures Sharpened." Obviously, officials expect interested parties to fight to keep the bases open for economic reasons, if nothing else. However, the continuation heading, "BASES: California Officials Plot Against More Closures," has a definite sinister bias.[19] Webster defines plot as "to plan or contrive especially secretly," and a plot implies an evil or unlawful scheme. I ask, Why are the California officials' efforts to keep bases open a plot? It seems to me more like an honest effort to help California's economy.

While many Americans did not agree with ex-President George Bush's policies or political persuasion, very few ever thought of his efforts as evil or of sinister intent. However, *Time* magazine headlined an article, "Two Faces of George Bush: The President woos Democrats, while his evil twin fights them."[20] Just because Bush was a Republican President who naturally tried to win Democratic support while opposing their efforts to pass conflicting legislation does not make him a Dr. Jeckyl/Mr. Hyde combination. What an insult to our nation's highest office!

Sensationalism is also often used with no regard for others. An article about Richard Esquinas' book claiming Michael Jordan is addicted to gambling was headlined, "Book: Jordan lost $1.2M in golf bets."[21] While the headline is stated as fact, the article itself deals with allegations, none of which have been proved.

The tragic deaths of Cleveland Indians pitcher Tim Crews and Steve Olin were headlined, "Indians' Crews ruled drunk:"[22] a smear of Crews to attract readers rather than a report of the tragedy of the deaths of two men who were greatly admired by their teammates.

It is interesting to note that much was made of ex-Presidential candidate Bob Dole's alleged request for federal funds for a boathouse in Wichita, Kansas, while the truth of the matter—his request was in reality for a clubhouse for senior citizens in an area of the city that is undergoing revitalization—was virtually ignored. Could it be that this was a conscious effort by the Democrats to smear Dole's efforts to block the Administration's economic plan? The reason for this is because the original reference to a request for a boathouse was made by President Clinton and picked up by the newspapers that were supporting him at that time. Remember, Clinton was just beginning to experience his fall from the press' grace. I wonder what the reaction would have been a month later? Would Clinton have been thoroughly chastised for his statement-in-error?

The glorification of violence is all too evident when you see a feature article with headlines such as "Man Fatally Shot in Chatsworth Carjacking" accompanied by two large color photos. The bravery of an off-duty police officer rated only the second sentence under a subheading of Crime, Law and Order. Law and Order, which the public as a whole admires and respects, was not thought of as newsworthy as crime, which most Americans abhor.

One of the old saws about journalism says not to let facts get in the way of a good story. As the newspaper industry tries to remedy falling readership in the millions, Al Neuharth, *USA Today* Founder, cites these reasons as responsible for the fall in readership: fiction printed as fact; a "gotcha" mentality; unfair, bizarre, and gutter journalism; and huckster leadership. Jean Gaddy Wilson in *New Directions for News* states, "Our research shows that publishers' No. 1 concern is reader-ship and circulation; No. 2, advertising; and No. 3 editorial quality. Publishers understand readers are leaving newspapers because of content."[23]

What kind of mentality headlines an article about the economic impact of the bombing of the Word Trade Center, "Trade Center blast helped NYC economy"?[24] Are we to conclude that things like a terrorist attack that kills six and injures over 1,000, to say nothing of the tremendous amount of dam-age, is a good thing—a thing to be desired—be-cause it is going to supply jobs for those who must rebuild it? Of course, there was a slight caveat, "city and authority officials did not suggest that news of economic benefit would undo the tragedy." Since when, was there ever any way to replace lives with money?

Some newspapers do have a clear concept of their role and have no fear of publicly stating it. One such newspaper is the *Miami Herald*. In a full-page spread, they examined the watchdog role the media must play in political affairs. Tracing the political/press conflict back to the enactment of the Alien and Sedition Acts of 1798, they pointed out that politicians like to feel secure from public scrutiny; but scrutiny from the press that is made public is the watchdog the public needs to ensure honest government.

They then cited two events, Hurricane Andrew and a probe into court-appointed lawyers who were overcharging for their services. These events resulted in the public being served well by the newspaper's exposure of the need to tighten South Florida's building codes and scrap the judicial appointment system in favor of an impartial, rotating list of qualified lawyers and an audited payment approval system. Had the Herald not pursued these investigations, the public would not have been aware of the need for reform.

In defending their obligation to uncover and report the truth, they quoted Thomas Jefferson, "Our liberty depends on the freedom of the press, and that cannot be limited without being lost."[25]

Some of you readers who can remember newspapers twenty years ago are thinking, "Sure, there were biases shown because the family who owned the paper supported certain candidates and issues, but by and large we thought the news was honestly reported. What's so different today?"

Dudley Clendinen, writing in *Lear's* magazine, may have provided the key when he asserted the election of Ronald Reagan signaled the shift of news from the newspaper to the television set.[26] At about the same time, newspapers realized they could increase their profits by going public, so you saw the transition from the family-owned newspaper to stockowner-controlled paper.

At about the same time came the shift from the family-owned newspaper's being supported by sales to receiving most of its income from advertising. As companies became part of conglomerate, fewer companies controlled where the money would be spent. Many corporations saw television and other media as a better place to spend their advertising dollars and dropped newspaper ads.

This, in turn, caused publishers to merge and stop publishing many afternoon editions. In fact, many metropolitan areas now have only one main paper. As a result, often newspapers no longer consider themselves as purveyors of news but as dissimulators of information instead. This brings a subtle change. Information, unlike news, can be moulded and packaged to meet the needs of advertisers. They feel this choice is forced by two needs: the ability to market a paper to an audience that is no longer predominantly male, white upper-middle-class; and the need to maintain the profit margin the marketplace expects.

In what has been termed "the biggest TV scam since the Quiz Scandals," NBC allegedly rigged test crashes of GM pickup trucks for a Nov. 17, 1992 segment on safety. Remote-controlled incendiary devices were hidden under the trucks to insure they would burst into flames on impact.[27] Falsifying information destroys any hope a network has of being thought of as a source of accurate and impartial news or information.

Accusations of tabloidism have also been made against NBC for programs such as these: the one naming Patricia Bowman as the accuser of William Kennedy Smith prior to Bowman herself coming forward with this information; airing footage of a woman being gunned down by her husband at the graveside of their daughter; showing footage as it occurs of police pursuits; canceling anti-nuclear crusader Helen Caldicott's appearance; and passing off five-year old footage of *Today* show as current in a story about Betty Friedan.

Unfortunately, NBC is not the only network that seems to have trouble with the truth. Despite charges that "The Incredible Discovery of Noah's Ark" was substantially false, CBS refused to comment on its authenticity months after the program was shown.

To quote *Los Angeles Times* reporter Howard Rosenberg, "If the network had integrity, a story about the controversy would have appeared on 'The CBS Evening News' by this time, and CBS would have purchased ads in major newspapers setting the record straight. By no doing this, CBS cavalierly ignored a dangerous phenomena in contemporary television: the blurring of traditional lines between news and entertainment. News, 'reality' and entertainment programs increasingly join each other in broadcast schedules that are designed by networks and individual stations to be perceived as giant blocs of information. That one component may come from CBS News, as in the prime-time series '48 Hours', and another from an outside producer of pseudo-documentaries a la "The Incredible Discovery of Noah's Ark," is a distinction lost by most viewers. If CBS cannot be trusted to be straight with America on its 'Noah's Ark' program, how can it be trusted to be forthright in labeling its programs under the coming system of 'violence advisories' announced by the networks?"[28]

As if this weren't enough, Washington state apple growers sought compensation for the losses caused by CBS's 'Sixty Minutes' program that alleged alar, a substance used to keep apples crisp and bruise-free, was a dangerous carcinogen, especially for children. In the panic that followed the program, the apple industry lost millions of dollars and some orchard owners went bankrupt.

The truth of the matter is that a 40-pound child would have to eat 1,000 apples a day for the rest of his or her life to get enough Alar to equal the dose that caused cancer in laboratory mice.[29] It appears that again there was irresponsible reporting.

Where does this leave the American public? Obviously searching for a source of news, not pre-digested information. Are there such sources available? Yes, but sometimes you have to search diligently to find them. Why are there no protests about such reporting?

Well, obviously there are objections, but the media quickly counters with the cry of, "It's freedom of the press. The Constitution guarantees it."

Is it freedom of the press or is it abuse of the right our Constitution guarantees to freedom of the press? Later in this book, we will take a look at some examples and then analyze and evaluate them to determine whether we have responsible mediamakers. After you have read the evidence, you can make your own decision about the reports you see and hear every day.

WORKS CITED

[1] "Voices From Across the USA." USA Today 9 April 1993 12A.

[2] Donahue, Diedre. "Modern Journalism gets a bad 'Review'." Los Angeles Times 4 June 1993 M2.

[3] Olasky, Marvin. Prodigal Press: The Anti-Christian Bias of the American News Media. Westchester, IL: Crossway Books, 1988.

[4] 9 April 1993.

[5] Williams, Walter E. "We need a moral reawakening in the US." Orange County Register 8 April 1993 Commentary 3.

[6] Koblyt, John. "Forget the Ideology—Radio's a Business." Los Angeles Times 31 May 1993 F5.

[7] Booth, William. "David Duke's Show is Dull, Owner Says." Los Angles Times 31 May 1993 F9.

[8] "Times-Globe merger: a media powerhouse." Orange County Register 12 June 1993 News 8.

[9] "Murdered Books." Los Angeles Times 10 June 1993 A2.

[10] Brislin, Tom. "Beyond Conflict." The Honolulu Advertiser 18 April 1993.

[11] Kramer, Staci D. "Comics explore real-life issues like gays, drugs, condoms." The Salt Lake Tribune 18 April 1993 F6.

[12] Scott, Janny. "Patrols by 'History Plice' Urges." Los Angeles Times 20 April 1993 A5.

[13] "Saving Marriages at Candlestick." San Francisco Chronicle 18 April 1993 A1.

[14] "Anaheim." Orange County Register 9 May 1993 Commentary 5.

[15] Gutirrez, Kathleen S. and Cacciola, Dr. Roseann. "Register covered student protest with a closed mind." Orange County Register 9 May 1993 Commentary 5.

[16] Crenshaw, Albert B. "More couples taking financial 'vows'." The Arizona Republic 2 May 1993 H6.

[17] "Generation X Singing Amour Blues." Los Angeles Times 4 May 1993.

[18] Randal, Johnathan C. "Ex-Premier of France Kills Himself." Washington Post 2 May 1993 A29.

[19] Bornemeier, James. "Tactics to Fight Base Closures Sharpen." Los Angeles Times 19 April 1993 A9.

[20] "Two Faces of George Bush: The President woos Democrats while his evil twin fights them." _Time Magazine_ 2 July 1990.

[21] Shuster, Rachel. "Book: Jordan lost $1.2M in golf bets." _USA Today_ 4 June 1993 1C.

[22] "Indian Crews ruled drunk." _Dallas Times_ 24 March 1993 1B.

[23] Neuharth, Al. "Why do newspapers turn you on or off?" _USA Today_ 23 April 1993 11A.

[24] "Trade Center blast helped NYC economy." _Orange County Register_ 8 April 1993.

[25] "Some politicians have no problem with their local press coverage." _Miami Herald_ June 1993.

[26] Clendinen, Dudley. "Yesterday's Newspapers." _Lear's_ December 1992 68.

[27] Harmon, Amy. "New Stance for General Motors." _Los Angeles Times_ 11 February 1993 D3.

[28] Rosenberg, Howard. "CBS on 'ARK': Mum's Still the Word." _Los Angeles Times_ 7 July 1993 F13.

[29] Williams, Walter. "Tasty tidbits for the populace to chew on." _Orange County Register_ 28 July 1993 Metro 9.

Chapter 1

THE REAL INTENT OF
THE FIRST AMENDMENT

When *The Las Vegas Review-Journal* decided to remove the comic strip, "For Better or For Worse," from its pages because they felt it advocated a gay lifestyle, there were angry accusations of violation of the First Amendment. But as journalist Rafael Tammariello asserted, "The First Amendment, among other things, says Congress shall make no law abridging the freedom of the press. It does not say newspapers shall print everything they purchase through a syndicate or wire service or receive in the mail. The First Amendment says you can publish what you want. It does not say you have a right to use somebody else's press to publish what you want, no matter who you are."

In light of conflicting views about the guarantees of the First Amendment to the Constitution, let's take a look at it.[1] Yes, it does guarantee that "Congress shall make no law respecting an establishment of religion, or prohibiting the free exercise thereof; or abridging the freedom of speech, or of the press; or the right of the people peaceably to assemble, and to petition the government for a redress of grievances." Let's look a little more closely at what the makers of the Constitution meant by the thought, "abridging the freedom of speech, or of the press." Introduced in June 1789 by James Madison of Virginia, the first ten amendments, or Bill of Rights, were generally modeled after the existing states' Bills of Rights. Congress approved them in September 1791, and they took effect in December after being ratified by the required number of states.

When citing the need for such guarantees, Thomas Jefferson wrote from France where he had been during the Constitutional Convention, "The people are the only censors of their governors; and even their errors will tend to keep these to the true principles of their institution. To punish these errors too severely would be to suppress the only safeguard of the public liberty.... The basis of our government being the opinion of the people, the very first object should be to keep that right; and were it left to me to decide whether we should have a government without newspapers or newspapers without a government, I should not hesitate for a moment to prefer the latter."[2]

Undoubtedly, part of the reason for Jefferson's concern was the bloody history of persecution in England of those who had dared to oppose the crown through either the written or spoken word. Even after the establishment of the colonies in the New World, censorship continued. The first book burned publicly was *The Meritorious Price of Our Redemption* by William Pynchon, and the event took place in the marketplace of Boston in 1650. Pynchon's religious assertions differed from those of the colony's established religion and so had to be eliminated. The first newspaper in the colonies, published by Benjamin Harris, had been silenced after a single issue. The reason? Harris had printed it without authority. In 1690, Harris again printed a newspaper without a license as required by a 1662 Massachusetts law. He was immediately closed down. It was no secret some of his articles had been criticized by both the government and the church.

After ten years of no new paper in Boston, James Franklin began to publish without a license. He was allowed to continue until the government became insulted by his criticism of their defense against pirates in the area. While James Franklin was imprisoned, his to-become-famous brother Ben took over the paper. Ben was more careful in his choice of articles, publishing excerpts on liberty, freedom of speech, and freedom of the press written by two London essayists who used the pseudonym Cato.

Although no formal licensing laws had been in effect in the colonies since 1695, James Franklin was forbidden to print or publish. James, however, fought the royal governor's attempt to reestablish licensing until the authorities finally gave up. This capitulation let Franklin establish the principle of no government censorship before publication, which was upheld by the grand jury. The concept of a press responsible to the public rather than the government was now affirmed.

ESTABLISHING OUR FREEDOMS

Although Franklin's efforts were the cornerstone of freedom of the press in our country, it remained for publisher John Peter Zenger to build the foundation. In his *New York Weekly Journal,* he had been extremely critical of the royal governor and his administration. Among the most serious criticisms were accusations they had tampered with trial by jury and had rigged elections. A grand jury was urged by the Chief Justice to indict Zenger for "seditious libels." Twice the grand jury refused to do so. After the elected assembly would not bring charges against him, the governor's council issued a warrant for his arrest for "raising sedition."

At his trial, he was defended by Andrew Hamilton, a lawyer of renown in the colonies. Hamilton had refused to accept a fee because he thought the case so critical to the future of liberty.

Zenger was to be tried under the British rule of libel which prohibited any criticism of the government, whether true or not. Whether it was seditious and tended to stir people up would be decided by the court. The Chief Justice refused to allow Hamilton to define whether the libel was true, but he successfully presented to the jury the concept that the government can be criticized and the press has a right to do so even if it makes the public distrust the government. Zenger went free.

So the concept of freedom of speech was established and incorporated into the constitutions of the individual colonies. After ratification of the national Bill of Rights, it would become binding on those states that subsequently entered the union of states.

BLEEP! BLEEP!

As the years progressed, the Supreme Court has felt that certain forms of pure speech and expression fall outside the protection of the First Amendment because they are not essential to the communication of ideas and are of little social value. These include obscenity and "fighting words." The Court has subsequently had difficulty in defining obscenity while having no difficulty in defining what inflames a person. In the cases of obscenity, they have issued guidelines that permit the banning of works that do not meet the standards set in the guidelines.

The case of the FCC v. Howard Stern is an example of action taken based on these guidelines. Not only was Stern accused of airing indecent material by the FCC, the agency also notified radio stations that air the program during a time when children may be listening that they may be liable for large fines.[3] As evidence of their belief that freedom of speech is important to them, some chose to pay the fines rather than remove the program from the air.

There is no doubt about it. Howard is vulgar, obnoxious, and sexually explicit. The question is, however, does he have the right to express himself as he chooses, or is he being singled out for prosecution?

I have listened to Howard's show many times. I have laughed uncontrollably at times due to his obscene, disgusting pokes at the male and female anatomy. He clearly tests the limits of freedom of speech and the press on each show. I am not saying I agree with Howard's method of delivery, and I certainly would never want or allow my children to listen to his program. However, the question remains, should our government be allowed to selectively exercise restrictive limits on this freedom? Is this language really any worse than the sex scenes that bordered on soft porn in the movie *Rising Sun*?

Jurist Robert H. Bork states, "If there is a bedrock principle underlying the First Amendment, it is that the government may not prohibit the expression of an idea simply because society finds the idea itself offensive or disagreeable." Colin L. Powell, U. S. General Retired, has also affirmed this concept by saying, "The First Amendment right of free speech is intended to protect the controversial and even outrageous word, and not just comforting platitudes, too mundane to need protection."

FREEDOM BUT NO LICENSE

The intent of the freedom of the press provision was to guarantee that the government not overstep its bounds. The idea that it gave the press free license was never intimated, only that the government could not step in and censor the press for its own purposes. Through the years, the majority of the court has viewed freedom of the press as subject to certain restrictions. Among those limitations are continued publication of documents that incite others to violence.

Think back to the second trial of the officers in the Rodney King beating. Could it be the media's constant reminder that another Los Angeles riot was imminent that incited the black community to violence? It certainly anchored the thought of a riot in all our minds. I was angered by the amount of media coverage and the unnecessary sensationalism of the case.

I second the opinion that the fear of another riot was already there because people were acting on a given event, the first trial and its outcome, the conflagration and riot. All of us, including Korean, Hispanic, black, and white, were saying, Can there be a fair trial? Most of us drew the conclusion that there could not be one. The media fed that thought by reaffirming in the minds of most people, "Don't expect a fair trial because it's not going to happen." The reporting was such that it inflamed our emotions, and a reasonable outcome would not be forthcoming. How could any juror sit on that panel and come out with a really honest verdict in light of the pressure from the community and the press that if they voted a certain way, there would be another riot?[4]

When asked if Freedom of the Press is being used today as the Founding Fathers intended it, Dr. Irving H. Ahlquist, Professor Emeritus of History, California State University, Long Beach, stated in a recent interview, "I think if the Founding Fathers had been concerned that freedom of the press would injure the good of the whole—the society—then they undoubtedly would have agreed to have restrictions added. But in the general realm of daily living, I tend to believe those bright men of the 18th Century really saw that in a republic, people should know what is for their good, but that society has a right to restrict it if it is destructive to the group as a whole. That's how I see freedom of the press. And if we translate that into modern terms, why should freedom of the press be an exclusive privilege of a certain group?"

My answer to, "Why do we have such blind reverence for a 217-year-old document (the Constitution) that doesn't necessarily fit in today's lives?" the question posed by John and Ken on KFI Radio on July 22, 1993, is that it meets the country's changing needs because it can be amended as those needs change. The Constitution, which British Prime Minister William Gladstone named "the most wonderful work ever struck off at a given time and by the brain and purpose of man"[5] would not have served the American people so well had it not been capable of being amended periodically.

That the first ten of these amendments were needed almost immediately prompted some to ask, "Why didn't the Founding Fathers recognize the need for them at the time the Constitution was framed?" The fact is they did, but the majority of the delegates felt their only duty was to create a strong national government. It was not until the fact became evident that the states' own bills of rights did not protect the citizen from the newly formed federal government that they were included as additions to the Constitution.

Largely through the eloquent rhetoric of Patrick Henry at the Virginia convention to ratify the constitution, people like Edmund Randolph and

James Madison, who previously had not supported a Bill of Rights at the Constitutional Convention, saw the need for it. Until well into the 20th Century, they were regarded only as safeguards for individuals against violations by the Federal Government. At this point, the Supreme Court began making decisions that also applied them to state violations.

HOW WOULD YOU VOTE?

When asked if the First Amendment were put to a vote today did he think it would pass with the present wording, Dr. Ahlquist commented, "I think there would be modifications. I think the preciseness of it is what we like about our Constitution, but I'm afraid a lot of people would say, 'No, I don't want freedom of the press as it is presently worded in the Constitution.' Now, whether it would be more restrictive, I don't know. Again, it's speculation on my part to say what might happen, but I feel, just from a personal point of view, the intent of the Constitutional makers was designed to let each of us be an intelligent participant as a citizen, a voting citizen. To do that, I need as much information as possible. And yet, I've also come to another conclusion. There are some things I shouldn't know–that I don't need to know–if they involve national security.

I think our Government has hidden a lot behind the idea that for national security purposes, we cannot allow this to be said, or we cannot permit these documents to be read or to be researched. And it is essential at times because of embarrassment either to people who are living or to the families of those involved. Many times, papers cannot be opened until a given year, so it can be 50 years after a person's death before you can look at the papers.

"When I was in Washington, DC at the Library of Congress and the National Archives in the late 1940s doing my doctoral research, a man from the National Archives said, "We're in the process of going through the papers relating to Pearl Harbor, but, you'll never probably really get to know the truth. I am sworn, of course, to secrecy, and when these documents will ever be available to the general public, I don't know."

The majority of American people would probably *not* vote for the First Amendment as it was originally written. Most of my colleagues are disgusted with all the hype, the instant news without thought, and the biased, one-sided viewpoint most journalists expound.

James Madison, our fourth president, was a staunch supporter of freedom of the press. It was not until one hundred years after his term of office that the first case involving freedom of speech was brought before the Supreme Court,[6] the conviction of Charles T. Schenck, general secretary of the Socialist party, for sedition. Even during the Civil War, when the constitutional right of freedom of the press was being violated, no cases were brought. Freedom of speech and freedom of the press had to be balanced against the situation that found our nation being torn apart by the fighting among its citizens.

Schenck and his fellow party members had mailed some 15,000 leaflets to draftees urging them to resist conscription. Justice Oliver Wendell Holmes wrote in upholding the conviction of Schenk, "We admit that in many places and in ordinary times the [defendant] in saying all that was said in the circular would have been within constitutional rights. But the character of every act depends upon the circumstances in which it is done. When a nation is at war many things that might be said in time of peace are such a hindrance to its effort that their utterance will not be endured so long as men fight and that no Court could regard them as protected by any constitutional right."[7]

As you remember, one of the reasons freedom of the press was deemed necessary was that for many years the government of England had exercised what is termed prior restraint through its power to license publications. In 1931, in the Near v. Minnesota decision, the first involving freedom of the press, the Supreme Court reaffirmed that a publication cannot be prohibited before it is published. There may, however, be punishment after publication if it violates libel laws. In 1936, in the case of Grosjean v. American Press Company, the Court determined that publications opposing the point of view of the authorities cannot be taxed unfairly because that constitutes an effort to limit circulation and was thus a violation of freedom of the press. In 1988, the court also stated that locations of newspaper boxes may be limited, but which newspapers were to be sold there could not.

It should be noted that in certain instances, publication of news has been limited by the Court so a free trial of the accused person can take place. Most notable is the case of Dr. Sam Sheppard in which the doctor was accused of murdering his wife. The press practically took over the courtroom.

The flashy-trashy trial of O. J. Simpson was a perfect example of media-run-rampant. The violations of court procedure, the grandstanding of the lawyers, and the barrage of media coverage caused Judge Lance Ito on more than one occasion to threaten to bar the press from the proceedings.

In recent years, the First Amendment has been cited as a defense in certain court cases. Peter DeNigris was sued by Medphone Corp. for posting a series of downbeat comments about the company on the bulletin board service run by Prodigy and causing the publicly-traded stock to drop in value. DeNigris claimed he had protection under the First Amendment's guarantee of freedom of speech to express his opinions. When the case was settled without a decision by the court that favored either side, DeNigris claimed that, "Freedom of speech [had] prevailed." However, lawyers warned users of bulletin boards to use caution in expressing their opinions.[8]

Katherine Power, the former anti-war radical wanted for 23 years following a deadly bank robbery, is fighting a court order that would bar her from selling her story. Power is claiming it violates her First Amendment right to free speech.

Newspapers have received a measure of protection against libel suits due to *The New York Times* v. Sullivan decision, in which the Court ruled a newspaper is not responsible for errors appearing in articles regarding public officials unless they are published with malice: that is, the newspaper had knowledge the information was false or recklessly disregarded whether it was false or not. The general public, however, could still win their cases by proving there was negligence shown in libeling them. In 1967, the definition of public officials was extended to include public figures. In 1988, the Court rendered a decision that public figures who are victims of satire—even if it is outrageous and pornographic—may not sue for damages.

When the federal government, under the leadership of Richard Nixon, tried to prohibit publication of the Pentagon Papers, which traced the history of the U.S. involvement in Vietnam, the Court ruled the government had failed to meet the heavy burden of showing justification for restraining further publication of the Pentagon Papers.[9] As a result, the American public was able to understand this event more clearly and hopefully, make better decisions when voting for their public officials.

FREEDOM OF INVESTIGATION

A discomforting concept is that personal papers cannot be opened for a given period of time so the privacy of those involved can be protected. The press seems to feel no such restraints when it digs into a person's past. Witness the ruin of Gary Hart's presidential bid, the invasion of all three candidates' privacy during the 1992 presidential campaign (George Bush, Ross Perot, and Bill Clinton), and the sensational headlines every time a leading church leader or evangelist has an indiscretion uncovered. The hidden good things a person has done are never uncovered. Only the embarrassing, scintillating, and scandalous actions are thought newsworthy.

Take the alleged affair of Bill Clinton and Gennifer Flowers. Who really cares? If the affair really did happen, perhaps we should question Bill Clinton's character, but does this give the media the right to question Clinton's ability to be a good President? Does a marital indiscretion really make a person unfit for office? Let's say Clinton did not have the affair. Should the media be allowed to report it without conclusive evidence? Should they perhaps be chastised for making Ms. Flowers a household name and Penthouse Pet?

Think back to when you were in your early teens. Would you have liked being treated by your local newspaper as the press treated Chelsea Clinton? They all but destroyed her with their ugly jokes, etc. Their treatment of Chelsea was disgusting!

It is my opinion that the media keep many great men and women from pursuing the Presidency and other elected offices by their irresponsible journalism. Witness the decision of Colin Powell not to run for the presidency because he ostensibly did not want to subject himself and his family to media scrutiny. What gives a reporter the right to dig up information that people would rather keep concealed and secret? Too often, we have seen on our television screens the invasion of privacy that occurs during a tragedy: families of victims of an airplane crash; the parents of Baby Jessica; families being notified of the death of a loved one; survivors, victims, and families of victims of an apartment or high-rise fire; families trying to pick up the pieces after a disaster; and mourners at a funeral. Worse yet is the instant coverage that permits a family to learn of the death of a member on the evening news.

WHO WILL WE BE?

The real questions, of course, are, Does the press have a right to know? and Have they taken that right too far? Are they, in fact, invading privacy, exposing past misdeeds that no longer figure in the life of that person, and bringing events to light that really do not relate to the issue at hand?

Another consequence crucial to this point is that our mediamakers today are establishing what will be evidence of life in '90s for the historians of tomorrow. What kind of a picture are they painting? Will we be thought of as a generation of all types of valueless, amoral perverts with no real statesmen willing to lay aside selfish pursuits to seek the good of the nation? I, for one, am glad our forefathers did not have to run the gauntlet of Monday morning TV quarterbacks that our leaders have to face today. They were left free to debate issues, not past misdeeds.

What will historians record based on television footage? We all assume that what we are seeing must be the truth just because we are seeing it. Remember that information can be just as selectively presented by the camera as by the spoken word. Important caveats may be edited out of an interview, selected views or old footage from days past may be shown, or only one side may be presented. The comments presented with the footage may or may not represent what is being shown.

In addition to the question of sensationalism, we need to look at the issue of the position of the media. Is what they are feeding the American public biased? Does the media truly have a liberal point of view? Bias may mean a judgment reached without a commitment to a particular belief, position, or cause held so strongly that it precludes consideration or even awareness of contrary evidence and opposing views.

"Few scholars would claim to be free of all bias. We cannot eradicate all bias, but we can do much to minimize it."[10]

"Historians' personalities and private views are a fact of life, like the weather, and like the weather, they are not really worth worrying about as much as in practice they are worried over. They cannot be eliminated, nor should they be."[11]

"Frankly, it is doubtful if any reporter could say he or she is free of bias. The important thing is to admit it, so the public can evaluate what is being said. I hate to generalize because historians are afraid of generalization, but much of the media is coming from a biased tendency of the liberal side rather than the conservative side. It's evident in the way certain issues are treated. I believe the majority of the American people, fundamentally, tend to be somewhat conservative. I don't think the media is reflecting that as effectively as our society holds to these given values."[12]

Studies indicate the majority of the media are secular in outlook, see themselves as liberals, feel they are professionals who translate the news rather than transmit it, have moved away from biased constraints on sex and sex roles, and belong to the cosmopolitan upper status groups in America today. Competing for influence in the direction the nation is to take, they have now joined business, labor, government, and other elite groups. Based on studies at the prestigious Columbia University's School of Journalism, this profile is not likely to change. Students there place themselves to the left of current mediamakers in political philosophy and moral standards.[13]

THE MEDIA GEPETTO

A study in *Newsweek* by Kenneth Woodward cited a study by the Center for Media and Public Affairs in Washington, DC that showed people at the top of television and movie making have views, attitudes, and ideas on various subjects that differ dynamically from those held by the average American. One hundred and four top television writers and executives were surveyed. The Center found that their attitudes toward moral and religious questions aren't shared by their audiences. Of the 104 mediamakers, 40% believe adultery is wrong while 85% of the populace says it's wrong; 45% of the mediamakers have no religious affiliation as opposed to 4% nationwide; 76% nationwide believe homosexual acts are wrong, while only 20% of the Hollywood execs do. Because we see this garbage over and over, as individuals, we are being convinced we're the only ones who don't believe it is OK. This is happening nationwide and thus altering our perception of what is acceptable and what is not.

Film Critic Michael Medved has expressed his concern for the young people of America and the plague of depression that seems to be devouring them. Stating that they stand to lose a great deal from prolonged exposure to the dysfunctional elements of our current culture, he specifically cited lost faith, lost confidence, and lost resistance to pessimism.

One of the greatest forces in contributing to this addiction to despair, in his opinion, is an immersion in mass media and its underlying message of hopelessness conveyed by ugly, consistently dysfunctional images, which encourage both self-pity and fear. Citing movies such as *Bladerunner*, *The Terminator*, and *Waterworld*, he accuses Hollywood of suggesting the world we will pass on to our descendants will be inevitably and infinitely worse than the one in which we live.

Not limiting his criticism to fictional accounts, he claimed the news business should really be called the bad news business, because "killing is always covered, while kindness is almost always ignored. The more alarming a news item may seem, the more attention it automatically receives."

At a time when overworked parents are not spending as much time with their children as is needed to influence their beliefs, young people are retreating more into the lurid images that flicker across their TV screens and this media's ability to redefine reality and alter their expectations of what constitutes normal life.[14]

METAMORPHOSING BRAINS

This absorption with television should be of major concern to all Americans in light of the recent studies that indicate the brains of young people today are biologically different from those of past generations. Why? It is because of the different types of stimulation they are receiving. Television viewing causes the brain to register a preponderance of slow (alpha) waves, which denote a lack of mental activity. This is in contrast to reading, which causes the brain to register high levels of beta activity, indicating active alertness.[15]

Scientists know the brain has the ability to change (plasticity), and the type of change that occurs is a reflection of the type of stimulation it receives. Both functional and structural changes occur. They also know that the more neurons are stimulated, the more dendrites they build to connect with other neurons; and the more connections there are, the better the brain functions.

Because there are peak times in physical development when the brain is best suited to learn certain skills, persons can often lose out on developing certain areas fully if learning is not accomplished during the prime time.

Today, we are seeing declining literacy, falling test scores, undeveloped oral expression, and ineptitude with the written word. Why? One reason advanced is that young brains are not being shaped around language, which is an essential tool for analytic thinking. Instead of conversing with others, young people have retreated into their headphones. Children are bombarded with noise and frantic schedules from birth, which leave little time for reflection.

Instead of carrying on conversations with others or inner conversations with themselves to develop their reasoning skills, they are becoming zombies in front of a screen letting whatever comes from the tube fill their hours. They are not analyzing content, nor in most cases are they coming into contact with anyone else who is evaluating it.

In a culture dominated by the written word, public discourse is generally coherent and the facts are arranged and presented in an orderly fashion. As children are exposed to these logical presentations either in print or by hearing them, their neurons are not only actively responding to stimuli, they are also developing the ability to also logically organize and present ideas.

However, in a television-dominated society, logical skills are not developed by watching the screen. The linguistic quality is often poor to abominable, and children do not learn the subtle differences in word structure or complex grammar and vocabulary. As the television set teaches children language skills, it also teaches them a way of thinking and reacting socially.

If the period passes in which peak learning occurs, a child often loses out entirely on being able to achieve to his or her fullest capability. In the past, children often had only their own families as companions during the pre-school years. During this time, conversation was often their primary entertainment simply due to the lack of radio, television, and animated toys. It was also during this prime learning period that children developed their ability to think and organize logically.

They came to school better prepared to learn

and understand. They did not expect to be entertained. They were even better prepared to learn to read because their ears had prepared their eyes for the melody of language. This is in stark contrast to the child today who has been prepared for school by passively watching the frantic images on the television screen.[16]

Today's children, for the most part, have passed a prime learning period without developing these logical skills. While skills can be learned at other periods, if the best learning period for a specific skill is passed, it will never be learned as easily or as completely. It may become more of a tragedy than we can even dream of if we do not turn around this trend of absorption without discernment.

Chuck Wooley, of the Calvary Chapel of Palm Springs, asks, "Can you imagine how this country's founding fathers would feel if they could view the decadence, degradation, and filth and corruption of our society? How much longer can we sing 'God Bless America' and be involved in the decadence, filth, and corruption in our society and the stuff that we laugh at."[17]

The nomination of Robert Bork to the Supreme Court was another instance of media bias. It was obvious from the moment the nomination was announced, the press was determined that he would not be presented in a favorable light. Because he differed from the liberal press in that he believed the court should only interpret the law, not make it, he was subjected to an incessant barrage of negative advertising and media coverage. He was slandered by the liberals in a vigorous campaign led by Ted Kennedy; journalists who were sympathetic to his stand were, in effect, gagged; and news reporters on the three major networks were completely negative in their coverage.

At the hearings before the Senate Judiciary Committee, furniture was arranged so that the camera shots would only present him in the worst possible light. False charges were hurled at him. Charges that were so absurd, Senator Humphrey even stated, "the charges against Bork were pure political poppycock, 99.9 percent pure, so pure it floats." Bork defended himself and his views with dignity, but the press presented an entirely different picture to the public. Friendly witnesses were not on television or reported in the papers. Appearances were scheduled so that only the unfriendly witnesses would make the news deadlines. In fact, by and large, the media reported only the accusations and not the facts that refuted them.To add insult to injury, when the press thought he would be pressured into withdrawing his name, they began to harass his home by setting up camp in the street. He was followed everywhere he went by two motorcyclists and a motorist employed by the three networks. He was even interrupted by a reporter while having lunch with friends after his nomination was rejected by the committee.

I find myself completely outraged that a handful of mediamakers have the power to destroy the career of someone who, prior to the nomination, was a jurist who had earned the deep respect of those who knew him and his work. That they could and would slander him because he represented a viewpoint more conservative than theirs is totally abhorrent to the American way of thinking. What they demonstrated by their withholding of and distortion of facts was not freedom of the press but abuse of their privilege.

We have always prided ourselves as having tolerance for other philosophies. We have elections so the populace can decide which philosophy best fits the majority. When so few can determine the course of the nation, we have become a dictatorship.

INSTANT EVERYTHING

Dr. Ahlquist also reflected that one of the problems facing our media today is instant reporting. Much of what is being said is not being examined carefully. Everything is on-the-spot and verbal, and this kind of oral reporting gets distorted. Even the president is faced with questions like, "Mr. President, what did you think of this or what did you mean by that? It requires an instant response, not a carefully thought out response, because it can't be." He continued by commenting that most of us get our news from television instead of from a newspaper, where we can sit down and at least think things through.

You know, as I reflect back on my childhood days, the instant oatmeal of today is not as good as old-fashioned cooked oatmeal. With some things, you need to wait for them to be good. This "Information is Power Age" is exacerbating the situation with the fax, car phone, overnight mail, E-mail, and the Internet all making it worse. I wonder if we are stopping to think about all we hear, or if we're just soaking it up and saying, "Well, that's the news." Are our values being subtly changed by those with whom we really don't agree because they're mostly who we see and hear, and we're not stopping to reflect on what they're telling us...just absorbing it.

WORKS CITED

1. Hentoff, Nat. *The First Freedom: The Tumultuous History of Free Speech in America*. New York. Delacorte Press. 1980: 57-68.

2. "The Supreme Court and Individual Rights." *Congressional Quarterly*. December, 1979: 51.

3. Michaelson, Judith. "FCC Delivers a Stern Warning." *The Los Angeles Times* 13 August 1993 F38.

4. Taped interview. Dr. Irving F. Ahlquist, Professor Emeritus of History, California State University Long Beach.

5. Lindop, Edmund. *The Bill of Rights and Landmark Cases*. New York. Franklin Watts. 1989: 11.

6. Evans, J. Edward. *Freedom of Speech*. Minneapolis. Lerner Publications Company. 1990: 31.

7. Friendly, Fred W. and Elliott, Martha J. H. *The Constitution: That Delicate Balance*. New York. Random House. 1984: 77.

8. Vogelstein, Fred. *Newsday* correspondent. "Computer Bulletin Board Libel Suit Settled for $1." *The Los Angeles Times* 28 December 1993. D7.

9. Lee, Martin A. & Solomon, Norman. *Unreliable Sources*. New York. Carol Publishing Group. 1992: 107.

10. Shafer, R. J. *A Guide to Historical Method*. Homewood, IL. Dorsey Press. 1969: 149.

11. Elton, G. R.. *The Practice of History*. New York. Thomas U. Crowell. 1967: 105.

12. Taped interview. Dr. Irving H. Ahlquist, Professor Emeritus of History, California State University Long Beach.

13. Lichter, S. Robert. et al. *The Media Elite: America's New Powerbrokers*. New York. Hastings House. 1990: 294.

14. Medved, Michael. "Protecting Our Children From a Plague of Pessimism." *Imprimis*. December 1995: 2-3.

15. Healy, Jane M. *Endangered Minds: Why Children Don't Think and What We Can Do About It*. New York. Simon & Schuster. 1990: 202-203.

16. Ibid: 50-92.

17. Wooley, Chuck. "What's Ahead for America." Calvary Chapel of Palm Springs. May, 1993.

18. Bork, Robert S. *The Tempting of America*. New York. Free Press (Macmillan, Intl.). 1990. 295-321.

Chapter 2

MEDIA SENSORY OVERLOAD

The war for our minds has raged relentlessly since the beginning of time. However, for the first time in history, the tools are so sophisticated, the mind often cannot comprehend it is being assailed. Early man had his clan leaders and wanna-be clan leaders who said, "Follow me and I will..." Then nations had rulers and aspiring rulers who said, "Follow me and I will..." Today, we have a new kind of leader who covets our eyes and ears and constantly beckons us to "Look and listen, and I will mold..." How this new leader molds will be examined in this chapter.

Yes, I know you are telling yourself that you decide what you want to believe, who you will vote for, what direction your actions will take. You and you alone make those calls. That's true; but tell me, what are the things that influence your thinking? Is it something you saw on TV, a program you listened to, or a book you've read? It's my bet all those things influence you. We are products of our environment to a certain extent, and all those things are part of our environment. When you stop to think about the amount of time the average person spends in front of a TV, this medium alone is a major force in molding opinions and attitudes. Add to that the commute time people use to listen to the radio, and you have two prime forces in many lives.

Before you become too complacent in your assurance that you are immune to this type of conditioning, let me share the experience of an older friend with you. She was a young adult during the peak of the atomic bomb testing program. She was firmly convinced of the necessity of it, including the tests in the Pacific. After all, there was the Russian menace and no one was being hurt by the tests. The people were given a new home that "everyone" said was just as good, and soon they could return. She watched the TV special, *Return to Bikini,* not too long ago, which raised serious doubts as to the veracity of those earlier claims. Her comment was, "Were they playing with my mind then, or are they playing with it now?"

VIOLENCE BEGETS VIOLENCE

The results of respected studies establish that there is a definite link between the violence seen on television and the rise our society is experiencing in violent actions. When seven sixth grade students were arrested for trying to murder their teacher, James Fox, dean of the College of Criminal Justice at Northeastern University, was quoted as saying murder and violence often aren't real to children today. "It's so commonplace in their lives, largely from television, it's lost its meaning."[1]

Ted Turner, cable TV magnate, says, "Television violence is the single most significant factor contributing to violence in America."[2]

Even more conclusive is the testimony given at the May 12, 1993, hearings before the House Energy & Commerce Committee's Telecommunications & Finance subcommittee and the Senate Judiciary Committee's Constitution subcommittee. Dr. Brandon S. Centerwall, professor of epidemiology at the University of Washington, testified, "The U. S. national homicide rate has doubled since the 1950s. As a member of the Center for Disease Control violence research team, my task was to determine why. A wide array of possible causes was examined—the 'baby boom' effect, trends in urbanization, economic trends, trends in alcohol abuse, the role of capital punishment, the effects of civil unrest, the availability of firearms, exposure to television. Over the course of seven years of investigation, each of these purported causes was tested in a variety of ways to see whether it could be eliminated as a credible contributor to the doubling of the rates of violence in the U.S. And, one by one, each of them was invalidated, except for television. It is estimated that exposure to television is etiologically related to approximately one half of the homicides committed in the U. S., or approximately 10,000 homicides annually, and to a major proportion—perhaps one half—of rapes, assaults, and other forms of interpersonal violence in the U.S."[3]

Dr. Centerwall also stated the results of two surveys of young male felons imprisoned for violent crimes including murder, rape, and assault showed that 34% reported having consciously imitated crime techniques learned from TV programs.[4]

Sherrie Mazingo, chair of the Broadcast Journalism Sequence, School of Journalism, University of Southern California, also has grave reservations about the ultimate effects of the violence to which audiences are constantly being subjected; and that is not her only concern. News reports that focus on the violence in life also present a distorted image of life in many areas. Singling out Los Angeles, she points to the fear she now feels while driving through the South-Central area (scene of the riots); fear that is by far greater than it was on the evening of the riots as she drove through it because of the reports since that time telling her of the violence that awaits her. Even though she knows there are many law-abiding citizens from diverse cultural and ethnic groups who are not a threat, her perception is now radically different due to the television broadcasts, and she is afraid.

Mazingo charges that real life activities are not being covered because of the media's preoccupation with violence–especially from the black community. That the Watts community is now predominantly Hispanic is not general knowledge. No television station seems to feel it is worthy of coverage, so the public continues to have an image of a black Watts in their minds when violence there is covered. She mourns the passing of responsible news presentations and changing personnel policies. No longer are editorial positions being filled by people from news backgrounds. They are now occupied by individuals whose first concern is financial success. These *money types* are content with a hit-or-miss coverage of violent acts but are not interested in probing into the depths of the story to give it the background that has meaning and interest for residents of the area.

The explosion in technology also affects coverage, Mazingo feels, in that live, on-the-spot coverage is now commonplace for even the most insignificant incidents. This coverage includes interviews with witnesses, watching law enforcement or emergency personnel in action, and often inappropriate questions or remarks from the newsperson. Instead of using this new technology to enhance what should be the central focus of the news, the media now use it to drive the presentation. This, in turn, is leading the media to emphasize negative stories.

According to the National Institute of Mental Health, 80% of all TV programs contain violent acts. Because violence acts like a drug, viewers require more because they develop a tolerance for it. In that sense, the media acts like a pusher because the current trend is for the networks to offer more and more violence. Prime-time programming averages 8-12 violent acts per hour. The Annenberg School of Communications finds violence in children's programming at an all-time high–32 violent acts per hour.[6] Programs like ABC's "Tales From the Cryptkeeper," cartoons scheduled for Saturday morning, awaken children to werewolves, mummies, vampires, zombies, and murders. These are not done in a Casper the Friendly Ghost manner. Characters use razor-sharp fangs and claws that slice through stone. I have friends who did not like to view the original HBO version of "Tales From the Crypt," because it left them feeling very uneasy and afraid. One cannot imagine small children truly enjoying this type of programming or benefiting from it in any way. Oh, by the way, the program's redeeming feature is supposed to be that each episode has a child doing something wrong that unleashes a monster to teach him or her a lesson. Some lesson!

One Saturday morning offered the following movies for our children to watch: *Nowhere to Run*, which tells the story of a teenager who becomes entangled in organized crime, *The Brighton Strangler*, the story of an actor who turns into a mad killer; *What Kind of Woman*, which related the love story of a prostitute and a paratrooper; *Norma Rae*, a movie full of violence as a woman tries to unionize a southern mill; *FX 2, The Deadly Art of Illusion*; *Hurry Sundown*, which chronicles social and racial tension in a southern town; and *Natural Causes*, whose plot features the mysterious death of a woman and a plot to sabotage diplomatic relations between the United States and Vietnam. Do I even need to say this is not kid stuff?

Other movies, which would probably be suitable for the older set watching Saturday morning

TV, included *South of the Border*, featuring Gene Autry; *Home Alone 2*; the musical version of *Lost Horizon*; *Abbott and Costello Meet Frankenstein*; *The Last Outpost*, starring Ronald Reagan; *River of No Return*, the Marilyn Monroe/Robert Mitchum classic of action and Indians; *The Bridal Path*, a comedy about a young Scottish islander in search of a bride; *Skyjacked*; and *The Legend of Lochnagar*. Frankly, I do not think that the movies listed, however good, are truly suitable for the pre-school set.

The argument that parents can exercise control over the TV set is not really viable in a society where on a Saturday morning, all of the children in the family are often watching TV before Dad and Mom are up and running. To keep this program and others like it from ever being aired or making its life extremely short, we can hope there are enough parents of the type who canceled their subscriptions to the *LA Times* when TV Times featured a photo of the Cryptkeeper that frightened their children. In what I feel are extremely user-unfriendly terms, executives for the show contended they were "braced for some sort of critical backlash."[7]

A TV Guide study counted 1,845 acts of violence in 18 hours of viewing time. That's an average of 100 violent acts per hour—one every 36 seconds![8]

It was broken down further into 362 scenes of gunplay, 389 assaults, 673 scenes of punching, pushing, slapping or dragging, 226 scenes of menacing with a weapon, and at least 175 fatalities. The programming was compared to that of a year and a half earlier. They noted very little difference; 63.3% of the programs contained violence, 4.2 acts of violence per program, and 5 acts of violence per hour. The most disconcerting aspect of this survey is that considerably more violence occurs in the early evening at a time when more children are watching.[9] Is this what we really want our children to be watching?

Dr. George Gerbner, who heads the Cultural Environment Movement, a Philidelphia-based advocacy coalition calling for a more responsible media, is concerned about targeting younger viewers with violent programming. As cartoons and comedies depict it, it is even more insidious because it is "happy" violence; that is, it appears as swift, cool, painless, effective, and always leads to a happy ending. It shows none of the pain and suffering that accompany real-life violence.[10]

Others, such as William Dietz of the American Academy of Pediatrics state, "The effects of such programming have been studied for so long there is no doubt that it leads to violent behavior. Many pediatricians now include counseling parents about the effects of TV on children as part of their annual visit.

Violence sells. Non-violent shows can attract an audience too, but they cost more to produce because they have to be good."[11]

Well, that about sums it up. If it's violent, anything will draw an audience, and it takes creativity, sensitivity, and effort to create something good. Have too many of our television producers been so desensitized they can no longer produce something good?

In fact, in a summit meeting on television violence between national legislators and the entertainment industry, mediamakers have insisted that with few exceptions, none of their new or continuing programming is violent enough to warrant parent advisory warnings. How much more violence do you need than a U.S. Marshall and four out-laws killed in a single segment of "Briscoe County Jr.," a comic Western aimed at children?

In reviewing past offerings that will continue and new shows that have been announced, it seems the parade of violent acts will continue. Mediamakers are quick to point out that no guide-lines have been established as to what is accept-able violence. Therefore, they cannot be in viola-tion and thus do not need to be labeled. In other words, if it doesn't have a skull and crossbones on the label, it can't kill you. Producers of westerns and gangster dramas are quick to point out that you have to show violence when dealing with these themes.

I think they have forgotten such shows as "The Lone Ranger" and "Sergeant Preston of the Yukon" that, episode after episode, righted wrongs. The big difference was they did it without killing peo-ple and without taking the law into their own hands. The bad guy was caught and brought to the proper authorities for justice to be served. Did these shows suffer from bad ratings? Absolutely not! Year after year, large audiences followed each episode and waited eagerly for the next.

Even though there was an industry-wide Lead-ership Conference on Violence in Television Pro-gramming with speaker after speaker deploring the proven effects of violence in television on children–especially smaller ones–the public did not see much in the way of changed programming as a result. Some programs were labeled to alert par-ents to the violence contained in them, and TV Guide published a special "Parents' Guide to Chil-dren's Television"; but the producers continued to defend violence in their programming as honest[12] and refused to accept responsibility for the increase of violent acts in our society.[13] Six months after the conference while visiting Hollywood, President Clinton again urged the industry to look at the effect of violence on young people—especially those from an impoverished background.[14]

It apparently had little effect because as of the date of this writing, programming shows no appreciable improvement.

I was especially disappointed in "Due South," which aired, was canceled, and then resurrected. The hero, a Dudley Do-Right Mountie, is delightful, and the show features wonderful subtle humor. However, the level of violence is much too high to make it anything that you would prefer your children watched–even though there are many good lessons they could learn if the program were more suitable for a younger audience by having less violence.

Steven Bochco, producer of "NYPD Blue," exemplifies the mediamaker who does not take the findings of the study groups on violence and television seriously. "I personally don't think violence will be an issue on this show. The "Hill Street Blues" series in the 1980s was a significantly more violent show."[15]

Hmmmm. Are we seeing some of the fallout from that series today? His latest offering, "Murder One", is also of the same genre.

He denied feeling any pressure from the public to stay away from violence. He said that if he had felt it, then he would be in the television business not television art. Come on, Steve! You're in business and you know it. You are not donating your services for the sake of art. Let's be honest. You just don't want to feel the pressure. You want to do your thing, but you're not stopping to think that you are hurting a lot of kids in the process.

Angela Lansbury is to be commended, however, for her willingness to ensure there will be no gratuitous violence in murder scenes. She uses earlier cutaway shots. My only question is, is "Murder She Wrote" being shown too early in the evening? Can a program that has murder as its theme week after week be reduced enough in violence to still be acceptable to a younger early evening audience?

The FBI and census data show the homicide arrest rate for 17-year-olds more than doubled between 1985 and 1991. The rate for those one to two years younger increased even faster than that of the 17-year-olds. As an answer to this increase, psychologists say children are being taught society is normally violent, and they have become frightened of being victimized. They are less likely to help victims of crime and have become more aggressive and violent themselves.[16]

It is frightening to think that the average child sees 8,000 murders and 100,000 acts of violence before they are out of elementary school. It is interesting to note that the homicide rates among whites declined in South Africa during the period between 1947 and 1975, when TV was banned there.[17]

No wonder parents today are interested in installing devices on their TVs that will block out violent programs.[18]

Equally interesting is the Canadian study that found following the introduction of television into two northern Manitoba communities, inappropriate physically aggressive behavior in boys increased 160 percent.[19]

One of my peers recently said he bets Walt Disney is turning over in his grave with the violence that is in the Disney-produced movies of today. We have people being killed like Ursula in *The Little*

Mermaid and Gaston in *Beauty and the Beast*. Adult humor and sexual innuendo is injected into other films that are targeted for the child audience. What has happened to the delightful world of make-believe and humor based on innocent happenings?

I wonder whether a movie such as *The Lion King*, which specifically targeted the small-child audience, contains more violence than a small mind can handle? At the matinee I attended, one little boy, who was about three, kept crying to go home because he was scared. Perhaps that brings out a question of deeper significance, Why does every recent Disney movie have a death?

Personally, I do not think Scar's duplicity was sufficiently explained so that children understood that not every adult is to be trusted–even if they are a member of your own family. Yes, I agree that is a sad commentary on life today.

Companies such as MCA who have taken a beloved child's book like *The Little Engine That Could* and turned it into a tale of violence also contribute to the feeling children have today that the world is indeed a violent place. The story of Tillie the little switch engine's courage and mega-effort to take toys and food to the children on the other side of the mountain has been perverted in the on-sale-everywhere video that turns the mountain into a vicious killer that tries to destroy the little train. One car actually is pushed off the side of the mountain, and the only way the panda is saved is by grabbing the elephant's trunk. This does not teach children the message of bravery and perseverance the original story conveyed. It has been twisted and destroyed. What a loss for our children.

Not only is it a loss for our children, but it is also evidence of the attitude of the nouveau-mediamakers who feel they are not responsible to anyone. One grandmother purchased this video for her grandson. After viewing it, she determined it was not suitable because of the violence. She sent the video back to MCA with a letter explaining why she would like her money refunded. MCA returned the video to her along with a letter that told her she was wrong in her evaluation and an explanation of their refund policy, which extends only to manufacturing defects. What an in-your-face attitude!

RESPONSIBLE ROLE MODELS

Recent movies such as *Mortal Combat* and *Judge Dread* perpetuate the idea that "violence is cool," and the only way to solve a problem or right a wrong is through force. We have been bombarded with this idea for fifteen years, starting with the movies, *The Terminator* and *Rambo* and karate action heroes such as Jean Claude Van Damme, Jeff Speakman, Chuck Norris, and Stephen Segal. If children are constantly exposed to role models such as these, will they be able to learn that problems can be solved through mediation or that violence hurts–even the bad guys? Will they be able to see that you want to right the wrong, but that hurting someone in the process is not necessarily the best way? It is encouraging to note that Arnold Schwarzenegger, famed for his violent roles, stated at the Cannes Film Festival, "Maybe we should see less violence." He continued as he discussed his role in *Last Action Hero*, "The movie shows what effect violence has on me, and how I change." He is now trying to make films that are "acceptable for the whole family...I ask myself what kind of movies do I want to show my kids?" If Schwarzenegger doesn't think his earlier movies are what children should watch, maybe we should listen to his counsel.[20]

That the people in charge of programming and promoting toys for children are not taking their responsibility to make programs and toys that will encourage good qualities to emerge in the users is evident in the remark made by Stacy Botwinick, editor of *Playthings* magazine, "While guns and holsters are out there for the possible pre-school set, there are stores out there that will not sell them. I think the kids are more sophisticated now. They don't want a cap gun–they want a submachine gun or Supersoaker."[21]

Responsible parents do not let their children have everything they want. Neither should responsible mediamakers or toy makers make things available "just because kinds want them." Of course, they want them. They've been conditioned by the media to want more and more violence. It is conceivable that had programming evolved with less and less violence, children would not even want the cap guns they now allegedly reject.

IT'S NOT THE MUSIC MAN ANY MORE

How many parents say, "Oh, I really don't like my kid's music, but gee, I can't take it away." I ask why not if they are watching rock videos such as MTV's "Jeremy"? Are the parents really aware it's about murder in the classroom? The video is based on a true-life incident according to the performers, Seattle's Pearl Jam, but contrary to what is shown on the video, the main protagonist commits suicide. What's even worse, this morbid, violent, gory offering isn't even eligible for labeling because it is not shown on network prime time.

You think that's the only bad one out there? Have you watched "Livin' on the Edge"? The *heroes* in this video take guns to class, steal cars and wreck them, but guess what? They aren't hurt because the car has airbags. After all, they're livin' on the edge! Parents everywhere will be happy to learn that both of the videos were nominated for four Emmys. Anybody else out there ready to revise the nominating system?[22]

Another problem that is being widely addressed today is the increasing violence toward women. The proliferation of graphically violent attacks on women as featured in network programming is a prime factor. Not only are women being murdered, their body parts are also strewn about and shown in such a way as to numb any sense of compassion for these victims. Prime time emphasis on abused women leads the public to believe this is the norm for our country.

No wonder the dating scene has changed. Men have been conditioned to mistreat women, believe they mean yes when they say no, and then throw them away when they've been used. Instead of being conditioned to view lovemaking as something to be accompanied with tenderness and affection, they think it must include violence. After all, that's the way men act. It's been proven to them over and over through the years by television and the movies.[23]

HOOKED ON VIOLENCE

One even wonders if the media itself has become hooked on the violence and no longer feels for those who suffer. They seem to need a violence fix to continue. The front page of a leading metropolitan daily had as its feature stories the Gay March on Washington and the closure of El Toro Marine Air Station. Other front page headlines were about the Russian elections, sports news, and an article about the closure of a drug counseling program because the service also offered family planning services. You may say, Those are all newsworthy stories. And so they are, but buried on page 16 was a squib about two girls being killed in a drive-by shooting. Those girls were children aged 11 and 14, and that was murder! Two girls walking down the street were gunned down. I suppose the media's rationale was that, after all, it appeared to be gang-related, and there have been so many gang shootings recently, it's just another happening. Think about this incident in the light of the headlines a week later. The death of one man at the air show at El Toro was accompanied by pages of four-color photos, on-the-spot interviews, crowd reactions, etc. Just because the death of one man accidentally occurred before a crowd at an entertainment event, does that make it of more news value than the deaths of two girls who really never had a chance to live? I think there was a time in our nation when people would have grieved over the death at the air show but been utterly incensed at the deaths of the two girls. What has caused this change in values?

If television violence exercises so much control over violent behavior, does it not also stand to reason television also controls the many other changes in behavior and attitude that have taken place and are continuing to take place in America? Don Feder, columnist for *The Boston Globe*, declares, "But simulated mayhem isn't the industry's only sin. Television distorts, manipulates, and indoctrinates." He goes on to show how TBS has consistently presented environmental and abortion issues only from Ted Turner's viewpoint. Worse yet, he says, is TBS's friendly view of communist dictators, presenting them and their accomplishments as noble and benefiting the people of their countries. Feder closes with the thought, "Televised violence is undeniably harmful. So is deliberate distortion in the service of agenda (environmental hysteria, apologies for despots)."[24]

A recent study about how the way children are learning today is actually biologically changing the brain's structure and its ability to think along organized, logical lines indicated that television is one of the prime causes of this change. In addition, violence on television was cited as a chief reason for the disturbing trend primary school teachers are seeing among their students–the inability to discuss and resolve differences. Instead they are resorting to violence as a first option.[25]

VALUES FOR SALE

There are those who admit the media can serve their particular cause. Marketing consultant Phyllis Z. Miller, who is responsible for many products you see in movies, including the U-Haul van used by Tom Cruise in *The Firm*, seeks to have movie makers portray safer sex by showing such products as condoms and spermicidal jellies during love scenes. One survey that shows those in the pre-teen to early-twenties age group are among the most frequent moviegoers and receive most of their information about AIDS from the mass media, is supposed to be the motivation behind this campaign. However, many people such as Lou Sheldon, chairman of the Traditional Values Coalition, object. "We know there are social, emotional, medical and psychological consequences to this kind of promiscuity." Marketers state this type of marketing could be a way to improve the image of product placement (not just for money, but for social value) since abstinence, which is rarely portrayed in popular films, is next to condoms as a symbol of safe sex.[26]

That raises a question. Why isn't the campaign for the use of both symbols? I guess I sympathize with the recent cartoon that showed the words, "Just Say Yes, Just Say No, Be Sure to Have Safe Sex." What's the real message being presented by the media today?

In a recent issue of a local newspaper, a lead article claims people are not thinking about sex because thinking means bringing the power of the mind to bear. It asks if anyone would wish to argue that today's sexual liberation has led to truth and happiness, to full and rich lives, strong families, wholesome communities–in short, to the enhanced dignity of men and women. The article goes on to point out that over the past 30 years, illegitimate births have increased from 5.3% to 28%; children with single mothers from 8% to 28.6%; children on welfare from 3.5% to 12.5%; the teenage suicide rate from 3.6% to 11.3%; violent crimes from 16.1 to 75.8 per 100,000 people; and SAT scores have dropped from 975 to 899. We now have the highest teenage pregnancy rate in US history as well as the highest abortion rate in the Western World, record child abuse, rape and incest and the AIDS epidemic. It specifically cites television as saturating its programming with sex.[27] It closes with the admonition we really should be thinking about sex. Who can argue with that reasoning?

Newton N. Minow, former FCC chairman and now director of the Public Service Television project of the American Academy of Arts and Sciences and Craig L. LaMay, associate director of the project, which is funded by the Carnegie Corporation, say the airways are a public property, and like any other public property, the users are subject to certain restrictions. Public broadcasters and media executives do not own the airwaves and cannot subject us to whatever is their whim of the moment. They owe the public, the true owners of the airways, promotion of the general welfare and protection for their children from harmful programs, not the individual pursuit of self-interest. They feel these people are the ones who will cause government intervention and censorship if they do not begin to exercise individual moral responsibility. "Make no mistake–it is those broadcasters and Hollywood producers who speak ominously of censorship who through their moral negligence are the greatest of the dangers to our 1st Amendment freedoms."[28]

If the airways really belong to us and not the executives, then it's time for us to assume control of them.

FOLLOW THE LEADER

You may ask, What direction is this new leader taking our nation—this leader that can infiltrate our belief and value system without our even being aware of it? As I pointed out in the previous chapter, the majority of the those in leadership positions in the media do not share the values and opinions of the average American. Are they trying to persuade us to their point of view? I think so.

I agree with Supreme Court Justice nominee Robert H. Bork that we have lost sight of our integrity in our quest for bringing about the "correct" political outcome. "The political coloration of news reporting is easier for the public to see than is that of judicial decision making, and, as the press has in fact become more political, it has lost legitimacy with large sections of that public."[29]

As I try to rear my children with values that place authority in a place of respect, they are assaulted by network programming, both television and radio, that is anti-established values. By that, I mean adults and parents in particular are painted as inept, out of step with the times, and in most cases, pretty useless to the child, who has the situation under control.

To what extent is this responsible for the too prevalent attitude that casts older family members on the trash heap of public assistance when life begins to get more difficult for them to handle? It is the result of an attitude that derives its values from movies or TV rather than a mentor who is a family member or close friend, and an attitude that says, I can say whatever I want to whomever I please. Freedom of speech, you know. That we should exercise respect because of the position of the person, whether parent, teacher, law enforcement person, or elected official, seems to be forgotten in the rush to get off a clever, smart-mouth retort.

My son loves movies, TV, and music. It's a constant struggle for us–giving him some independence while at the same time limiting his exposure to violence, sex, and a view of our "value-void" world. Do you find this is also a dilemma in your home? When you stop to examine the values most of us hold, have you ever asked yourself, Why should this be a problem? Why should I be put into this Catch 22 situation? What's wrong here today?

When I was growing up, the biggest problems to be solved in entertainment were whether the movie lasted too late, if my choice of program conflicted with my parents' choice, or which program was the better choice. Why should the parents of today be subjected to screening programs for conflict of values? I don't think they should have to be forced to make such choices. The programming should be on a higher level.

As I think about explaining how sex is a beautiful experience best saved until you are an adult, I see that my children will be assailed by teenagers on TV who at best have a mom who says, Be careful. Here's a condom, instead of a mom who talks to them about the reality of sex–how there is emotional upheaval in a relationship once sex enters it and how kids are not really ready yet to handle this dynamite. Afternoon talk shows that debase a beautiful relationship, focus on the perverted, and emphasize abuse are directly in opposition to the view I want my children (of both sexes) to learn about the relationship between men and women. And it's not like these are isolated instances of programming. It seems as though there is nothing out there that addresses the issue of the wholesome family, the healthy relationship, and the beauty between men and women.

It's ironic that one new program that appeared to fit this bill, "The Road Home," didn't even start until 9 p.m. and was canceled after its initial run of a few episodes. Why not schedule programs such as this in the earlier time slots when the entire family can enjoy them?

Other similar programs, such as "Christy" and "Hawkeye," which at least received an earlier time-slot, were also canceled after their initial first few episodes.

When I get discouraged by actions such as these, I can take some satisfaction in knowing there are those who still care about young people and the values their parents are trying to instill in them. Programs such as "Dr. Quinn, Medicine Woman," "Lois and Clark," and the "National Geographic Specials" all air in prime time, and for the most part, do not contain objectionable material.

Most encouraging of all was the Family Channel's rerunning of "Christy" because of the flood of listener requests for it to be shown again. It makes you wonder how the ratings could be low enough to justify canceling the program if so many people wanted it on the air.

When was the last time you saw a movie, watched a TV program, read a modern book, or heard a radio program that extolled the virtues of honesty, respect, self-control, unselfish love, and strength of the family unit? If you are thinking that would be pretty boring programming, ask yourself, When did I start thinking that? Have I always thought that way? What made me change? Have I been so conditioned by what I see and what I hear that I have changed my value-set? Am I a better person for this change?

Of course, all the changes that have occurred within the American populace have not been bad. We can look around and see a program that was started in response to needs that were presented in a media special or covered in regular programming. Many humanitarian projects that bring help to those in need were started as a result of concerned citizens' efforts after they were made aware of a need. In discussing this matter with a friend, he indicated the media had made him more compassionate about the suffering of others, and that generally the media had helped to make us all aware of others' needs. "In that sense, the media has served us well."

A CALMER, GENTLER TIME

Rick Du Brow, writer for the Los Angeles Times, laments that television and radio talk shows are now gone that present issues in the calm, rational atmosphere that encourages understanding of the issue and searching for a solution for the betterment of man. I would agree with this evaluation, with the exception of Rush Limbaugh's program. The conservative public has finally been given a spokesman who is willing not only to look at the issues but also to present possible solutions that do not involve additional taxation or government control of the problems at hand. The ideals of our founding fathers are respected and offered as goals which we should seek.

In an article deploring the now-existing moral void of Sunday morning programming, programs such as "Lamp Unto My Feet," "The Eternal Light," and "Look Up and Live" were cited by Du Brow as examples of programs that gave a reassuring human perspective to television. He further states, "Times are meaner all around us and on TV too—which is why prime-time drama has turned into the killing fields; why nasty, leering and exploitative reality shows harden what is left of the soul of the medium; why slimy, suggestive dating shows and snake-oil infomercials pollute and cheapen the human environment, and why, alas, spirituality has little or no place on the networks."

He continues by lamenting that everything on network TV today has to make a buck, or forget it; and such programming is not a profit center. He goes on to say that network TV also seems to avoid religious programming because of a bogus fear of being accused of proselytizing in a politically correct age. "The end result is a failure of the networks to deal, except sporadically, with a part of life that is important to many viewers and helps sustain them through the worst."[30]

My response to this comment is three questions. Does the media only reflect today's times?

Or are they responsible for today's times? Did they abdicate their responsibility and help bring these times upon us?

Du Brow continues his reminiscing. "The gaping hole at the networks may not be obvious to a generation that can barely recall, or doesn't remember, the earlier era on TV when cultural programming was made for special Sunday daytime viewing along with such news series as "Meet the Press" and "Face the Nation" aired. But those who do remember know what is lost in terms of civility and the calmer, higher road." He then comments on how nice it would have been to have heard the Dan Quayle-Murphy Brown dispute discussed in a calm Sunday morning arena and the Rodney King case presented removed from the "Hard Copy" approach. He closes, "It never ceases to amaze me that there once was an Emmy Award for 'best cultural, religious or educational program.' It was in TV's earlier days, but of course now we've become so smart and sophisticated that we don't need stuff like that anymore."[31]

I counter, Has network control passed from those who cherished those values to those who see them as of no value and not relevant to their lifestyles (perhaps even opposing them), and so have simply eliminated them from what the American public will be able to see on their home screens?

What direction will the technology developed by Scott French take? French used an Apple Macintosh computer endowed with artificial intelligence to write a book that reads like a bestselling novel. Will the new leader take such technology and develop books, scripts, and speeches that have been shown to provoke the best response to an idea? Or will he or she simply enter an idea and have output generated that will be in terms that will insure public acceptance and support? Will there be teachers and mentors who have taught the public to think independently to resist these tactics or will the people surrender to the easy way out—how they feel after they hear or view the event–because of the conditioning they received without pausing to think of the source?

I think back on the axioms I heard as a child while seated at the top of the stairs listening to my Dad, "Whatever is true, honorable, right, and pure, think on that"; "If you can't say something good, don't say anything at all"; "You become what you think." Have we so filled our minds with the bad, the violent, and the perverse, we are becoming that kind of nation?

I can remember my father talking about the rise of Hitler and how he seized the schools early on so he could mold young minds in his plan for world domination. I'm sure if Adolf Hitler were living today, the first thing he would seize would be the media so he could begin to brainwash the people.

By the same token, I believe that many in control of media programming have used it in the past and are using it now to try to change the attitudes and moral values of the American public. I also think if we do not make a concentrated effort to stem this rising tide of counter-moralistic programming, our children will not cherish the same values we do because they will have been conditioned to think and believe in another way. They will see the world from a totally distorted perspective.

WORKS CITED

1. Watson, Tom and Castenada, Carol J. "Reading, writing and murder plots," USA Today 10 June 1993.

2. Feder, Don. "The Wasteland Revisited," The Orange County Register 5 July 1993, M9.

3. Lamson, Susan R. "TV Violence: Does It Cause Real-Life Mayhem?" American Rifleman July 1993: 32-33.

4. Jackson, Robert L. "Panel Voices Frustration on Continued TV Violence." The Los Angeles Times 13 May 1993 F5.

5. Scheer, Robert. "The Bottom Line is Also Tied to Credibility." The Los Angeles Times 17 January 1994 Editorial Section.

6. Ibid, 89.

7. Cerone, Daniel "Abracadaver! New Toon Too Gory for Kids?" The Los Angeles Times 19 June 1993: F1.

8. Knight-Ridder Newspapers, "Violence drenches children's television." The Orange County Register 10 May 1993 News 18.

9. Jackson, Robert L. "Panel Voices Frustration on Continued TV Violence." The Los Angeles Times 13 May 1993 F5.

10. Miller, Greg. "Number of Violent Scenes on TV Drops by Half." The Los Angeles Times 28 July 1993 F4.

11. Duston, Diane. "Congress takes a critical look at TV violence." The Orange County Register 13 May 1993 News 7.

12. Braxton, Greag. "Producers Defend Violence as 'Honest.'" The Los Angeles Times 31 July 1993 F1.

13. Duston, Diane. "A word from sponsors of violent TV: Don't blame us." The Orange County Register 30 July 1003 News 4.

14 Richter, Paul. "Clinton Appeals to Hollywood on Film, TV Violence." The Los Angeles Times 5 December 1993 A1.

15. Herbert, Steven. "Producers Defend Violence as 'Honest'," The Los Angeles Times 31 July 1993 F1, F14.

16. Lamson, Susan R. "TV Violence: Does It Cause Real-Life Mayhem?" American Rifleman July 1993, 89.

17. Scanlan, Christopher. "TV, Kids and Violence." The Orange County Register 10 May 1993 News 18.

18. Editorial, "Block out violent TV." USA Today 14 May 1993 12A.

19. Will, George. "Turning into an aggressive society." The Rocky Mountain News 11 April 1993.

20. "People," USA Today 17 May 1993 2D.

21. "Entertainment," USA Today 19 May 1993 6D.

22. Duff, Marilyn. "The uphill battle against MTV's sordidness." The Orange County Register 17 July 1993 Commentary.

23. Stephenson, June. "Media Violence," Lotus Summer 1993 65-67.

24. Feder, Don. "The Wasteland Revisited," The Orange County Register 5 July 1993: M9.

25. Healy, Jane M. Endangered Minds: Why Children Don't Think and What We Can Do About It. New York. Simon & Schuster. 1990.

26. Horovitz, Bruce. "Hollywood May Add 'Safe' to Its Sex Scenes," The Los Angeles Times 6 July 1993: D1.

27. Farland, Norman F. The Orange County Diocese Newspaper. July 1993 1.

28. Minow, Newton L. and LaMay, Craig L. "From Wasteland to Land of the Wasted," The Los Angeles Times 4 July 1993.

29. Bork, Robert H. The Tempting of America (New York: Macmillan, Inc. 1990) 2.

30. Du Brow, Rick. "A Spiritual Void on the Small Screen," The Los Angeles Times 17 April 1993: F15.

31. Ibid.

Chapter 3

SPECIAL INTEREST GROUPS HYPE

As the Fox Network special documentary on 1968 closed, narrator Martin Sheen summed up what had happened to our nation during that momentous year. "A consensus with compromise [on both sides] is no longer possible. We have become a nation of enclaves."[1]

Instead of being the great melting pot with people of all nationalities and interests working toward a common goal–building a better America– we have become a nation of special interest groups with each seeking its own agenda. The nexus of the assassination of John F. Kennedy and the arrival of the Beatles had brought about the altering of traditional institutions.

Nineteen sixty eight marked the beginning of recognition by the media of the power wielded by special interest groups. Featured "entertainment" on the television that year included the riots following Martin Luther King's death, portrayals of the Flower Children, the assassination of Robert Kennedy, seizure of Columbia University by students, scenes of worldwide student rioting, the marches on Washington by the poor and veterans of the conflict in Vietnam, scenes from Africa where 300 a day were dying of starvation, the Democratic Convention where there were riots and demonstrations by the Yippees followed by Gestapo tactics by the police, the Republican Convention where Afro-Americans rioted, graphic portrayals of the fighting and its aftermath in Vietnam, and finally the truce.

Since that time, the media has allowed itself to be used increasingly by special interest groups to promote their objectives. The media has seized the opportunity to sensationalize demonstrations and thus bring national attention to the protesting group. The media rarely observes it is only a small percentage of the populace that has this specific goal. It often sounds as though everyone supports the effort. Whether it is intentional or unintentional, the media is helping the organization achieve its aim. We also see how these pressure groups often prey on guilt and human frailties to create rage and violence against the very people they purport to protect.

WHO ARE THEY?

Who are these groups and where did they originate? The census taken by the United States Government every ten years continues to try to identify citizens by ethnic groups. Presently, you have five choices of race—White, Black, American Indian/Alaskan Native, Asian/Pacific Islander, or Other.[2]

Somehow, I had always thought there was only one race–the human one. Could that also be the reason over 10 million Americans chose Other? That question aside, as a nation we seem to be intent on becoming a part of some small group instead of a part of the larger group, and the government and media are intensifying this trend.

These organizations recognize the great power the media wields. In discussing the media, "[Latino leaders] know it is the media that sets the trends that will determine whether Latinos are largely ignored or stereotyped."[3]

While asserting the media consistently portrays them as problem people, I'm sure they cannot deny the media was invaluable to their efforts to obtain a Chicano Studies Department at UCLA. However, in the same way they used the media to help their efforts, the media used them to provide another breaking story for the news while ignoring the basic issues. The purpose of each side was the same–to grab the headlines.

In the same article that discussed the Latino leaders' evaluation of the media, the author asks a probing question that all Americans should ponder, "If the key questions about an incident can be shelved, what does this suggest about how the media reports on everyday issues?" In other words, Does the media use integrity in their reporting?

We can expect other groups to profit from the experience of this special interest group in trying to achieve its goals. They will use the same tactics to force this or some other institution to give in to their demands. Statesman Arthur Schlesinger Jr. aptly describes such events as "the disuniting of America."[4]

They ignore the basic reasons institutions are established and their tenets as they seek to impose their small agenda on the institution. The recent flaps over the Boy Scouts, a private organization, are evidence of this lack of respect for the reason this organization was established.

More specifically, the hunger strike at UC Irvine by a group of students who wanted to force the UC Board of Regents to restore and expand affirmative action in the entire UC system showed how the media features these actions and, thereby, gives them more momentum .

When the strike finally ended, fortunately none of the strikers had died, but neither had their demands been implemented. Although they tried to capitalize on the tactics Cesar Chavez had used in implementing better working conditions for the farm workers, they were neither striking for such a noble cause nor able to muster the support he did. They were simply trying to force their will upon an educational system that has the ability to determine for itself the types of policies that should be in effect.

At the same time on the same campus, there was another "controlled fast" staged by students who were aiming at pressuring the school to accelerate the creation of an Asian-American studies program. Although it raised campus awareness, it did little to move administrators. I find myself wondering when agitators will learn to differentiate between just causes and simply something they want. Although the tactics used are the same, the results are entirely different.

I understand the position of wanting their heritage passed on, but in the past, hasn't that been the job of family groups or perhaps organizations that are specifically created for preserving a specific ethnic heritage? Because I am of Italian heritage, I want to see this passed on to my descendants, but I certainly don't expect the university of their choice to be the vehicle for this information.

I will pass on the stories my parents and grandparents told me. If I am really conscientious in this effort, I will preserve the stories in writing. I will not expect the media to focus on a small group who are agitating for a major educational change in a large educational system to pass these stories on.

However, I have seen from the efforts of a few at UCLA how the media creates an interest by a large group of the same ethnic background to agitate for an educational goal that is not in the best interests of the whole community. Please understand this is not an effort in any way to negate the contributions of any of the many different groups that contribute to the make-up of our country. I simply do not think that demonstrations of this sort and pressure from the media are the best ways to achieve a change in curriculum—if it is really needed.

WHAT I MEAN IS...

Not only do these special interest groups ignore the foundations on which institutions are built, but they also develop their own vocabulary. This is transparently evident in the media. They use words that have a specific meaning in a different context in ways that blur their true meaning, and they invent new phrases that actually change the meanings of the individual words. Of course, the audience often perceives an entirely different meaning simply because each of us has our own set of connotations we attach to words.

On the political scene, the media now uses such phrases as a "trust fund established for reducing the budget deficit" for what we used to call paying off the debt; and "investing in the future" when they really mean we will have higher taxes now. If we are unfortunate enough to have a physical handicap, we are "physically challenged." We can no longer be poor, we must be "economically disadvantaged." The ignorant and illiterate have become "educationally deprived." Oh yes. When you want to call in sick, the government has said you can no longer be sick. You are now being "medically challenged."

We can laugh at the pretentious language used to describe sad situations, but remember, while they are clothed in warm fuzzy connotations, these words have a definite, hard as steel goal—never say what you really mean.

It has even come to the point where certain

airlines have been forced to change the First Class label on the curtain that separates the first class passengers from those in the coach section. It now must read First Cabin. Have we gotten so hypersensitive that we misconstrue an airline's attempt to distinguish classes of service as an attempt to separate people into classes.

If no one can understand your intent, you can make as many speeches as you wish to tell people what you plan to do, but no one will catch on. I believe this is exactly what the media is promoting today. They are clothing the true goals of special interest groups in warm fuzzy words that we can't quite grasp. It all sounds so good that we nod and say, "Bless their hearts. Look what they're doing for the country." It's time we woke up and took a long hard look at what they are doing to our country.

Word usage does evolve over a period of time. That is natural, but this is a deliberate choice of words that implies one set of images but in reality is only masking an entirely different intent. Words and phrases are being coined that change or blanket the true meaning of what the person plans to do.

A reader wrote to columnist Jack Smith (recently deceased) asking for his help in defining some words and phrases she did not understand that kept turning up in her newspaper. They included ethnic cleansing, affirmative action, significant other, and substance abuse, as well as several others. She complained, "I thought it was the [media's] function to communicate. Instead we receive the news in code. They invent words and phrases and use them without bothering to define them." Smith agreed with her and added, "The media takes to vogue words the way kids take to candy. One is supposed to get their meaning by textual inference, a highly unreliable method."[5]

COMING TO YOU LIVE FROM...

The Latino community of Los Angeles, however, is not the only group using and being used by the media. The media did not just report the student riots of the '60s. In many cases, they tried to provide a realistic story for their readers and listeners by having the students recreate incidents so they could film them for their audience. While doing this, the media ignored the orderly students throughout the rest of the campus going about their school-business.

A professor during that time at California State University, Long Beach, recalls one particular incident. Some students went into the library, overturned the card catalogues, and dumped books all over the floor. When the media heard of the incident, the converged on the campus and had the students re-enact the demonstration. This re-enactment was then shown on television as live coverage.[6]

SAVE MOTHER EARTH

Mother Earth has spawned many different special interest groups. Among them are those who would trade the logging industry for the spotted owl, those that would outlaw cars, and those that say we'll be out of natural resources in less than a quarter of a century. Probably the group that has been around the longest is the Flat Earth Society, but not many of us are willing to say their claims have much validity. While some groups have legitimate concerns, many of them attempt to force their agenda on the American people whether or not their tenets have merit. Too often, we see the media helping them by featuring their demonstrations or spokespersons in either primetime spots or headline stories.

There even seems to be evidence that science has gone political.[7] Unless we pay careful attention, we will be misled by false information that is being passed off as science by some group in support of a political agenda. While not being entirely to blame for this situation, the media seems to blindly trust scientists as persons of integrity who will provide trustworthy information instead of carefully examining the information to be sure it doesn't reflect the agenda of the scientist.

There is increasing evidence that the environment of both Prince William Sound and Mt. St. Helen's are recovering—an event that wasn't supposed to happen for at least 100 years. While reporting the Forest Service efforts to antique the rocks that show signs of this recovery, neither the network news nor CNN mentions that this recovery belies the claims of environmentalists. Can that be because it doesn't fit their agenda?

A recently released report from scientists after discovering a 3,613 year old tree indicates there is no evidence of global warming from the industrial age. Throughout history, there have been periods of warming and cooling. This tree shows evidence that during the last 100 years, the temperatures were not higher than they were in previous times. In fact, 2,000 years ago, the temperatures were much higher than they are now.

The researchers who examined the tree tell us, "Global warming may not be a generalized problem. We need to know more about atmospheric circulation of temperatures before science can draw any final conclusion about the effects of industry on global climate."[8]

FREE WILLIE

Many families enjoy going to Sea World, San Diego Zoo, Marineland, Wild Country, and other places that bring nature to them. They use these outings to see how birds, animals, and sea inhabitants live and teach their children an appreciation of these creatures. Increasingly, animal rights activists are pressuring wild life parks to release their captives back into the wilds. The parks are arguing that many like Shamu of Sea World probably would not be able to survive the change. They have been in captivity for too long.

The movie, *Free Willie*, fueled much of the public sentiment when activists passed out pamphlets urging the release of Shamu. In an apparent disregard for Shamu, also known as Corky, whale researcher and animal rights activist Paul Spong says, "I know Corky could die this way, but I'd prefer that she die in the ocean, hearing the sound of her family, than sink to the bottom of a concrete tank at Sea World."[9] Needless to say, Sea World says they have no intention of releasing their star performer to almost certain death. The chief veterinarian there likens releasing Corky to turning a family pet loose in the forest to survive.

In an effort to present a more reasonable approach that could possibly satisfy both sides, Dennis Kelly, a marine biologist at Orange Coast College in Costa Mesa, California, suggests conducting "whale sabbaticals." Wildlife parks would capture the whales, keep them in captivity for five or six years and then slowly reintroduce them to the wild. Kelly commented, "Paul Spong has raised an issue worth exploring, but Corky isn't the right candidate. She's too old. Spong is just using *Free Willie* to push people's buttons. What we need is a well-though-out plan."

Unfortunately, too many other special-interest groups are also pushing people's buttons and needing a well-though-out plan. They think noise and publicity will create acceptance for their agenda instead of searching for a workable solution.

CONFLICT OVER THE SECOND AMENDMENT

In another instance of special-interest groups applying pressure for legislation to implement their agenda, President Clinton holds the dubious honor of being the first president in history to ask for anti-gun legislation to be passed so he could sign it into law. The anti-gun lobby groups have ignored a Constitutional right guaranteed to the American people by the Second Amendment in painting what some feel is a very distorted picture of the threat to personal safety posed by firearms. Many feel this is especially disturbing in light of the fact that more people are killed by automobiles than guns each year.

The special interest group, Handgun Control, Inc. recognizes the value of the media in supporting their efforts. One of their newsletters stated, "HCI must devote special resources to keeping the terrible toll of gun violence constantly in the headlines and on the news so that politicians will be forced to respond to this pressing national issue."[10]

A "breaking" news story shocked audiences as it featured a man who went on a shooting rampage in a San Francisco high-rise building. By the time peace returned, eight people were dead and six others wounded. The media made sure the public knew exactly what type of firearm was used, gave the story top coverage, broke into regular programming, and appealed to their listeners to wake up and start working on the elimination of weapons in urban settings.

The media released statements like, "There is absolutely no reason in any urban setting to ever have a weapon like this legalized and have it available,"[11] while ignoring the fact that even severe gun control will not prevent murderers and other criminals from getting guns on the black market. No doubt, had the assailant not committed suicide, he undoubtedly would have been tried for murder.

In contrast, just two days later on July 3, 1993 in a Los Angeles suburb, a man driving under the influence hit a pickup truck, causing the driver of the pickup to lose control. The truck careened over the guard rail and fell fifty feet into a railroad yard. The accident left seven passengers in the bed of the pickup dead, and three other persons were severely injured. The driver of the car that hit the pickup was charged with gross vehicular manslaughter instead of murder.

This tragedy rated only a spot on the evening news and a story in the next day's newspaper. No public outrage was voiced; there were no demands for the removal of automobiles from the streets of cities; and there was no clamour to penalize drunk drivers.

It is especially ironic to note that neither perpetrator was guilty of prior criminal actions; both were in a deranged metal state (although from different causes); and both possessed their weapons legally. The driver had even legally purchased the liquor that rendered him unable to drive safely.

The problem is not the legal ownership of objects, but rather how they are used. We do not hear any clamour from the media to cut the horsepower of car engines to the point they could not possibly travel fast enough to harm anyone. We do not hear cries of, "Back to walking everywhere." Why? Because we really don't want to return to a more simplistic way of life.

However, the idea of gun control is being put before the public by an extremely vocal group of people who belong to many different special interest groups. This fact may even veil the true motive behind their efforts. Can it be they think it would be easier to enforce their agenda on a nation that has been deprived of its right to defend itself?

We need to look at the root problem—violence—and not at the tools. Why are we being faced with violence? Is it starting with our children who are parked in front of the TV watching totally unsuitable programming—programs that fill them with the need for their own violence-fix? Yes, I think we are seeing the fulfilment of a legacy we are permitting to be handed down to our children. Its message, however, is being overshadowed by the voices who have another agenda.

GOING! GOING! GONE! FOR $24 IN TRINKETS

Too often we see special interest groups who are lobbying for actions long since resolved. Twenty-four dollars in trinkets for Manhattan is admittedly a paltry price for such real estate; however, it's a done deal and both sides seemed to be satisfied at the time. There have been many injustices in the past, but bringing them up again for yet another resolution often brings unnecessary conflict.

A few years ago, a 22-acre parcel on the grounds of California State University, Long Beach, became the site of a dispute between some American Indians and University officials. In 1972, workers digging a trench on the land, then being used by a group for organic gardening, unearthed Indian remains. Officials assumed it was the site of a Gabrielino Indian village called Puvungna, the birthplace of a deity called Chunquichnish. No longer a major tribe, fewer than 1,000 of these Indians remain today.

The officials buried the remains across the street and posted a sign declaring the site was that of the village. In 1974, the area around the organic gardens was listed on the National Register of Historic Places.

The University wanted to develop the property. The media told us the Indians assembled and were keeping a vigil declaring they must protect the land–land the University obtained legally. They vowed to keep the University from using it for other purposes.

Another special interest group, the American Civil Liberties Union, also became involved. They said that unless the University abandoned its plans, they would take it to court. The University countered it would conduct an archeological survey to see if the site merited preservation, but the ACLU representative said no such survey was necessary. "If [the Indians] believe it is a sacred site, then it is a sacred site. It's not a question of historical or scientific significance, the question is one of religious significance."

University officials claimed they were the victim of a "disinformation campaign," and that only recently did the Indians claim the site was sacred.[12] Who helped disseminate the disinformation? Look at the facts. The media spread the story, and the media certainly helped to make it a big issue.

Something like this blows my mind. How many modern cities are built on the sites of previous cities? How many burial grounds have been discovered and then respectfully moved to make way for progress? Our national highway system would not exist if every time a grave was discovered during its construction, the builders had been forced to alter the route.

The media shows its bias when it features and thus supports the protesters at the expense of the good of the whole. We should not ignore groups that protest, but featuring them instead of insisting the issue be taken to a place of arbitration where the best solution can be resolved borders on sensationalism. Again, it is anything for a story.

THE GAY AGENDA

Demands from certain militant elements of the gay community besiege us today. Somehow, these people think they have rights that go far beyond those accorded to others. I am not talking about gay people as a whole. I am speaking about the fanatics. I am not homophobic. I have gay friends and believe that whatever two consenting adults do behind closed doors is okay. However, these fanatics not only want to be treated equally, but many of them also seem to feel they deserve preferential treatment in employment. They are clamoring for special protections.

We saw marches to end the ban on gays in the military even though everyone acknowledged there have been gays in the military all along. These marches were held despite the opinion of then-Chairman of the Joint Chiefs of Staff, Colin L. Powell, and other top military advisers. In a letter to Patricia Schroeder, Powell said in part, "The presence of homosexuals in the military is prejudicial to good order and discipline." In reply to her assertion that it was the same type of issue as blacks in the military, he stated, "Skin color is a benign, non-behavioral characteristic. Sexual orientation is perhaps the most profound of human behavioral characteristics. Comparison of the two is a convenient but invalid argument. I believe the privacy rights of all Americans in uniform have to be considered, especially since those rights are often infringed upon by the conditions of military service."

However, the militant gay community continues to press for open acceptance in the military. If a vote were taken, how many homosexuals would say they really want to be in the military? Can it be that the media is creating the desire to be in the military?

Even though a person may not agree with the decision, any group that is basically unique in purpose has a right to set its membership standards. Can you recall hearing of demonstrations by flat-footed people against the infantry because it wouldn't let them participate? No one seems to argue about the fact that pilots must have good eyesight, or that physically unfit people are not accepted by the services.

It appears that this special interest group is seeking to force its will on another group that is maintaining inclusion of an openly gay lifestyle would be detrimental to its avowed purpose. The objection by military advisers is not to the lifestyle but to overt behavior that could possibly affect platoon and barracks morale.

The accounts of those military personnel who have been disciplined for their homosexual activities are top news. Their most outrageous quotations are dutifully carried by the media, for example, "I think clearly, some members of the Republican party have a vested interest in demonizing

lesbian and gay people for fund-raising purposes."[13] Any time a gay person is considered for a
position, the media focuses on that aspect instead
of whether he or she is otherwise qualified for the
job. The issue of sexual orientation blots out all
other concerns.

The media also featured the trial of a service-
man for the beating death of a gay shipmate. Although during the trial he testified he had not killed
him because he was a homosexual and he reiter-
ated this fact to the victim's mother following his
sentencing,[14] the media seemed to ignore it when
covering the proceedings. Had the motive been
presented as something else, would there have
been equal coverage? The sad fact of the matter is
that the alleged motive is what made the story for
the media.

Leaders of militant gay and lesbian groups have
stated they will continue to challenge President
Clinton in court, in the military, and on the streets
for accepting a "Don't ask, don't tell" compromise.
What has happened to the idea of respecting another's decisions even though we may not agree
with them? Does any special interest group have
the right to threaten civil unrest if its demands
are not met?

Because this is exactly the position taken by
some in the black community with respect to the
trial of the officers for beating Rodney King and
the trial of the youths who beat Reginald Denny,
it appears these militant groups are developing a
terrorist mentality; if you don't give me what I want,
I'm going to make you wish you had! This is a sad
commentary on one of the most precious freedoms
we enjoy here in America–the freedom of choice.

The media, of course, fans the fire of these demands by its constant and sometimes sensational

coverage of demonstrations. Has there ever been a Gay March that didn't receive front-page publicity? The media also does the public a disservice in not telling the truth about these parades. When you view them in person, you see not only a bunch of people "just like you but with a different sexual orientation," but also many people who are obscenely dressed and demonstrating pornography in the flesh.

When observers object to these participants, they are accused of depriving the participants of their civil rights. This appears to be at the expense of the rights and values most Americans hold. Historically gay people have been treated terribly, but I am sick and tired of being blamed for something my father's generation did–not mine!

It is most objectionable that any special interest group should be given immunity from suffering the consequences of their actions. There is not another group in the United States today that could behave in this manner in public without being prosecuted! Gay people should not be oppressed or discriminated against; however, neither should they be given a license to be angry.

David Mixner, a gay political strategist and longtime friend of President Clinton, triumphantly observed after a Gay March in Washington, "We are now a civil-rights movement that America can't help but recognize."[15] Comments like this cause those of us who hold heterosexual beliefs and values to wonder whether we will also have to demonstrate in order to maintain our lifestyle. If we were to do so, we would probably be censured and called a bunch of right-wing extremists.

Unfortunately for those everyday, average citizens who happen to be gay, their lifestyle is being sensationalized not only by the militants and exhibitionists but also by the media who is using them to gain headlines and top stories. I fault the media and its sensationalism with causing increasing distrust and widening the gulf between the two lifestyles.

HEALTHCARE FOR ALL

Hillary Clinton's healthcare reform proposal was also the target of special interest groups. The Health Insurance Association of America earmarked $4 million dollars for an ad campaign designed to influence the proposal. They kicked it off with what appeared to be a talk show. In reality, it was a carefully engineered "infomercial."

Other groups including drug companies, physicians, distillers, chiropractors, occupational therapists, some major health insurers, and the AARP, hoping to be influential in the decision, bought time to air their views. They hoped to reach the public with their message if they failed to influence lawmakers.

To understand the value these groups placed on the power of the media, remember all of this was before the contents of the proposal were even known. They knew all too well they needed support for their position–no matter how it was treated in the proposal, and so used the media to try to gain it.

IT'S ALL YOUR FAULT

Sadly for our country, the media often drives wedges between groups by its coverage. An educator who came to our country in 1956 was asked to speak at a Prep School. A group of students accused him of being responsible for bringing Afro-Americans to the United States to be slaves. He pointed out the absurdity of such an idea; nevertheless, the students declared him guilty of slave trading just because he was white.

He went on to voice his concern that so many in our country blame the earlier mistakes and injustices of individuals on the community to which they belonged. However, he noted that this philosophy is not working in reverse. Many of these groups are not willing to assume responsibility for any past injustices committed by those of their community. The scholar closed by mourning the fact that in our country a start had been made in rejecting such unjust lumping of people and guilt by association, but that today it seems to be returning.[16]

IT'S NOT UTOPIA YET, BUT...

The United States certainly is not Utopia yet, but we can safely say it is the country that allows the largest measure of freedom for its citizens. In return, most of its citizens try to use that freedom wisely.

When the injustices to minorities were brought to light at the beginning of the civil rights movement, the nation went to work to rectify these wrongs. Laws that repressed these groups were repealed, and laws that guarded their rights were enacted. Today, people in all parts of this country continue to work productively toward equal rights for everyone.

The portion of the media that emphasizes the areas that need improvement while ignoring the progress that has been made only feeds the hatred that some people still feel. It does nothing to build a better future.

They should learn the lesson that Eddy Harris, author of *South of Haunted Dreams: A Ride Through*

Slavery's Old Back Yard, has learned. In his journey through the South, he grew "from an angry
black man looking for racism in every state pa-
trolman's smirk to a black man willing to admit
the South might just be where he feels the most
comfortable."[17]

In his efforts to understand why the blacks,
and especially the slaves, had put up with what
they did, he found a new respect for them and
how much they endured just to survive. Says
Harris, "I think now that they must have been doing
it for my sake. And that makes me think about
what I should do for the generations coming behind me." Harris learned that he must build for
the future, not tear down the present with memories of the past.

It is not just the news media that becomes a
sounding board for special interest groups. The
literary media as a whole is often used to present
a particular viewpoint or agenda. The man who
related the following incident told me, "I know a
professor from Columbia University by reputation.
He's a fine historian, but I know what I'm going to
read before I ever read it. He was a radical student
at Columbia and is racially biased in favor of
African-Americans.

"Recently, he wrote a very fine volume about
the Reconstruction Period, but you don't read
about anyone except the African-Americans. The
whole reconstruction is seen through their actions,
and they're painted as demigods. During that time,
quite a number of African-Americans served in the
United States Senate, the House of Representatives, and State Legislatures, and he's correct in
saying they've been overlooked in the past; but
when you read this book, it seems as though they
hardly did anything wrong.

"It was always the other people who helped themselves to the state coffers, but never the African-Americans." I'm sure there are quite a number of Caucasian authors who have written about a subject only from their limited viewpoint, but this is the type of literary near-sightedness that often distorts the historical perspective.

We need to be sure to discern the position of the author before we accept everything we read as fact. We have to realize they are writing not only from their viewpoint but also are often working toward achieving their own agenda. They write books because a pamphlet may be viewed with skepticism, but a book is usually accepted as fact.

AND THEN THEY BURNED THE BOOKS

Any small group pushing for adding their special interest to a school's curriculum or taking something from it is given exposure all out of proportion to the event. When a majority of the school board in a Southern California community approved adding creationism to the curriculum, it rated front-page coverage in Los Angeles' largest newspaper.

We were "treated" to all the concerns state officials, interested parents, and the ACLU had regarding the defiance of the state guidelines by the school board and the illegality of teaching about creation.[18] That the author of the article was opposed to the decision came through very loudly in its language. By the end, one might have almost thought Christianity was a crime, and the board was advocating teaching the children how to become criminals.

From time to time we also learn that certain books either have been banned or are under fire by some special interest group. That particular group may be concerned parents, self-appointed guardians of morality, or one of the larger organized groups. I am constantly amazed when I see that someone wants a particular book banned that I have read and not found objectionable. Even such classics as Mark Twain's *The Adventures of Huckleberry Finn*, Dicken's *Oliver Twist*, and the fairy tale, *Snow White*, have felt the ax of censorship.

While I think teachers and parents should guide children toward books suitable for their age and interests, I do not think a few people should inflict their prejudices on the whole group. This would not be so easy if the media were more responsible and did not give the protesting group out-of-proportion coverage, thus permitting the appropriate persons to handle the situation without pressure.

The press often headlines small groups who instigate such actions for the sensationalism. This publicity can intimidate school or library officials who will then remove the offending book rather than face a fight and the resulting publicity. Perhaps this is the reason "People for the American Way," a political action group that monitors book bannings formed by TV producer Norman Lear, recently reported censorship in public schools rose 50% during 1993.

It's too bad we don't hear the media reminding its audience instead that freedom of speech is something we have in this country; and with so many special interest groups that have active agendas, it is almost impossible to author anything that does not offend someone somewhere. While writing this book, I realized how much all of this has affected me because I was careful not to offend certain special-interest groups.

It is particularly ironic that the Banning, California School District removed Maya Angelou's book, *I Know Why the Caged Bird Sings*, from classrooms after complaints from some parents because the book contained the true-life child molestation incident that left the author mute for five years.[19]

This comes at a time when officials are urging parents to educate their children about this outrage because of the increased incidence of molestation. I can hardly think of a better way to tell children about a danger than to let them read about another child's experiences. Granted the subject is distasteful, but one of the best ways you can warn children about it is with the truth.

ROE V WADE?

Periodically, we are subjected to demonstrations outside of birth control clinics, allegedly because of the Roe v Wade decision. Does either side really understand that decision? It did not suddenly legalize abortion or make it available to the public. The Supreme Court simply said the decision of whether to allow an abortion was no longer up to the individual states. It was a right guaranteed by the Constitution and, therefore, had to be available in all states.

For some unknown reason, the decision caused the militant factions on both sides of the issue to mobilize. As a result, our country has seen killings, people jailed for religious reasons, and media-produced propaganda on both sides. Some of it is subtle, using primetime entertainment television as the vehicle. Other methods are obvious–pamphlets or documentaries supporting a particular position.

Another arena born of this conflict is the political one. Candidates for almost any office are forced to declare either their support of or opposition to this decision. Unfortunately, many pro-choice supporters seem to feel that those who are pro-life are a deterrent to human rights. Most of those who defend the pro-life position are doing so because of religious convictions. The pro-choice groups seem to want to ignore the fact that freedom of religion is also guaranteed under the Constitution.

In *The Way Things Ought to Be*, Rush Limbaugh states abortion is an action that cheapens the value of life. He adds, "When we cheapen life, we are contributing to an overall decline in our society's moral values."[20] The rights that the pro-choice faction so vocally say they support do not apparently include those of the unborn child. How much poorer the literary heritage of our nation would be if there had been no James Michener? His birth mother had enough compassion for him to carry him, bear him, and leave him on the steps of a church where he would be found almost immediately and given a home.

However, the media continues to feed the flames of conflict between the two by featuring the latest confrontation. Pictures of demonstrators make the front pages of newspapers and are guaranteed top spots on the nightly newscasts. The women's rights groups are closely tied to this movement, so any time there is a demonstration, look for representatives of these groups to capitalize on the publicity. These groups are those militant feminists who are warring against traditional American values and fundamental institutions such as family and marriage, not those who simply favor equal rights for women. Their tag-along use of other movements has given them a visibility far greater than they could have had on their own merits. The media aids in this by including them in its reports and, in some cases, featuring them instead of the group actually making the protest.

A report from the Center for Media and Public Affairs, states that among the editors and reporters for the three major networks and *The Washington Post* and *The New York Times*, all were distinctly biased toward the pro-choice faction.[21]

Not only were they distinctly biased, some asserted they were actually attempting to influence the public and political arenas with their bias.[22]

They accomplish this in a number of ways. One of the ways is to use biased language and show intolerance of opposing views. You can read how the media has done this with the abortion issue in the *American Spectator*.[23]

AND NOW FOR AN EXPERT IN THE FIELD...

Another way in which the media promotes its views is to feature "guest experts" who are selected because they share the same point of view as the mediamaker. The consultant will then find "documentary" proof for his or her position, even though their own bias is often misleading in the selection of evidence and documents. An opposing point of view is never selected because then it becomes a debate, and that is not the intention of the media. Yes, it is just like a business. People can make an analysis and arrive at the conclusion they want by using selective data sources.

NEWS MAKERS?

When you examine how the media both features and uses these groups, a pattern begins to emerge. The media uses these groups to create their news. If the real story isn't good enough, they falsify the report, adding whatever is needed to make it "real news."

Such is the case of Wendy Bergen of Denver's KCNC, who exposed the story of vicious pit bull dogfights. When the truth emerged, the tapes, which supposedly had been sent to her anonymously, turned out to be dogfights staged for the television crews to record. She had apparently mailed the tapes to herself to make the story appear authentic. While the interests of animal rights activists may have been served, the media chose an untruthful method and the result was a hoax foisted on an unsuspecting public. Another station, KCCO-TV in Alexandria, Minnesota, showed scenes of teenagers downing beers at a party as part of a special report on underage drinking. They failed to tell the public the TV crew bought two cases of beer for the kids to drink and then filmed them while they consumed it.[24]

The groups, in turn, use the media to disseminate their stories, which may or may not be true. When *NBC Nightly News* featured a story on the environmental dangers of logging in Idaho's Clearwater National Forest, Dick Jones, an experienced hydrologist in the forest, happened to watch the footage. He was shocked to see dead fish floating belly up in a stream. He knew logging did not cause that kind of devastation. As it turned out, the film was shot in a forest more than 400 miles away and sent to the station by an environmental group committed to ending the logging of ancient forest on public land.[25]

As Pulitzer Prize-winning TV critic Howard Rosenberg points out, "When viewers become seduced by TV's aura of authenticity, the potential exists for distorted reality to become society's reality." The special interest groups have seized that knowledge and are using it today to force acceptance of their agendas. As intelligent citizens, we must be aware that this mutual co-dependency exists and carefully evaluate what we see and what we hear in order to sift out the grains of truth and discard the chaff of subterfuge.

WORKS CITED

1. "1968." Fox Television network. Aired on Channel 11 in Los Angeles on 11 May 1993.

2. Barringer, Felicity. "Ethnic Pride Confounds The Census." *The New York Times* 9 May 1993 E3.

3. Munoz, Sergio. "Media, Beware: L.A.'s Invisible Majority Is Giving Up Its Silence." *The Los Angeles Times* 6 June 1993 M6.

4. Dallek, Robert. "A Political Assault on Academic Values." *The Los Angeles Times* 9 June 1993 B11.

5. Smith, Jack. "Words You're Entitled, Empowered to Substantially Abuse." *The Los Angeles Times* 10 May 1993 E1.

6. Ahlquist, Irving H., Professor Emeritus of History, California State University Long Beach.

7. Smith, L. Neil. "Weird Science." *The Orange County Register* 23 May 1993 Commentary 1.

8. Villalba, Ricardo, University of Colorado, Boulder in an article by Paul Recer. "Study: Ancient tree rings show no evidence of global warming." *The Orange County Register* 21 May 1993 News 21.

9. Robbins, Gary. "Free Corky." *The Orange County Register* 3 August 1993 News 8.

10. Brady, Sarah. Handgun Control, Inc. Summer, 1993 3.

11. San Francisco Mayor Frank Jordan

12. Dillow, Gordon, Special to the *Times*. "Indians Call Site Sacred but University Disagrees." *The Los Angeles Times* 19 June 1993 A30.

13. King, Gregory, spokesman for a homosexual lobby group, by Leslie Phillips. "Lesbian confirmed for No. 2 HUD post." *USA Today* 25 May 1993.

14. Jameson, Sam. "Sailor Gets Life in Prison for Killing Gay Shipmate." *The Los Angeles Times* 27 May 1993 A1.

15. Sadownick, Doug. "Coming-Out Party." *LA Weekly* 6 May 1993 10.

16. Machan, Tibor. "They're trying to make us cogs on a wheel." *The Orange County Register* 21 May 1993 Metro 9.

17. Wilson, Craig. "A black man's journey to a truce with the South." *USA Today* 11 May 1993.

18. Granberry, Michael. "Board in Vista Orders Teaching of Creationism." *The Los Angeles Times* 14 August 1993 A1.

19. Granberry, Michael. "Besieged by Book Banners." *The Los Angeles Times* 10 May 1993 A1.

20. Limbaugh, Rush. *The Way Things Ought To Be*. New York: Pocket Books (Simon & Schuster), 1992.

21. Leo, J.. "Is the press straight on abortion?" *U.S. News and World Report* 16 July 1990 17.

22. Cowden-Guido, R.. "The post-Webster press." *National Review* 19 November 1990 36.

23. Eastland, T. "The new intolerants." *American Spectator* September 1990 27.

24. Levine, Daniel R. "The Truth About TV News." *Reader's Digest* November 1993 88-89.

25. Ibid.

Chapter 4

EVENT SIGNIFICANCE INDEX

In the presentation of news events, there seems to be a distinct difference in the importance of the event to the public's well being and where it is ranked by the mediamaker. Stories that are sensational or scandalous in nature receive major headlines and full coverage–often taking a majority of program time–while serious stories that affect political integrity or the public welfare are scarcely mentioned or buried in the back pages. In other words, as the integrity of a story decreases, the hype used to present it increases; and as the integrity of a story increases, the less likely it is to be featured by the media.

Is there a distinct difference in the way liberal mediamakers present the news and the way in which more conservative mediamakers make their presentations? The following news items gathered over a period of time prove there is a significant difference in the way in which events are presented by the media. Sometimes it is evident that it is not the sensationalism or scandal that is attached to the event that characterizes the difference in the way it is handled, it is because of the political agenda the mediamaker is trying to implement.

AIDS

AIDS is a subject that seems to separate the differing viewpoints instantly when the word is mentioned. Officials are often characterized as either extremely supportive or heartless, while victims are regarded as innocent sufferers or people who deserve their fate. There seems to be no middle ground from which an intelligent assault on the terrible disease can begin. The media has played an important role in widening this chasm by its manner of reporting. In a report of a demonstration that disrupted a meeting of the New Jersey State Assembly, *The New York Times* devoted a good share of its article to quotes from one of the defendants. It made no effort to qualify these statements or to explore the fact that Diana McCague is an activist who has chosen a disruptive way of trying to enforce her will on the government rather than work within the established framework of the democratic process.[1]

The *Times* was careful to report her rough handling by the state police and the negative effect her activism has had on her life, but they made no attempt to chronicle how the efforts of Act Up (AIDS Coalition to Unleash Power – the activist group with which Ms. McCague is affiliated) have disrupted public life within the schools, government, and healthcare facilities. They also failed to analyze her assertions that unless a candidate's viewpoint agreed with that of Act Up, he or she could expect opposition from them and demonstrations against their candidacy.

Although the product of another arm of the media, advertising plays an all-important role in the dissemination of information regarding the AIDS epidemic. The alcohol and sex, cigarette and sex, sex and jeans ads are sending a clear message today of sex without consequences. Ask the unwed mother, the teenage father who must forego his dreams in order to support his new family, or the person who has just received a diagnosis of HIV positive if these ads are truthful. I think, down to the last person, they will tell you "No." These pictures of false security helped entice them into a situation they had not expected to happen.

In marked contrast, *The Boston Globe* published a thoughtful analysis of the decision by the Massachusetts Supreme Court, which refused to reverse the conviction of two men for giving away clean hypodermic needles. The newspaper pointed out the rise in the number of AIDS cases and the fact that, although possession of a hypodermic needle is against the law, it was time to rethink public policy. There were no sensational quotes from involved persons – just an orderly report of findings and recommendations.[2]

This same newspaper also published an analysis of a report issued by the National Commission on AIDS. In addition to criticizing the federal government for its tepid efforts to treat victims of this epidemic, the newspaper pointed out the problems that would probably arise when an effective vaccine is discovered unless lessons from the past are learned by the Federal Government. (Such as the swine flu fiasco of 1976 in which two million doses of vaccine were made from the wrong virus in the wake of a crash program to inoculate the entire population by the end of the year.) The article also cited the areas in which the media would probably "make the atypical seem typical."[3]

Then, somewhere out in the media position-haze, you have newspapers such as *The Chicago Tribune* that, on the one hand, tastefully report what one group is doing in the way of support for AIDS victims ("Season of Concern"[4]), while on the other hand, publishes without comment an analysis of "The Janus Report on Sexual Behavior," which seems to condone attitude and behavior patterns that some medical authorities claim have led to the increase in AIDs cases.

The report indicates that heterosexual

Americans are now increasing their sexual activity to a level above that of three years ago after a period of abstinence brought about by the fear of AIDS. According to this report, although 80% of those surveyed said although they remain concerned about AIDS, they consider it primarily a problem of the poor and gay communities.

This report, offered without comment or contradiction, almost fosters an attitude of, *It's OK to have lots of sex again. AIDS is not a problem.* Of course, this is in direct contradiction to the facts that continue to emerge that support the charge the epidemic is spreading, that AIDS is not only a national crisis, it is a worldwide one.

We have the World Health Organization issuing statistics regarding the magnitude of the epidemic, but few other media outlets bring them to the attention of the general public. Too often the statistics, such as those stating that AIDS is rapidly becoming the No. 1 killer of young men throughout the United States, are buried well back in the newspaper or news report.[5]

If any other disease had an incidence from a high of 8 million in sub-Saharan Africa to a low of 25,000 in Australia, with almost 13 million people infected worldwide,[6] the headlines of most metropolitan dailies would reflect the danger to the general population. Witness the hysteria generated by outbreaks of the flu virus and the news coverage urging the population to take precautions to avoid it.

Although this conclusion seems almost impossible to accept, it seems as though the liberal media with its cavalier attitude toward sex has closed its eyes to the threat presented by this disease when there is irresponsible sex.

The Houston Chronicle is an exception to this

trend. This newspaper presented an insightful section on the problems created in Zambia by the large number of AIDS victims. These problems range from uncared for children who, in some cases, are also victims of the disease to the secondary infections caused by the disease–diarrhea and tuberculosis. Clearly documenting the scourge, it also presented the assistance these unfortunate people have received from native physicians and researchers and from those in other countries, notably the United States.[7]

While presented in understated terms, the threat to not only the people of Africa but also to the world as a whole was clearly defined. I found this honest, clinical appraisal more chilling and awakening than any amount of sensationalism.

Then there was the young AIDS researcher who became a media star as a result of his studies with a drug therapy that was heralded as a cure for the disease. When the so-called cure proved ineffective in clinical tests, he was forced to apologize to his colleagues at the 9th International Conference on AIDS for the sensation he had caused.[8] How unfortunate the media overplayed what turned out to be a test that fizzled.

Unfortunately, we continue to see only sensationalized headlines almost every day regarding this disease. Whether it was the media hysteria provoked by Ryan White's insistence that he be permitted to go to public school, the media hype surrounding Magic Johnson's announcement and Arthur Ashe's death, or the hope of a new drug that may be effective against the disease, too often we see it treated with sensationalism rather than rationality. It is presented in the manner that will make the most sales or hook the most listeners. It is rarely presented as simply another story.

It is cloaked in hushed tones punctuated by solemn pronouncements or given the headline treatment.

THE GULF WAR

A different type of sensationalism greeted the American public with the advent of the Gulf War. Almost without exception, mediamakers everywhere supported the effort of the United States to rid the Middle East of the Evil One–Saddam Hussein–as a threat to the whole world. Sending troops to Kuwait and the barrage of air attacks against Iraq were cheered and lauded as patriotic, unifying efforts–the first seen in decades.

As the troops went off to war, yellow ribbons blossomed everywhere as a token of the support offered by those left at home. No one stopped to wonder why there wasn't more of a dissenting voice, one that was asking why we were becoming involved in the affairs of independent countries half a world away.

The joint Soviet-US stance on the resolution of the conflict was hailed as a milestone–the first since 1976 that indicated unity on an issue.[9] The government warnings of a world economic crisis after the Iraqi invasion of Kuwait with Hussein as the powerful aggressor who had a world-class arsenal at his disposal began to be put into proper perspective toward the end of February, 1991, when *The Chicago Tribune* commented, "But an objective history of the Persian Gulf War will write that [the young Americans] were ordered to battle while Saddam was maneuvering to quit the war."[10]

Later analysis of the war indicated that the Bush Administration had, in all probability, used the Armed Forces and the local threat of Saddam Hussein as a rallying point for the American people–a unifying factor to bring together a country that had no common purpose. This ulterior motive was cloaked in patriotism, flag waving, and a constant barrage of positive feedback from the media.

Ultimately, the Bush Administration admitted they had grossly underestimated Saddam Hussein's power and ability to stay in charge. Ex-President Bush even admitted that perhaps it had been a mistake not to see that he was removed from power. Yitzak Shamir, Israeli Prime Minister, claimed that he and his cabinet "almost fell out of our chairs" when they heard that Hussein was not to be dethroned. "We were certain that the defeat of Iraq would bring an end to the rule of this crazy man."[11]

Those of us who closely watched the progress of the conflict were motivated for several reasons. In a masterstroke of programming genius, soldiers on the front lines were featured in interviews with live reports on the scene showing anticipation for the next action–even troops under attack (complete with interviews of those being shelled).

Telephone conversations were arranged between the soldiers and the families they left behind. Never before in history had the public been made such a part of the action. Even in Vietnam, the reports were not so personally inclusive.

What caring person could see a relative or friend on the television and not immediately be thrown into an empathetic relationship? Somehow, the separated families joined those in the desert in spirit. Eagerly they waited for the next glimpse of a loved one to share another moment in time. All the while, the propaganda hammered away that this was a just war. The Americans "needed" to be there. These brave, young soldiers reflected the "inner spirit of the country."

Although I did not oppose the action, I was able to see how the public was being manipulated by the media. The government needed the support of the people. To get this support, the government also needed the backing of the media.

How did this unequivocal support come about? One extremely important way was the control of the press that was exercised by United States officials. The importance of abiding by the rules that had been set up was emphasized when those smaller news organizations who would not agree to them were barred from being part of the press pool that was established.[12]

In order to reinforce the feeling of family involvement, the airwaves were filled with reports of "our" attacks and how "we" accomplished this objective or that objective. General Schwartzkopf became "Our General," and in a short time everything became identified by an "ours" or "theirs" tag.

One pilot's destruction of an Iraqi bridge was described by his commander who barely suppressed his pride that the achievement had been accomplished by a gravity bomb rather than a laser-guided smart bomb. He went on to say the pilot's ability to drop bombs guided by his coordination, "is a source of joy to combat pilots."

This is hardly the picture that is normally presented to the public; one of sober, responsible pilots who must at times destroy property and sometimes as a result, also take lives. It is rather an image designed to promote a mob reaction, Come on, join us. It's fun to tear things up! I must ask if this was truly the motivation for presenting such a picture.

Most chilling in the management of media

reporting was this statement made by a Pentagon official, "We lie by not telling you things."[13]

What did this official mean by that statement? Let's look at the explanation.

The public was shown high-tech photos of bombings that eliminated the actual carnage in human losses. Almost without exception, the public saw an antiseptic, bloodless conflict. Iraqi missiles were terrorist weapons while American bombings became "surgical strikes resulting in collateral damage." *Time* magazine defined collateral damage as a term meaning dead or wounded civilians who should have picked a safer neighborhood.

American weapons were touted not as destroyers but as savers of life. Almost without exception, the term casualties meant loss of American lives. Iraqi lives were not taken into consideration. Any Iraqi loss of life was claimed to be the direct result of Hussein's deliberate attempt to place his people in harm's way.

Even *The New York Times*, noted for its responsible reporting, offered a generally one-sided analysis following the end of the hostilities. They reported that allied armored units trapped Iraq's vaunted Republican Guard and cut it to pieces in a ferocious tank battle. Casualties among coalition forces were light and Iraqi losses heavy, with the destruction of more than 200 tanks out of a force of 300. No reports of tank loss were reported among the 800-tank allied force. Overall, of 4,230 tanks estimated to be in Hussein's arsenal, 3,700 were knocked out, and 29 divisions (300,000 men) had been put out of action. While 50,000 Iraqis were reported prisoners of war, no numbers were given for the dead, although estimates were in the tens of thousands. The Iraqi Air Force was reported as completely destroyed.

In contrast, when commenting on the Allied losses, the extremely low level of American casualties was termed almost miraculous. For the entire campaign, 79 were reported dead, 213 wounded, and 44 missing, although the public was told the totals were expected to rise later. In addition, a total of 28 from other countries had been killed.[14]

This overly optimistic and widely hailed report was later corrected by a sober count of the final casualties. However, this final report was buried among the back pages of most newspapers.

In a continuing mode of gathering public support for the war even though it seemed to be won, a metropolitan daily featured the story of how school children had compared Saddam Hussein to the Biblical villain, Haman, who long ago threatened to annihilate the Jews. The children likened Hussein's threat to Israel during the Gulf War to Haman's threat to the same people during Old Testament times.[15]

Further emphasizing the villainy of Hussein were the reports of the oil field fires wantonly set by the Iraqi forces. These fires were aimed at destroying the entire oil production system–part of a scorched earth policy and to serve as a smoke shield against air bombardment.[16] These fires were predicted to burn for years before they could be extinguished.

Graphic descriptions of the fires were presented on television as well as a sober analysis of the loss of oil production to the western world. These reports created the impression that because of Saddam's villainy, irreversible harm had been done to the world's oil supply and it was a situation we would all have to suffer through together. The problems of extinguishing the fires were emphasized.

Not much hope was offered that there would be a speedy resolution to the apparent ecological disaster.[17]

There is no way I can excuse Iraq's actions in releasing such an economic and ecological nightmare on the world; however, it has been interesting to follow public television documentaries on these same fires. The last fire was extinguished slightly over a year after the hostilities ceased. While conditions are still terrible in the oil fields, they are beginning to recover and production is resuming. The picture is indeed much more encouraging than the one presented in the earlier reports.

This media manipulation of the Gulf War was the direct result of an effort to offer unequaled and unanimous support for what was then a very popular administration. The positive hype foisted on the American public was an unparalleled effort to gain the unswerving loyalty and support of the American people over an issue that could have just as easily been turned against the Bush Administration, had not the media positively sensationalized and distorted the news presented to the public. In the words of *U.S. News & World Report*, "[It] was the smartest PR offensive the Pentagon ever mounted."[18]

VIETNAM

We all remember Vietnam and the horrifying images that came into our homes via television broadcasts. We saw the corpses, the effects of napalm bombing, and the mutilated American soldiers night after night. There were also graphic portrayals of the apparent lack of regard for human life the American soldiers exhibited.[19]

These broadcasts still burn in my childhood

memories. It was no wonder that popular opinion went from a generalized lack of support for the war to active opposition to it. Never before in history had there been such organized opposition to a military effort. This opposition was documented and also brought into homes throughout America. As the conflict dragged on, the public began to say, "Enough. Let's get out of Vietnam."

As troops streamed home, very little support was offered to them; and as a result, a dichotomy began to emerge among the people that has not healed to this day—twenty-five years later. A distinct distrust developed between the media and the military (who felt they had been betrayed by the media presentations). This probably accounts, in part, for the censorship imposed on the media during the Gulf War by Pentagon officials. However, this tit for tat attitude does not make a right from two wrongs.

Memorial Day dredges up memories of Vietnam—almost with a vengeance. In Washington, DC, there was a rowdy disturbance when President Clinton tried to address a group at the Vietnam Veterans Memorial. Why was the President of our country treated in such a disrespectful manner?

The simple fact was that he had refused to serve in the Armed Forces during the Vietnam era. In fact, he had opposed the war, demonstrated against it, and according to some reports, actually dodged the draft. Those who had served in the military resented his being asked to address their group. He was widely regarded by them as a hypocrite.[20]

The issue of MIAs as a result of Vietnam also created a charged atmosphere. The families of soldiers who have never been accounted for claim many men are still being held as prisoners. Photographs of alleged prisoners that appear from time to time in the media seem to lend credence to this belief. For the most part, the media does not seem able to treat these reports dispassionately. Witness the headlines that occurred recently when a news release indicated there was a Soviet report that Americans were still being held as prisoners of war in Vietnam.

The author's own preconceived notion of whether the report was authentic or not and his feelings about Vietnam were evident in the way the information was presented to the public. Obviously, he had distinct opinions about whether all of the prisoners had been released or whether some are still being held in a camp somewhere in communist territory.

"Clinton Envoy Cites Doubts on POW Report,"[21] "Viet general denies writing POW report,"[22] "U.S. Doubted Defector's POW Claims, Data Shows,"[23] "POW document complicates dispute over Viet embargo (a different story by the same author about the same set of facts),"[24] "Did Hanoi keep hundreds of American POWs?" (with the sub headline on the continuation page) "POWs: A smoking gun on Hanoi's lies?,"[25] "A Researcher's Dream Find on U.S. POWs Turns Into a Nightmare,"[26] " Vietnam Report on Prisoners A Fake, Reputed Author Says,"[27] "Duplicity documented,"[28] "Document resurrects POWs-for-cash theory,"[29] "U.S. Given Hanoi's Full List of POW Pilots, Vessey Says,"[30] and "U.S. POWs: Pawns for global communism."[31]

As Robert McNamara's memoirs were published, many veterans of Vietnam and their families reacted to his apology regretting his policy in Vietnam with anger. "What's sad and regrettable is that defense secretaries, Pentagon officials, Administration leaders and patriotic flag-wavers never consider the human toll of carrying out flawed policy."[32]

The question I must raise is, At the age of 78, why did McNamara feel he must take the last vestiges of the feeling that "loved ones did not die in vain" away from the families of those who suffered the most during this "police action" by his irresponsible use of the media?

I see a parallel each time I read an article or hear a story that relates to Vietnam; I am reminded of the Civil War. There were those then who could not forget or forgive. They went on remembering (sometimes for generations) what had happened. They were marked forever. Their cause, whether victorious or lost, was never to be forgotten as the new country that emerged from the great conflict took shape. It would forever be brought to mind as either the reason for their actions or the reason they could not act.

CLARENCE THOMAS/ANITA HILL

In a period when sexual harassment and racial bias were buzzwords, the Senate hearings for the nomination of Clarence Thomas to the Supreme Court created an arena in which no holds were barred. Anita Hill charged that Thomas had sexually harassed her over a period of years. These hearings featured two successful, well-educated, articulate African Americans engaged in a debate over incidents that no one else had evidently witnessed.

Mediamakers across the United States immediately took sides in the issue. The pictures that emerged from their reporting differed so greatly, the public often questioned whether the same hearings were being reported.

The day after Anita Hill made her charges, *The New York Times* published an article that assumed Thomas' guilt and portrayed Hill as a victim of his

unwanted sexually explicit descriptions of pornographic films. Citing cases where other successful
women in fields dominated by men had submitted
to sexual harassment in order to succeed, the
newspaper assumed this was the case again. It
urged lawmakers not to believe Thomas' denials
and to delay a decision.[33]

Two days later, the paper ran an article stating Thomas should step aside and allow the nomination of Judge Amalya L. Kearse of the U.S. Court
of Appeals to proceed. They alleged that Thomas
was, in fact, unqualified for the position and while
the truth underlying Hill's accusations would probably never be known, the charges would cast a
shadow over Thomas.[34]

On the same day, this newspaper published
another story that accused the Senate Judiciary
Committee of not taking Hill's charges seriously
enough. They pointed out the charges, if verified,
were enough in themselves to keep Thomas from
the high court bench.

The fact that both the White House and the
Committee stood squarely behind Thomas with
counter-charges of "character assassination" was
offered by the newspaper as evidence why people
who have had an experience similar to Hill's are
reluctant to speak out. They fear an assault on
both their motive and their character. The article
concluded that this is the usual fate of women who
accuse men of sexual ill treatment.[35] No consideration was given to whether the charges of character assassination were accurate.

Other newspapers, such as *The Boston Globe*
and *Newsday*, tried to keep their reporting at a
more non-judgmental level by discussing the issues involved. However, occasional glimpses of
the sympathies of reporters crept in. One such

headline, "Hill's friends bolster her account," appeared on the same day that witnesses on both sides testified and brought reader reaction.

They criticized the *Globe* because it had no right to make a judgment before all the facts were in. Reporters for the *Globe* defended their coverage by stating the majority of the testimony was for Hill on that day, and that, "It was clear to us that Hill was compelling and told the truth. Thomas never added to the fundamental facts after Friday morning."[36] The newspaper did concede that, in all probability, the readers felt betrayed when they perceived a fall from the strict balance of news normally presented.

The *Globe* also pointed out the minor revolution in media reporting that evolved from the hearings: the trendy story with its lifestyle angle and first-person sidebar. This type of reporting overwhelmed the hard news. When reflecting on whether this was a healthy development, the author of the article rather bitterly pointed out that most media institutions are like the Senate–dominated by white males.[37]

A year after the hearings, PBS offered a documentary on them. However, the focus was not on the issue at hand–sexual harassment–but on what they believed was perceived by black America–racism. While white America concentrated on the gender war, interviews with a number of black professionals voiced the opinion that the hearings would never have captured so much attention had the subjects been white. They feared that racial sexual stereotypes had been reinforced by the hearings.[38]

A year and a half after the hearings, the issue was still alive in the media with the publication of *The Real Anita Hill* by David Brock. In a review of this book, *The Boston Globe* quoted Andrew Fishel, a former personnel officer of the Department of Education where Hill formerly worked, as saying, "Brock's account is absolutely true."

Harry Singleton, who succeeded Thomas as head of the department, said, "Hill's testimony is a lie."[39] Needless to say, Hill supporters prepared a point-by-point critique of the book because they believed Brock's statements were "flat wrong."

In a charge of media bias, L. Brent Bozell III, Chairman of the Media Research Center in Alexandria, VA, claimed that Anita Hill was the best example of a media cover-up in the 1990s.[40] Following the unproved charges, almost no one in the media questioned her.

He then went on to catalog the media's treatment of David Brock, author of *The Real Anita Hill*, first published as an article in *The American Spectator*. He was characterized as an ultraconservative with a prejudice toward Clarence Thomas who told outright lies in his book.

Bozell then contrasted this treatment with that afforded by the media to Anita Hill and Timothy Phelps, whose book, *Capitol Games*, completely supports Hill's accusations. Bozell closed his analysis with the observation, "Until these outlets give Brock his due, we will know that to them, honesty and fairness doesn't matter. Only politics does."

One of the few media voices supporting Clarence Thomas was columnist Cal Thomas (no relation). He termed the hearings the "public lynching of Clarence Thomas."[41] He shared Thomas' concern that the circus the hearing turned out to be increased the nation's lack of respect for law and the legal system.

He hailed David Brock's book as the vindication that has finally come of a charge unjustly made. He pointed out that everyone who knew both

Clarence Thomas and Anita Hill believed Thomas, not Hill. He also cited the integrity of those who testified for Thomas.

Those who continued to follow Anita Hill found it interesting to note the prominence given to her following the hearing. She received the Ida D. Wells Award from the National Coalition of 100 Black Women and became a featured speaker on many occasions. These speaking engagements reportedly brought her $10,000 apiece, and she became somewhat of a prima donna by refusing all questions about her testimony from both the audience and the press. All of this from a woman who supposedly had nothing to gain from her testimony at the hearings?

Three years after the hearings, when the furor was beginning to die down, *Strange Justice* by Jane Mayer and Jill Abramson was published. The authors contended that Thomas had perjured his way into the Supreme Court and that he was known for his sexual exploits and penchant for pornographic films and literature.

However, Thomas' supporters saw other motives for the new wave of attacks. The liberal arm of the government was attempting to destroy him because of his conservatism. Steve Smith, his law clerk, supported Thomas fully, saying, "What is being charged is not consistent with the man I know."[42]

NATE HOLDEN/MARLEE M. BEYDA

After a long, tough fight in court, Los Angeles City Councilman Nate Holden was exonerated of sexually harassing a former receptionist. The judge ruled that all extracurricular contact was initiated by the woman, who had welcomed his advances. However, lawyers for Beyda vowed to appeal the ruling and push for better complaint procedures regarding harassment at City Hall.

Spokespersons for Beyda claimed the decision for Holden was evidence that people are willing to stand up and that other women and minorities cannot be deterred from filing these actions. Other council members announced their intention of introducing anti-sexual harassment procedures that would apply to all elected officials, not just supervisors.

Holden then countered that the judge concurred Ms. Beyda had seen the opportunity to visit Holden in his apartment as some kind of opportunity to enhance her position. He then said he saw the verdict as a clear victory. Holden also claimed he saw victory in the cases two other women had brought against him for the same reasons.

I do not presume to claim to have inside information on the cases or to minimize the charges brought against Holden, but it seems to me the media has been used and has used these charges to increase their audiences and bring someone to the public's awareness who has no such reason to be in this position.

BOB PACKWOOD/SEXUAL HARASSMENT

After years of rumors that he sexually harassed female associates and engaged in official misconduct, Senator Bob Packwood was asked to resign his position in the Senate by the Senate Ethics Committee. Interviews on television and massive news coverage followed the news of his resignation.

The nation asked why he still was appearing on the Senate floor if he had resigned, and women's advocates, such as Barbara Boxer, characterized his appearance as "absolutely outrageous."

This featuring of an obvious faux pas so extensively by the media did not give our elected officials time to right Packwood's wrong of still assuming leadership when he no longer had authority.

Did the media then show how the Senate had remedied this error by Packwood? No, of course not; but they did make sure the faux pas was featured as an audience-getter. There was no praise of the Senate group who forced his resignation or of the way in which the ethics by which elected officials are supposed to perform was upheld. This obvious misuse of media coverage is yet another evidence of how the public is led astray by the manner in which information is emphasized.

CHERNOBYL

On April 29, 1986, the Soviet Union announced that a nuclear accident had damaged a reactor at an atomic power plant in the Ukraine on April 26, three days earlier. A radioactive cloud covered most of Northern Europe. In an effort to cover up the lethal nature of the accident, the government-controlled media played down the danger of the escaping radioactivity.

When the nature of the incident became known to western countries, they immediately called for complete evaluations and inspection teams to be allowed into the area. They revealed they had suspected a nuclear accident before the official announcement was made due to the increased levels of radioactivity monitored in their countries.

The official Soviet news agency, *Tass*, stated this was the first such accident in the Soviet Union; however, other unofficial reports indicated there had been at least one other accident in 1957 and one in 1967.[43]

The Russian press minimized the incident and stated the only fatalities had been firefighters. However, figures smuggled out of the country indicated hundreds died as an immediate result, with thousands dying later as a direct result of the radiation they received.

While the Soviet media downplayed the danger presented by this accident, the media of surrounding countries began to calculate the magnitude of the explosion and the resulting exposure to radiation that was being received by their respective countries. Unfortunately for the citizens of those countries, the news was in the past tense, and they simply learned the extent of the danger of the radiation to which they had already been subjected.

I will never forget the anger expressed years later by the wife of a U.S. soldier who was stationed in Germany at the time. The family, which included their daughter who was a baby at the time, lived in a small German village near the base. She told me of the helpless anger she felt at learning they had been exposed to such high levels of radiation without even having been told by the Soviet media there had been an accident. "We didn't even have a chance to leave the area or do anything to protect ourselves."

As the news reached the United States, headlines such as, "Soviet Reactor Spews Cloud of Death Fears,"[44] blazoned across the country. Because they did not know the magnitude of the nuclear reaction, speculation was wild as to what the results would be. There was even controversy among different monitoring groups as to what the levels of radioactivity were.

Unfortunately, for those who simply read the headlines and not the body of the articles, an alarmist attitude was often sounded. The headline, "EPA Says Air Worse but Still Breathable."[45] implies there is (perhaps great) danger, but it is not life-threatening. In reality, the article stated the amount of radioactivity (if breathed for a year) would only equal that received by one-third of a chest X-ray, which is not regarded as a dangerous amount by most authorities.

As time went on, the news of the explosion receded into the background because of the great political changes occurring within the Soviet Union. From time to time, the name Chernobyl was linked to other accidents within the country. However, the striking difference was that these new accidents were being reported promptly and apparently accurately.

Chernobyl again surfaced as a headline in 1993 with the return of many American citizens from visits to the Soviet Union. Now that foreigners were permitted to travel freely and report their journeys, there were frequent accounts of the many people sick and dying from the effects of radiation–not only at Chernobyl but also at divergent locations where there had been other types of radiation contamination. Especially touching were the haunting photographs of the affected children.

Headlines, however, were worded to evoke emotions and sympathy, not to just report the facts: "Victims of Silence," "Holding on to Hope," "Deadly Blast a Dark Secret," "Doctor regrets part she played in covering up cause of illness," "Radiation's Terrible Toll," "Lives Cloaked in Pain," "Opening Secret Doors,"[46] "Giving a Ray of Hope to Chernobyl Victims,"[47] "West's Help for Chernobyl Area Falls Far Short of Expectations,"[48] "Chernobyl fallout found on Mount Blanc in France,"[49] "Chernobyl Affects 800,000 Children,"[50] and "Cancer in Children Up Near Chernobyl."[51] The problem that originated as a direct result of the Soviet government-dominated scientific community and media had become a dilemma for which the United States must find a solution.

I am not minimizing the suffering of innocent children–one of the most heinous crimes ever committed–I am simply trying to point out that a problem for which our country was in no way responsible had been dumped in our laps. The media was taking the public on an extended guilt trip as a result of the plight of these suffering little ones. Somehow, it had become our fault the problem existed.

RODNEY KING v LAPD

The Rodney King/Los Angeles Police confrontation serves as a perfect mirror to reflect the efforts of the media to mold American opinion. The headlines, "Across US, public's confidence in police officers takes a plunge; Mistrust follows LA case, other reports of beatings,"[52] "Victim of videotaped police beating released without charges,"[53] "The L.A.P.D.'s Thin, Savage Blue Line,"[54] "Violence and Racism Are Routine In Los Angeles Police, Study Says,"[55] "The Uncritical Eye: Has the LAPD Really Changed?"[56] "Fellow Parishioners of Stacey Koon question fairness of the verdict,"[57] "L.A. still may face flash points when officers sentenced,"[58] "The Trial Is Ended; Now Ours Begins,"[59] "King Verdicts Let L.A. Turn Focus Back on Inner City,"[60] "Lesson of the King Case: The Risk of Shuttle Justice,"[61] "Was peace held hostage in Los Angeles?"[62] "After Verdicts, Hopeful Days Are Here Again,"[63] "The word that delivered L.A.: Guilty; Guilty, an ugly word–but not on this day,"[64] "Vivid video focused public on brutality, demands for reforms,"[65] and "A Badge Is Less a Shield When Police Go Too Far"[66] painted a picture far different from what was presented in the courtroom.

As you consider the opinions expressed about the trials, the outcome of the trials, and their reflection on the city of Los Angeles, please keep in mind the only point being made here is that the convictions of the authors of the articles are being injected into the headlines with an eye toward molding the opinion of the public at large to agree with theirs. Facts are not simply being presented; sides are being taken.

ELECTIONS – 1992

The Presidential Elections of 1992 saw the media reveling in the opportunity to play up the favorite son, boo the underdog, and pontificate on every subject. By and large, the media did not hold the debates in high regard. They were termed contrived and stage-managed with the candidates even stooping to schoolyard taunts. The media begged the candidates to deal with the issues that the average citizen faces. We saw headlines such as, "Tough Questions for Hard Times,"[67] and "Aides to Bush, Clinton discuss debate plans."[68]

President Bush was criticized for dragging the economy down (when in fact it was on a definite upswing). His smallest errors were played up, indicating that in all probability, his integrity should be questioned.

An honest misinterpretation of a term was taken as a deliberate effort on his part to lie about an issue. Bush had thought the term, arms-for-hostages, referred to the Iran initiative—not to arms being shipped to Iran in exchange for the release of hostages in Lebanon, with profits from those sales being used to finance the guerrilla war

by rebels in Nicaragua. Because Bush misinter-
preted the question, he answered the query incor-
rectly, indicating he knew of the diversion of money
to Nicaragua. He had consistently denied knowing about it, and no evidence has ever come to
light to indicate otherwise.

Even though when he learned he had misun-
derstood what was meant, Bush clearly stated the
facts to which he had testified many times previously, many mediamakers chose to use these statements as his effort to explain away a blatant lie,
citing members of Clinton's campaign team as the
source of their evidence.

Some newspapers chose to play up Clinton's
candidacy positively with headlines such as the
ones that follow. This headline, "Perot Upsets
Bush, Clinton Strategies; In shift, Clinton stresses
credentials as outsider,"[69] pointed out that Perot's
campaign had thrown a curve ball at both Bush
and Clinton, but also gave the readers a positive
assessment of Clinton's credentials as a possible
future president.

Most headlines indicated the support the paper offered to Clinton. For example, "Clinton Explains and Makes Voters Believe,"[70] "[Clinton] Won't
let up despite lead,"[71] "Clinton has answers on all
fronts,"[72] "Clinton sees damage in Florida; Declines
to blame Bush on cleanup."[73] Some papers even
offered advice to him for running his campaign:
"Clinton Needs to Stick to His Strategies."[74]

The press, as a whole, was so pro-Clinton it
caused some journalists to question why this was
so and why the media was so anti-Bush.[75] One of
the conclusions reached was that the reporter's
personal values actually colored their stories.[76]

GAYS IN THE MILITARY

Following closely behind the election came the issue of gays in the military. Clinton's pro-gay stance and promise to lift the ban on homosexuals in the military had given him many supporters from this community. His retreat from the issue because of congressional opposition and final compromise with a "Don't ask, don't tell" policy was widely regarded as a betrayal of the confidence gays had expressed in his administration. Newspapers and magazines featured articles on the issue. It was a top news story for many weeks.

The public saw headlines that often reflected the position of the paper rather than the issue's current status. Some of the headlines were appropriate–you decide. Among the headlines were: "Don't ask, don't tell, don't legislate,"[77] "Waffling, shuffling and invoking an unfair gay policy,"[78] "Compromise; Clinton's decision on gays in military pleases few,"[79] "The Real Reason Gays Want Services to Admit Them,"[80] "Hysteria in the military,"[81] "Retired top brass back ban on gays,"[82] "Gay sons, daughters lend 'a face' to debate,"[83] "Homosexuals Serve in Doubt and Secrecy,"[84] "Tufts [University] hit for ban of forum on gays in military,"[85] "Clinton's support of gays disputed,"[86] "Many see gays as predators,"[87] "Little-known policy suddenly captured national attention,"[88] "Schwarzkopf: 'A 2nd-Class Force' If Gay Ban Ends,"[89] "Gay Rights: Movement shows clout in capital,"[90] "Gay Sergeant Not Welcome in Army, for Now,"[91] "Servicemen Warn Panel Not to Lift Ban; Some Predict Violence,"[92] and "White House backs constitutionality of previous gay ban."[93]

Even though most editions of the major newspapers kept opinion out of the headlines, the story itself was featured, complete with photographs, as a major news item. The fact that the Gay and Lesbian Rights Parades in many cities coincided with the debate in Congress made the parades and demonstrations front-page news. What should have been an issue decided by calm hearings and rational Congressional debate was turned into a three-ring circus.

Not only were the parades and demonstrations treated as top news, most papers also featured in-depth profiles of some of the individuals involved. *The New York Times* even published a lengthy autobiography by Sgt. Jose Zuniga, who was discharged from the Army after his homosexuality was made public.[94] However, one headline stood out as a banner for sanity. It said, "Rational Thought Needed on Gays in the Service."[95]

Obviously, the media saw in this subject large dollar signs if it were sensationalized. All the stops were pulled out and every element explored for maximum coverage. The original issue of Clinton's support of lifting the ban and then backing off from this conviction was lost in the flurry created by other personages who became involved in the debate. This turnaround of the crux of the issue by the media serves as a blatant example of the media's willingness to take an event of lesser significance and sensationalize it by creating the aura assumed by a major occurrence. The event of lesser significance thus becomes a major news story, which people eagerly follow because of the way it has been sensationalized.

TONYA/NANCY

You do not even need last names to be able to know exactly who they are. The media so sensationalized the vicious attack on skater Nancy Kerrigan that it was impossible to escape from their

coverage. It rated the front page for weeks–often
the leading headline–and no news broadcast could
begin without a teaser that hyped the latest rumor
or action in the case. When her rival, Tonya
Harding, was implicated in the attack, the hype
reached a near-JFK Assassination level. Regular
programming was interrupted by the latest news
release, soon-to-be-made announcement, and
speculation.

Although rarely equaled in unsportsmanlike
behavior, this attack certainly did not merit the
position it was given by the media. Nancy was hurt,
but not badly enough to prevent her competing
for the Olympic gold medal at Lillehammer. The
real story that could have come out of the attack–
Tonya's behavior was the opposite of every trait
an Olympian is supposed to represent–never surfaced. Instead, for days we were subjected to stories of Nancy's sweet disposition and girl-next-door
wholesomeness in contrast to Tonya's bad girl
image.

The morning after the attack, *The Los Angeles
Times* chose to play down Nancy's comments and
hype the story by making it their lead for the day.
It was even accompanied by a 6'x5' four-color picture of her crying in pain shortly after the attack.[96]

In an ABC television interview, Nancy's comments indicating she had accepted the attack as
simply one of the bad things now occurring in the
sports scene clearly showed her wish to have the
incident put aside. However, the media again
showed its utter disregard for personal feelings and
began to sensationalize the story. Important coverage of national and international affairs was relegated to the inner pages of the paper because the
Tonya/Nancy affair rated the front page.

Although not remaining the top story, the news

of the attack continued to be among the top ten news items until almost a week later when Tonya's husband (or ex-husband–the media couldn't seem to make up its mind which) and bodyguard were implicated in the attack.[97] Then, when it seemed that Tonya also was involved in planning the attack, there was no turning back. Every day, the newspapers and newscasters had their top story assured–something about one or both of the principles. Most of the time, these stories were accompanied by photographs.

The public heard only good things about Nancy. She was a strong person who was able to overcome great difficulties. She was quoted as not understanding why the attack occurred because, "I can't think that viciously."[98] She was pictured as being dedicated and aloof from the controversy and concerned only with preparing herself for the competition. Her close-knit family with its obvious affection for one another was often featured when Nancy was mentioned. She was everything an Olympic champion should be and had been welcomed by major business interests to advertise their products or represent them in some other way.

I am not implying this is a false picture of Nancy Kerrigan in any way. I am just saying that we heard and saw nothing that presented her in anything but an unblemished state. She almost assumed sainthood. I feel certain she would be the first to say, "But I'm only human. I'm not perfect. No one is."

On the other hand, Tonya's dysfunctional family and economically-deprived childhood were presented as the reason she was such a "tough cookie." The news leaked that the media despaired before any press conference with her. She just didn't project the image they thought she should.

They had to remove cigarettes from her mouth, edit her comments, and smooth her rough edges. In an interview before the Olympics began, a group of businessmen were asked, "Why have you used Nancy Kerrigan so often in commercials since the last Olympics and not Tonya Harding?" They pointed out that Tonya simply did not project the wholesome image they wanted to accompany their products; whereas, Nancy made everyone love her.

Tonya's lifestyle was termed scandal-ridden, and most of her problems were considered her fault.[99] Stories of her childhood and earlier skating years pictured her as an outsider, never quite becoming one of the group. Instead of being featured as a hard worker who had overcome great difficulty to rise to the top of her sport, she was portrayed as the product of a hard life. Her behavior was "atrocious," and her language filled with swear words.[100] In contrast to Nancy, Tonya could do no right.

After the pair reached Lillehammer amid tremendous hoopla and predictions by the Olympic Committee of a media circus, they could not even practice in peace. In a town where the media outnumbered the Olympic competitors, every movement was covered. Connie Chung even managed to get an apartment next to Tonya's so she could buddy-up with her while she tried to get a "real scoop" on the other media representatives. Connie did get an interview, so it must have paid off. I was appalled, however, when the media stooped to the level of common thieves and broke into Tonya's electronic voice mail so they could gather gossip.

In a close-up look at the Tonya/Nancy rivalry, NBC offered a special, "Shattered Glory," during the Olympics. The narrator observed, "When there's a story like this, why is there automatically a media feeding frenzy?" Sandra Kaplan, Senior Editor of *TV Guide*, replied, "It's the biggest soap opera ever, and people tune in."

The other competitors were virtually ignored, even though their sports and their relative positions within them merited as much attention. Coverage of other sports was constantly interrupted by updates on Tonya or Nancy and promises of the next story about them. The media presented this one competition as the reason the Winter Olympics were held. All other ones were simply tag-alongs.

Needless to say, this sentiment is not in keeping with Olympic spirit and the games in general. My sympathies are certainly with all of those other deserving athletes who were ignored in the rush to cover Nancy and Tonya. They worked just as hard, many of them overcame equally difficult circumstances, and the media did not give their efforts the consideration they deserved.

After the competition ended, Tonya went home without a medal, and Nancy received the Silver. Reluctant to let go of a story, however, the media continued to try to keep Nancy in the center of controversy. They distorted her comments when she was asked her opinion about Oksana Baiul's winning the gold medal. Nancy had said that some people might have had a different opinion (a relatively neutral remark), but the media reported she had slammed the judges. Then they showed her remarks while in a parade at Disneyland out of context, which made her appear to put down Disney's characters. It's no wonder she chose not to compete in the next World Championships. Who knows what the media would have done there had she appeared?

Again, we see the media sensationalizing an incident that should have remained relegated to the sports section. It should have been only reported without comment until the Olympic Committee could determine whether Tonya Harding should be allowed to compete and law enforcement officials could determine what, if any, charges should be brought against her.

Because the media chose to put it into the spotlight and distort it all out of proportion, we saw what should have been another time of national pride in all of the athletes who had worked so hard to earn the privilege of representing our country in this world competition turned into a media feeding frenzy. A frenzy in which the real reason for the games was ignored and the other competitors obscured. The media's lack of integrity was again made all too evident. Another trivial incident was catapulted to the top as the most important news item of the day.

NATURE UNLEASHED

For those who live in areas that are ravaged by nature from time to time, the escalation of reports into accounts of an unequaled horror that is about to descend on them is nothing new. Often it is impossible to find out what else is happening in the world because of the domination of the news by this one event.

The citizens of the Los Angeles area were startled to hear the voice of a newscaster announce that the horrendous brush fires occurring in several areas were the only news for that day when it came time for the normally scheduled newscast. This might not have seemed so startling on an average night, but elections, including the tight race for Mayor of Los Angeles, had been held that day. Even though the fires were certainly prime items, other things of importance were also occurring in the area and should have received some air time.

Usually, in the location of the disaster, most regular programming is preempted for continuing coverage of the event. An interesting comment from a resident of such an area was, "I like to be kept aware of the situation, but I don't like having nothing but that when I turn on the TV or the radio. It's overkill. Finally, I just get to the point I turn it all off. I really don't think it's healthy to be hearing nothing but disaster."

The past five years have been especially notable years for violence, floods, fires, earthquakes, and random shootings. For the most part, when a news broadcast is turned on, the majority of the time is spent on events such as these. The newspapers also headline these events often without enough facts in the articles to present a clear picture of what really happened. The spectacular picture, catchy headline, and exaggerated facts invite people to buy and read or tune in to a particular paper or channel for news of their daily violence fix.

Does the radio or television industry even stop to contemplate how they are playing with the emotions of those who listen to their broadcasts? The experience of a friend who is in the military is evidence that would indicate they do not. He was in the Azores when the Northridge earthquake hit the Los Angeles area. The only television available in that area is the Armed Forces Network, which broadcasts for only a few hours each day.

It was well over twenty-four hours before he could be certain the quake had not rendered much damage to the area where his parents lived. Based on the reports he saw and being acquainted with the area, he realized where the major damage had occurred. The reports, themselves, would not have been too helpful to anyone who did not know the area. The maps that were shown were only of the local disaster area, not of the entire metropolitan area, so viewers could put the occurrence into its geographical perspective. Military personnel offered to try to patch him through to his parents (a difficult procedure), but he declined after finally learning where the major damage had occurred.

He laughed as he said, "That reminds me of the time I was flying home on leave. While I was waiting to board the plane, the TV in the waiting area interrupted its regular programming to announce that a major earthquake had hit the Los Angeles area (the Whittier narrows earthquake). Additional reports would be made as they were received. I made the entire flight home wondering if my folks were OK; would they be able to meet me as planned, just how bad was the quake? Hardly a relaxing flight."

Multiply this man's experiences by thousands throughout the country. How much unnecessary anxiety is caused by a media that refuses to accept responsibility for their actions? Getting the story first, hitting hard with it, and capturing the largest audience are far more important than presenting the story with enough facts to offer a somewhat clear picture to the public. It does not seem to matter to the media that they magnify the sensational aspect of each item rather than tell the story as it is.

HURRICANE ANDREW

Hurricane Andrew spawned dire headlines across the United States. There is no doubt that this storm was a horrifying spectacle of nature for anyone to experience. We have only to look at the video coverage to witness the violence it unleashed. However, the following headlines offer an interesting comment on the media's treatment of it.

On August 22, 1992, there appeared on one of the inside pages a short article titled, "Year's First Tropical Storm Gaining Strength in Atlantic."[101] Two days later, the same paper headlined news of the storm, "A Million are Told to Flee Hurricane in South Florida."[102] The article was filled with scare terms–"ferocious"; "risking suicide"; "resources exhausted"; "shelters packed"; "prepared for trauma"; "nowhere to sleep", etc.

For a storm of that magnitude, these terms were not out of proportion; however, these are the terms that are encountered in most accounts of any storm that causes a break in normal activities. The public then is forced to evaluate the account with what they know of the conditions, instead of expecting to encounter terms such as these only when hearing about a monster storm.

Almost unbelievable in its understatement was the headline of another daily, "Unusual Storm in an Unusual Year."[103] As the storm continued on its course after slamming into southern Florida, people were expecting the worst. Headlines mirrored that expectation, "Hurricane Andrew: When a Monster Is on the Way, It's Time to Get Out of Town."[104] Then we learned the "Rescuers [were] Ready, Restless."[105]

Because of the proximity of the presidential elections, politics soon became part of the scenario. "The Politics of Disaster Relief; A Subtle 'blame game' in Florida,"[106] "More troops ordered to Florida. U.S. Frees up $300 million to assist victims,"[107] "President to visit hurricane-scarred states today,"[108] and "US to pay hurricane cost; Bush urges public's help,"[109] were headlines that told of a shift in emphasis from the effects of the storm to the political analysis of the aid offered and other relief efforts.

It was not until some months later that concern for the people and the damage that was caused again became the focus of stories about Hurricane Andrew. As the area began to rebuild and people picked up what remained of their lives before the hurricane, stories of courage and strength in the face of adversity emerged. The media shared with the whole country the lessons the area had learned about building to adequate safety codes and the need for states to set up disaster funds for such "mega-catastrophes." In this instance, the media performed a definite service to the public.

TRULY IMPORTANT OR TRIVIA?

The lesson we can all learn from this examination of how the media treats news of importance to the public is that we should always look beyond the headline to find the real story. If, upon examination, we find the headline is misleading, we should disregard it.

The public should also remember that the headline serves mainly as the medium by which the public's attention is caught so the paper will be purchased. This headline may not even reflect the truth of an issue. If the importance of the issue can be inflated by sensationalism, reports of violence, or sexual overtones, then rest assured the media will exploit this aspect of the story and use it in the headline.

Often the public has to completely ignore some trivial aspect that has been featured as the major component in order to dig to the heart of the matter. This burial of the real issue in the trivia surrounding it is one of the greatest disservices the media does to the people of America today.

Even more disconcerting is the elevation of the trivial, sensational story over the truly important one because trivia is easier to sensationalize. Too often, the public must dig deeply into the newspaper to find the truly significant events of the day— the stories that tell of the things that will truly impact lives and our way of living.

The media have it all backwards. As shown on the event significance scale, the media tends to sensationalise the insignificant, and practically disregards the significant, less exciting, events in our lives.

I believe this inversion in the order of importance is often done by the media in an effort to keep important decisions from coming to the attention of the majority of the public. If this news is kept out of the television broadcasts and buried in the newspapers and magazines, then most of the people of the United States will not know anything about it until it is too late to do anything.

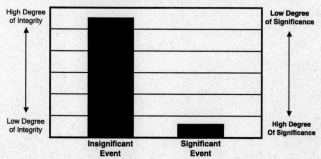

NEWS EVENT SIGNIFICANCE

High Degree of Integrity

Low Degree of Integrity

Low Degree of Significance

High Degree Of Significance

Insignificant Event

Significant Event

This reversal of the position assumed by news stories is not only a deliberate attempt by the media to veil significant actions within the liberal element of government but also an effort to take advantage of the sensation-fix the public seems to crave. If the media can fulfill that need, then they have every reason to believe the public's attention will be so taken with the trivial matter, they will not be searching for the subjects about which they should be seriously concerned. It can be compared to the young scholar who is so smitten with a pretty girl in his class that when she favors him with a smile, the lessons of academia flow right past his awareness as he basks in the attention she bestowed on him.

I believe one effort all of us can make is to skim past the eye-catchers that try to snare our attention and search diligently for the real news. When we find it, we should read it carefully to determine what has actually happened; and then if we feel the information is scanty or of such importance it should have made the front page, question the mediamakers responsible for the newspaper or magazine. This is the one effective weapon we have at our disposal–our displeasure with what we are being offered. The media today has every reason to be complacent with their actions. No one is really complaining–and we all know it is easier to flow with the status quo.

If the media is challenged by the public for their presentations and responds with change, then we should see a reversal of the present Event Significance Index. Instead of trivia or sensationalized news receiving top billing, we should see it relegated toward the bottom, as it should be. Events that are of importance to our way of life and well being should begin their climb toward the top of the Index. With a responsible media providing the news, these are the stories that should assume the upper places. There will always be a story now and then that is totally trivial but so sensational that it will assume a position completely out of place for its significance; but if we can stem the flow of garbage to the top, then the reports we see and hear should assume a more balanced positioning.

WORKS CITED

1. Liberman, Si. "New Jersey Q & A: Diana McCague; With Act Up in the War Against AIDS." *The New York Times* 18 July 1993 Section 13NJ, 3.

2. "A deadly ruling on clean needles." *The Boston Globe* 1 August 1993 74.

3. Turner, Robert L. "Hurdles for an AIDS vaccine." *The Boston Globe* 20 July 1993 15.

4. Obejas, Acht. "AIDS issue falls on Season of Concern." *The Chicago Tribune* 10 September 1993 2.

5. Tanner, Lindsey. "AIDS: a leading killer in cities." *The Orange County Register* 16 June 1993 News 27.

6. Merson, Dr. Michael. Science (World Health Organization) 28 May 1993.

7. Sorelle, Ruth. "The Ravages of AIDS." and "Seeking an Answer to AIDS." *The Houston Chronicle* 18 April 1993 1A, Texas 10.

8. Painter, Kim. "Researcher rejects claims about African interferon." *USA Today* 14 June 1993.

9. Curtius, Mary, Mashek, John, Oliphant, Thomas. "Questions follow US-Soviet statement on gulf war. Israelis seek assurances on Bush policy." *The Boston Globe* 31 January 1991 1.

10. Larsen, Leonard (Scripps Howard News Service). "Bush's war aims prolonging the agony." *The Chicago Tribune* 27 February 1991 C17.

11. Associated Press. "Shamir Tells of Shock That Bush Left Husseiin in Power." *The Los Angeles Times.* 15 January 1995. A4.

12. Lee, Martin A. & Solomon, Norman. *Unreliable Sources: A Guide to Detecting Bias in News Media* Secaucas: Carol Publishing Group, 1992 xvi.

13. Ibid. xviii.

14. Apple, R. W. Jr. in a Special Report from Dhahran, Saudi Arabia. "Allies Destroy Iraqis' Main Force; Kuwait is Retaken After 7 Months." *The New York Times* 28 February 1991 A1.

15. Goldman, Ari L. "Today the Villain of Purim, Haman, Is Spelled Saddam." *The New York Times* 28 February 1991 B3.

16. Royce, Knut. "Iraqis Fill Skies of Kuwait With Smoke." *Newsday* 23 February 1991 15.

17. Hayes, Thomas C. "The Job of Fighting Kuwait's Infernos."

The New York Times 28 February 1991 D1.

18. Gergen, D. "Why America hates the press." *U.S. News & World Report* 11 March 1991: 57.

19. Lichter, S. Robert, Rothman, Stanley, Lichter, Linda S. *The Media Elite: America's New Powerbrokers.* New York: Hastings House, 14.

20. Richter, Paul and Libit, Howard. "Cheers, Jeers for Clinton at Memorial." *The Los Angeles Times* 1 June 1993 A1.

21. Wallace, Charles P. "Clinton Envoy Cites Doubts on POW Report." *The Los Angeles Times* 20 April 1993 A4.

22. Shenon, Philip from *The New York Times.* "Viet general denies writing POW report." *The Orange County Register* 10 April 1993 News 1.

23. Ross, Michael. "U.S. Doubted Defector's POW Claims, Data Shows." *The Los Angeles Times* 27 May 1993 A26.

24. Ross, Michael. "POW document complicates dispute over Viet embargo." *The Honolulu Advertiser* 18 April 1993 A23.

25. Caldwell, Robert J. "Did Hanoi keep hundreds of Americans POWs?" *The San Diego Union-Tribune* 18 April 1993 G1.

26. Lippman, Thomas W. "A Researcher's Dream Find on U.S. POWs Turns Into a Nightmare." *The Washington Post* 25 April 1993 A4.

27. Shenon, Philip. "Vietnam Report on Prisoners A Fake, Reputed Author Says." *The New York Times* 25 April 1993 A1.

28. Editorial page. *The Arizona Republic* 18 April 1993 C4.

29. Engelberg, Stephen. "Document resurrects POWs-for-cash theory." *The San Jose Mercury News* 18 April 1993 5A.

30. Pine, Art. "U.S Given Hanoi's Full List of POW Pilots, Vessey Says." *The Los Angeles Times* 22 April 1993 A1.

31. Nguyen, P. Phuoc. "U.S. POWs: Pawns for global communism." *The Orange County Register* 21 April 1993.

32. Hart, Shannon. "McNamara Book on Vietnam." *The Los Angeles Times.* 17 April 1995 B4.

33. Jordan, Emma Coleman. "Why Rush to Vote on Thomas?" *The New York Times* 8 October 1991 A25.

34. Newman, Jon O. "A Replacement for Thomas." *The New York Times* 10 October 1991 A27.

35. Wicker, Tom. "Blaming Anita Hill." *The New York Times* 10 October 1991 A27.

36. Scharfenberg, Editor Kirk as quoted by McKibben, Gordon. "A perception of Globe bias on Thomas coverage." *The Boston Globe* 21 October 1991 OP-ED13.

37. Nolan, Martin F. "Glimmers of silver linings peek out from story saga." *The Boston Globe* 13 October 1991 16.

38. Koch, John. "PBS tells the 'other' story of the Thomas-Hill hearings." *The Boston Globe* 11 October, 1992 B6.

39. Tye, Larry. "New book on Anita Hill raises row." *The Boston Globe* 25 April 1993 2.

40. Bozell, L. Brent III. "Anita Hill's protectors in the media." *The Orange County Register* 17 May 1993 Metro 9.

41. Thomas, Cal. "Clarence Thomas sees the light of vindication." *The San Jose Mercury News* 18 April 1993 3C.

42. Mauro, Tony. "For Thomas, it's just business as usual." *USA*

Today 3 November 1994 2A.

43. Associated Press. "Radioactive cloud drifts over Siberia." *The Orange County Register* 8 April 1993 A16.

44. "Soviet Reactor Spews Cloud of Death Fears." *The Chicago Tribune* 29 April 1986 News 1.

45. "EPA Says Air Worse but Still Breathable." *The Chicago Tribune* 21 May 1986 News 5.

46. *The Orange County Register* 6 June 1993 Close-up Section.

47. Sala, Darlene. "Giving a Ray of Hope to Chernobyl Victims." *The Los Angeles Times* 29 April 1993 B11.

48. Seely, Robert. "West's Help for Chernobyl Area Falls Far Short of Expectations." *The Los Angeles Times* 27 April 1993 A6.

49. "Chernobyl fallout found on Mont Blanc in France." *The Orange County Register* 17 June 1993 News 31.

50. News Dispatches. "Chernobyl Affects 800,000 Children." *Newsday* 14 October 1993.

51. Cooke, Robert. "Cancer in Children Up Near Chernobyl." *Newsday* 3 September 1992.

52. Tye, Larry. "Across US, public's confidence in police officers takes a plunge; Mistrust follows LA case, other reports of beatings." *The Boston Globe* 15 July 1991.

53. "Victim of videotapes police beating released without charges." *The Chicago Tribune* 7 March 1991 News 10.

54. Anderson, David C. "The L.A.P.D.'s Thin, Savage Blue Line." *The New York Times* 21 July 1991 D16.

55. Reinhold, Robert. "Violence and Racism Are Routine In Los Angeles Police, Study Says." *The New York Times* 10 July 1991.

56. Davis, Mike. "The Uncritical Eye: Has the LAPD Really Changed?" *The Los Angeles Times* 9 May 1993 M1.

57. Cross, Jane, *The New York Times*, "Fellow parishioners of Stacey Koon question fairness of the verdict." *The Orange County Register* 19 April 1993 News 7.

58. Froomkin, Dan. "L.A. still may face flash points when officers sentenced." *The Orange County Register* 18 April 1993 News 16.

59. Levenson, Laurie L. "The Trial Is Ended; Now Ours Begins." *The Los Angeles Times* 19 April 1993 B11.

60. Lee, Patrick. "King Verdicts Let L.A. Turn Focus Back on Inner City." *The Los Angeles Times* 22 April 1993 A3.

61. Lindner, Charles L. "Lesson of the King Case: The Risk of Shuttle Justice." *The Los Angeles Times* 25 April 1993 M1.

62. Maglalang, Michelle. "Was peace held hostage in Los Angeles?" *The Orange County Register* 26 April 1993.

63. Flanigan, James. "After Verdicts, Hopeful Days Are Here Again." *The Los Angeles Times* 19 April 1993 D1.

64. Trotter, Jim. "Guilty, an ugly word — but not on this day." *The San Jose Mercury News* 18 April 1993 1A, 26A.

65. McGreevy, Patrick. "Vivid video focused public on brutality, demands for reforms." *The Arizona Republic* 18 April 1993 A17.

66. Berger, Joseph. "A Badge Is Less a Shield When Police Go Too Far." *The New York Times* 9 May 1993.

67. "Tough Questions for Hard Times." *Newsday* 17 October 1992 16.

68. Kranish, Michael. "Aides to Bush, Clinton discuss debate plans." *The Boston Globe* 1 October 1992 1.

69. Frisby, Michael K. "Perot Upsets Bush, Clinton Strategies." *The Boston Globe* 23 May 1992 1

70. Kamarck, Elaine. "Clinton Explains and Makes Voters Believe." *Newsday* 17 October 1992 73.

71. Goldberg, Nicholas. "Won't let up despite lead." *Newsday* 21 October 1992 3.

72. Goldberg, Nicholas. "Clinton has answers on all fronts." *Newsday* 29 October 1993 5.

73. Wilkie, Curtis. "Clinton sees damage in Florida." *The Boston Globe* 4 September 1992 6.

74. Mankiewicz, Frank. "Clinton Needs to Stick to His Strategy." *Nwsday* 27 October 1992 79.

75. Ailes, Roger. "What ails Roger." *U.S. News & World Report* 21 November 1988 21.

76. Henry, William A. III. "Are the media too liberal?" *Time* 19 October 1992 46.

77. "Don't ask, don't tell, don't legislate." *The Chicago Tribune* 26 September 1993 C2.

78. Greenberg, Paul. "Waffling, shuffling and invoking an unfair gay policy." *The Chicago Tribune* 23 July 1993 15.

79. Kasindorf, Michael. "Compromise; Clinton's decision on gays in military pleases few." *Newsday* 20 July 1993 5.

80. Mona Charen, Mona. "The Real Reason Gays Want Services to Admit Them." *Newsday* 30 March 1993 81.

81. Jackson, Derrick Z. "Hysteria in the military." *The Boston Globe* 12 September 1993 A7.

82. Howlett, Debbie. "Retired top brass back ban on gays." *USA Today* 3 June 1993 1A.

83. Howlett, Debbie. "Gay sons, daughters lend 'a face to debate.'" *USA Today* 1 June 1993 10A.

84. "Homosexuals Serve in Doubt and Secrecy." *The Salt Lake Tribune* 18 April 1993 A-1.

85. Solowsky, Adam. "Tufts hit for ban of forum on gays in military." *The Boston Globe* 25 April 1993.

86. Schmalz, Jeffrey. "Clinton's support of gays disputed." *The San Jose Mercury News* 18 April 1993 12A.

87. Tuller, David, *San Francisco Chronicle*. "Many see gays as predators." *The Orange County Register* 16 April 1993 News 22.

88. Powell, Stewart M. "Little-known policy suddenly captured national attention." *The Orange County Register* 15 July 1993.

89. Healy, Melissa. "Schwarzkopf: 'A 2nd-Class Force' If Gay Ban Ends." *The Los Angeles Times* 12 May 1993 A1.

90. Nagourney, Adam. "Gay Rights: Movement shows clout in capital." *USA Today* 23-25 April 1993 1A.

91. Warren, Jenifer. "Gay Sergeant Not Welcome in Army, for Now." *The Los Angeles Times* 28 April 1993 A3.

92. Healy, Melissa. "Servicemen See Danger in End to Ban on Gays" (continuation headline) *The Los Angeles Times* 11 may 1993 A1, A14.

93. Skorneck, Carolyn. "White House backs constitutionality of previous gay ban." *The Orange County Register* 31 July 1993 News 5.

94. Zuniga, Jose. "My Life in the Military Closet." *The New York Times* 11 July 1993 Section 6 40.

95. Greeley, Mary. "Rational Thought Needed on Gays in the Service." *Newsday* 9 February 1993

96. Harvey, Randy. "Top U.S Skater Attacked, May Be Out of Trials." *The Los Angeles Times* 7 January 1994 A1.

97. Elliott Almond. "Case of Attack on Skater Takes Bizarre Twist." *The Los Angeles Times* 13 January 1994 A1.

98. Randy Harvey. "3rd Man Jailed in Attack on Skater Kerrigan." *The Los Angeles Times* 15 January 1994 A1.

99. Reuters. "Arrests cause rift in Harding's hometown." *The Orange County Register* 15 January 1994 News 7.

100. Egain, Timothy. "Harding's hard life spent looking for a medal." *The Orange County Register* 16 January 1994 News 9.

101. AP News Service. "Year's first Tropical Storm Gaining Strength in Atlantic." *The New York Times* 22 August 1992 5.

102. Rohter, Larry. "A Million are Told to Flee Hurricane in South Florida." *The New York Times* 24 August 1992.

103. Cooke, Robert. "Unusual Storm in an Unusual Year." *Newsday* 25 August 1992 31.

104. Applebome, Peter. "Hurricane Andrew: When a Monster Is on the Way, It's Time to Get Out of Town." *The New York Times* 26 August 1992 D20.

105. Scott, Gale. "Rescuers Ready, Restless." *Newsday* 20 August 1992 7.

106. Kasindorf, Martin. "The Politics of Disaster Relief." *Newsday* 29 August 1992 4.

107. Wire Services. "More troops ordered to Florida." *The Chicago Tribune* 30 August 1992 C1.

108. Mashek, John W. "President to visit hurricane-scarred states today." *The Boston Globe* 1 September 1992 1.

109. Mashek, John W. "US to pay hurricane cost; Bush urges public's help." *The Boston Globe* 2 September 1992 1.

Chapter 5

MEDIA INTEGRITY INDEX

A Hollywood Madame makes front page headline news complete with a four-color photo showing her on the way into Municipal Court for arraignment. Is this the front page of a scandal sheet? No! It was the front page of the largest daily newspaper in Los Angeles, and *The Los Angeles Times* was not alone in this coverage. The headline told us that, amid a media crush, Heidi Fleiss pleaded not guilty.[1] Why was this story given such a spread? Plain and simple. Sex sells. The newspapers are interested in sales, and so what sells is featured day after day. It may be sex; it may be violence, but rest assured, it will be something that guarantees sales.

One columnist even claims the perfect lead for any story is sex. If the editor objects to a one-word lead, you can add other words like celebrities, money, or power. If you really want something powerful, add a religious overtone. He laments the fact that Heidi Fleiss did not make the cover of *Newsweek*, even though they gave her a three-page spread inside. Previous covers had featured "Sex and the Church," "Homoeroticism in the Military," and "Lesbian Couples." I had to agree when he suggested adding a third tenet to the familiar litany of *Don't ask, don't tell*–don't care. He wisely noted that Ms. Fleiss would follow her predecessors to obscurity in a short while, which is indicative of our media's preoccupation with boudoir behavior.[2]

What you see on your television screen and read about in your newspaper are not the stories that are of vital importance or will make the most difference in your life, but are those that are the most sensational. There is no doubt that a story of a woman who arranges sex for the fabled community of Hollywood with its recognized names grabs top interest. This top story was not a bare bones coverage of a dull day in court. She was described as "quaking in her spike-heeled pumps," wearing a Norma Kamali mini-dress (I wonder if they looked at the label to find out), which was described as the most conservative outfit she owned. Oh yes, her lawyer had on a pin-striped suit and drove a black BMW. Wow! What news! Her living room has a pillowy couch, and she lounged in a denim work shirt and exercise tights for the interview. Then we had two columns devoted to other key players in the drama.

The media, true to form, defended its coverage of the Fleiss story. Warren Cereghino, news director of KTLA-TV, said, "It's not a natural disaster, but it is a terribly interesting story and I think our viewers would like to know what she looked and sounded like in court." Would you believe KTLA thought the story was of such importance that it was one of two television stations that broke into regular programming to broadcast the arraignment live?

DO I REALLY CARE?

Do I care about such a story? No, personally I don't. It absolutely sickens me to see such stories featured as news. I abhor prostitution, but I think the sensationalism attached to this story simply highlights the depths to which too many mediamakers have sunk to make a buck. Suzanne Garment, Resident Scholar at the American Enterprise Institute, summed it up pretty well. "The real problem is that Heidi's story is so–well, bush league. Connie Chung and *Penthouse* may give a damn, but most civilians do not."[3]

Let's look a little more deeply into how disproportionately the story was featured. What other news happened on that day? The senseless murder of a beloved school crossing guard while on duty, national policy proposals, Middle East unrest, a review of American policy in Somalia after the deaths of four U.S. soldiers, the death of a U.S. diplomat in Russian Georgia, and the Pope's visit to Denver all rated inside pages. Somehow, I feel these stories were more important than the story about sex in Hollywood.

The media, however, saw this from an entirely different viewpoint. This was evidenced by the top newspaper and television coverage it received. I will never forget when, several weeks later, Heidi Fleiss was scheduled again to be in court. She appeared alone. The media had gone on to bigger and better things. The one reporter who covered her appearance was downright disappointed at the lack of interest shown by the media.

In an analysis of the media's actions, a team of peers evaluated the debacle. Here is what they found. One television channel had managed to unearth a 1975 magazine that featured an article on her family and their eating habits; CNN had sent four crews to cover the arraignment and interrupted regular programming with the proceedings as though they were as important as the Gulf War; and *The Los Angeles Times* had thought the story worthy of three front-page photos and a story every day for two weeks. In fact, they were responsible for touching off the media frenzy with the front-page story of her arrest and a detailed account of her early life and current activities.[4]

LOOKING INTO THE
SITUATION MORE DEEPLY

The media didn't stop with simply covering the court appearances and interviews with Heidi. Serious talk shows such as CNN & Co. had somber discussions on social morals, the reasons why men patronize call girls, and whether Hollywood is a modern-day Sodom and Gomorrah. Why did the media suddenly grab onto Heidi Fleiss this time when previously they had virtually ignored her antics and reputation? Some newsmen say it was only midsummer madness. They cite previous Augusts when other weird things happened: Elvis died, Nixon resigned, Saddam Hussein invaded Kuwait, Woody and Mia started their private war, and Pee-Wee Herman displayed unacceptable behavior in a movie theater. Others say the media has simply slipped its collective cogs. Tom Goldstein, dean of the Graduate School of Journalism at UC Berkeley said of the story that spread like a disease across the world, "It just seems wildly overplayed."[5]

Since Hollywood's early days, there have been stories about the major part sex plays in its life. Why the media should think it worthy of a top spot in their coverage of world events today is beyond me. It is a sad commentary on our entertainment industry, but the sensationalism the media used in capitalizing on this arrest is a sadder commentary on the integrity of our mediamakers.

As much as I loathe the profession of prostitution, I have to agree with civil liberties Attorney Edward Tabash. He says, "Let's stop jailing women for their own good." Whatever moral opinions we may have about sex for sale should have nothing to do with its legal consequences. Is the action something that should put a woman behind bars? Should we prosecute consenting adults who engage in sex for pay? Because we have religious freedom in our country, we can object to illicit sex on those grounds with reason, but that should not make it a criminal action.[6] Such a dichotomy in our thinking has given the media a golden opportunity to sensationalize stories about people like Heidi Fleiss.

AND NOW FOR THE REST OF THE NEWS

The argument that there simply wasn't any other news simply does not hold water. As we saw earlier in this chapter, there were a number of events that had been consigned to lesser positions in the paper so this sex scandal could be featured. Personally, I am much more interested in the present unrest in other parts of the world than I am in what goes on behind the bedroom doors–and I believe it affects my life in a much more significant manner. The events in Somalia affected the United States directly. We not only provided humanitarian help, we also deployed military forces,

I want to know why a diplomat was assassinated. What implications does his death hold for United States policies in the former Soviet Union? The Catholic population as well as other persons interested in religious issues were very interested in the Pope's visit to Denver. Not only had a large group attended from this area, issues vital to their personal lives were to be discussed.

Most appalling of all was that the arrest of a madam should be thought of greater news value than the senseless, violent taking of the life of someone involved in a public service. This shows the depth to which the media has sunk in providing its audience with news. It no longer serves our needs with more important types of coverage; it feeds our baser instincts.

This illustration is not an isolated event. It simply serves as an example of the type of distortion and sensationalism the media employs to sell its wares. It also serves as the perfect illustration of why we, as discerning citizens, must be very careful in our acceptance of what is placed before us. We must decide whether it is truly newsworthy, or whether it is there simply because it is sensational. Is it worthy of as much attention as it received? If it is not, then is it newsworthy at all?

OBSESSED

"Obsessed With Flash and Trash," read the headline on page one of the *Los Angeles Times*.[7] Who is obsessed? The sub headline continued the thought, "But as lines blur between journalism and sensationalism, media may give an increasingly distorted picture of society." Why did a leading U.S. newspaper probe this issue on page one? Is it because the media were undermining their own integrity and credibility by its irresponsible news making? Is it because the media by its obsession with sensationalism was giving readers and viewers an increasingly distorted picture of not only their society but of the media itself? It is because both of these results were occurring? No longer is the media respected by the public; it is suspect and held in contempt by many.

Pick any day of the week; pick any hour of the day, and you can receive the most up-to-date version of the latest tabloid headline—not from the tabloid staff, but from mainstream mediamakers. You can choose from "60 Minutes," "20/20," "Day One," "Now," "Prime Time Live," "48 Hours," "Eye to Eye," "Front Page," "Dateline," "Turning Point," "Hard Copy," "American Journal," "Inside Edition," and "A Current Affair" as well as lesser-known local programs. You will hear not only about the event, but you will also meet the participants "up close and personal" and hear the "human" side of the story. This story may have the person's permission to air, or it may be done without their permission.

A sad incidence of a such a story is that of Bill Sipple, who had saved Gerald Ford's life when the then-president was attending a San Francisco campaign rally. The media took it upon themselves to share his gay lifestyle with the public. Unfortunately, his family did not know of it. They broke off relations with him, and he died alone and broken. The families of victims of violent crimes are subjected to an almost inhuman invasion of their privacy. The media engages in badgering the friends of the grieving families, makes telephone calls at all times of the day and night, stalks the families as they come and go about their normal activities, and surreptitiously attempts to obtain information about the victim or the family.

Gone are the days when the subject of a story really had to be worthy of the honor. Gone are days when good taste and human sensitivities were taken into consideration. The definitions of news and newsmakers seem to have changed with the passage of time. While those who are considered respectable conservative news services appear to look down their noses at the tabloids and sensational programs, the fact of the matter remains that they own these papers and stations and do nothing to control or censor their coverage.

In their efforts not to be "scooped," so-called mainstream, respectable mediamakers often stoop to the same level they deplore in the tabloids. They leak names that only a short time ago would have been kept secret. This, in turn, causes the individual to become a celebrity and thus in great demand by all of the media. The public is then inundated by the flood of information about the person, soon learning more than there is to know about him or her. Some major commentators try to defend their use of the story or person on their program by claiming they are bringing balance to what the public is hearing.

As this type of media making continues to escalate and stories that once would have been sensational only in the local area in which they happened are now featured nationwide, a distinct pattern emerges. The more important the story is to the welfare of the public, the less likely it is to be featured. And conversely, the more trivial the event, the more likely it is to receive extended first-place coverage. If the event falls into a category that can be labeled as sensational or gossipy, then you can bet you will hear everything there is to hear—and then some—about it.

BEWARE OF THE BIG PRINT

How can we tell when the press has abdicated its position of reporting the news in favor of sensationalism as a come-on? Sex and violence are not the only indicators of the lack of integrity in the press. Sometimes we have other clues when their integrity is being breached. One warning signal is the headline that is out of proportion in size to importance of the subject. If type that is two inches high tells of something of national or worldwide significance, then it is probably being covered with integrity. However, if the same size type is featured for a subject that is trivial in the whole picture of life, then I would say it indicates the media's lack of integrity in presenting it.

TENSION, STRESS, AND MURDER

Newspapers across the nation headlined yet another killing spree by a postal employee. The media quickly seized the idea that the postal department was to blame for the rash of murders. Stress and bad management were cited as reasons for the violence.[9] We were then treated to an avalanche of stories about the pressure under which postal employees must work. I must admit I think this emphasis on stress in the workplace is out of proportion to the amount of pressure under which they actually do work. Ask anyone who is employed if they have pressure at work, and 99+% will tell you they are under a lot of pressure.

We must face the fact that this makes a good story; workers go berserk because there is so much pressure. What an angle! Everyone can relate to that, so we now have the public convinced that the Postal Service is a bad employer. People simply can't hack the pressure that is put on them. In reality, it appears to me that there may not be any more pressure in that job than in any other one where employees deal with the public. We cannot deny that there is more pressure on people in general today or that perhaps unstable persons were employed, but that does not indict the industry as a whole. Yet the media did not seriously take any of these other factors in consideration. This type of irresponsible and incomplete reporting serves only to force the wrong conclusions on the public and paint a false picture of the events that led to such a tragedy.

At the point in time when the reasons for such a rampage might be emerging from the investigation, the media did not even deem it newsworthy. They had already passed their verdict (unsupported by the truth of the matter), garnered their headlines, and were now ready to seize the next shocker with which they could hold the public's attention. The ironic part of it all is that probably one of the reporters will receive an honor from his or her peers for excellent reporting on the event even though neither the whole truth was honored nor the sensationalism condemned.

OUR TROOPS ARE...

I believe both the Gulf War and the crisis in Somalia also indicated a lack of integrity in the media. While I am sure some of what the media presented was done in innocence after having been fed false information, I think they intentionally presented programming they knew to be in error. Many veterans of the Crisis in the Gulf told of participating in staged news coverage, which was later presented as spontaneous.[10] Journalists had to sign papers agreeing to abide by the press regulations before they were granted visas. All dispatches had to be cleared through military censors, and no major network joined the several small news organizations in filing the suit that challenged the Pentagon on this issue. I think that failure in itself compromised the media's position to present an honest evaluation of the situation.[11]

They further compromised their integrity by failing to report on the events as disinterested parties on the crisis. Upbeat images and messages were shown on the nation's TV screens, and the public saw and heard the media become spokesmen for the government. Never before had military actions been reported in terms of first-person pronouns. Instead of the Air Force attacking Iraqi positions, "we" attacked them. "Our" personnel participated in the events. This usage of personal pronouns served to help rally support for the United States position in the Gulf War. We were shown bombing results that were absolutely fantastic in their accuracy; however, recently reports have begun to leak out that belie these results. I think Napoleon was right when he said you don't have to completely suppress the news; all you have to do is delay it.

In spite of continuing reports that chemical weapons were not used by Iraq, some veterans are now claiming they were attacked by chemical weapons but told by their wartime commanders not to discuss it. The Pentagon denies there were any chemical attacks during the war. Interestingly enough, Czech officials say their soldiers measured traces of Sarin, a nerve gas, while in the Gulf, but the levels were not health threatening. However, their military officials investigated symptoms similar to the American complaints among the Czech personnel who served in the U.S.-led operation against Iraq. There were also reports of British soldiers being affected by the same symptoms.[11] If our news teams had been free to report conditions as they actually were, I wonder if the families who have had to deal with this mysterious illness would now be receiving more support and sympathy from both military and civilian sources? I am sure it was very demoralizing to return home ill from a war and be told, "Yes, we know you are sick, but we're sure you didn't get it in the Gulf."

The major networks supported the Administration's decision to send troops into the Gulf region. Guests who were opposed to the decision simply did not appear. When ABC's Sam Donaldson was questioned about the lack of an opposing voice, he explained, "It's difficult to play devil's advocate, especially against such a popular president as

Bush." In other words, we've surrendered in our mission to present the truth. In an evaluation of the position of the mass media in relation to public opinion, Martin A. Lee and Norman Solomon state, "Analysts often wonder whether mass media shape opinion or merely reflect it. Coverage of the Gulf crisis showed that U.S. news media primarily reflect the opinions of official Washington, thereby shaping public opinion. American journalism surrendered to the U.S. government long before Iraqi forces did on the battlefield."[13]

WHERE IS THE TRUTH?

Forces returning from Somalia told a far different tale from what was being presented in the news.[14] They told of being placed on wartime status, exceeding legal service hours during peacetime, and fighting that was much fiercer than was portrayed in the newscasts. Troop build-up and weapons dispersal were much more concentrated than the public was told. As the returned troops said, "We knew we were at war, whether or not the public was told. We understood the orders were coming down from the top." I ask this question, Why were we not told the truth? Was this a cover-up by the administration of an illegal seizure of power? Was it a conspiracy between the administration and the media to bring about some part of their liberal agenda? Or was it a cover-up by the media for other reasons? I would like to know the truth. Wouldn't you?

TOM'S ADVICE

I like Thomas Jefferson's sentiments. He suggested that newspapers be divided into four sections: "Truth, Probabilities, Possibilities, and Lies."

Each section would be clearly labeled. He indicated the first section would be very short. I wish the mediamakers of today thought as he did. People deserve the truth and are capable of making their own judgments from it.

Acknowledging the importance of a free press, Jefferson said, "The press must be its own censor. Freedom of the press cannot be limited without being lost." However, he also believed in the inherent ability of people to be discerning. "The firmness with which the people have withstood the late abuses of the press, the discernment they have manifested between truth and falsehood, show that they may safely be trusted to hear everything true and false and to form a correct judgment between them."

STOP TELLING US IT'S WHAT WE WANT

It is imperative that the media stops using sensationalism, a pre-defined point of view, and cover-up in its reports. They must start using truth and integrity as the yardstick by which they measure the importance of the stories to be covered. The value they place on a story must not be determined by its shock value or its sensual appeal, and they must present all the facts. Its place must be determined by its value to our society as a whole and its position in the overall picture. The fact that the media seems to feed on the shallow and sordid aspects of our life indicates that they place a lesser value on important issues than they do on titillating stories. What is even worse is that the media has brainwashed us into believing we are all sexual, moral, and ethical deviates, so these stories are where our interests lie.

It may be that we are seeing the efforts of a

group with superficial interests in what we read and what we hear and see on the television. It may be that because of their own shallowness, they have lost the ability to discern what are the important issues of life and what should be covered as news. I simply do not buy the story that the reason they are filling the media with such trash is that the public "wants" these stories. Our human nature probably leads us to enjoy sensational accounts, but I think we also have a side that cares deeply about important issues and wants to know about them. This better side of our nature is not being served by a media that focuses almost exclusively on the scintillating.

The media cannot use the excuse that there is no other news that can be covered day after day. All you have to do is look at your daily paper to see that important stories are buried in back pages while the sensational story of the day is plastered all over the front page. This lame excuse is used to hide the real reason–the lurid or sensational story grabs the attention of people, and thus increases sales. The media has succumbed to the allure of gold at the expense of integrity and responsibility. They placed their credibility on the auction block, and it was purchased by the greedy to be used by the unscrupulous.

THE MEDIA INTEGRITY INDEX

To help you better understand what I am see-ing today in the media, I offer you the Media In-tegrity Index. This index plots the integrity of the media over time. Two facts seem to emerge. The first is that integrity in the media has diminished. In other words, as the years have progressed, the media have used less and less integrity in its re-porting. The second fact, as maintained in the previous chapter, is that the more significant, and hence the more controversial and sensational, the event the less likely the media is to report it with integrity.

Unlike the Dow-Jones Industrial Average, which has its highs and lows but over the long term trends upward, the Media Integrity Index has continued to spiral downward. The more significant or controversial the event, the more likely the media will distort the truth.

Insignificant events are reported with integrity, even though often it is in a perfunctory and almost aloof fashion. Small errors in insignificant matters are faithfully corrected, but the headline stories almost always remain as they are first reported. Unfortunately, when the truth is uncovered at a later date, the media often no longer considers the story important. Along with this is the penchant the media has for isolating the facet of the story that can be sensationalized and then blowing it all out of proportion.

It's rather like the man in a debate who knows his arguments are weak, so he substitutes volume. The media is short on documentation that will support the story, so they resort to sensationalism, thus revealing their lack of integrity. If all events were reported with integrity, they would stand on 1) whether they were honest in their content; 2) whether they could be documented; and 3) where they fit in the overall events of our lives. The Media Integrity Index illustrates this trend in the way in which events are reported.

MEDIA INTEGRITY INDEX

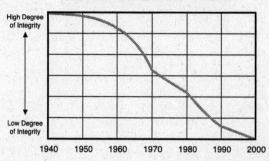

As you can see, the degree with which the media reports the news with integrity has decreased as time has passed. During the period of World War II and shortly following, the media prided itself on accurate reports. The truth was an important commodity. They clearly saw their responsibility to present the facts when they reported what was happening in the world. The fifties were a time of growth and prosperity in the United States. The media provided a sounding board for mainstream Americans and their values. While some of the stories that emerged during this period were sensational in themselves, the media in general did not try to take the trivial and turn it into a "breaking story."

During the sixties, however, the picture began to change radically. Special interest groups realized the importance of the media to their causes and began to solicit their support. Those in the media who agreed with the groups' agendas were only too glad to use their positions to assist. We began to see the proliferation of headline stories that highlighted special interest causes. Whether the story could be supported by facts began to assume less and less importance. The story was what really mattered.

During the Vietnam era, we watched the real power of the media emerge. The war erupted in our living rooms via the television tube. Various groups and their agendas were featured extensively. The public was subjected to a constant barrage of pressure to increase the war effort, pull out completely, let the UN handle it, and various other "solutions" to the conflict. Again, often the facts of the event were submerged under the plethora of special interest hype. Opinions instead of facts freely flowed.

As the seventies brought the close of the Vietnam Conflict and the emergence of the race for space with the Soviet Union, we were amazed as we watched men walk on the moon and shared some of the life they led in their spaceships. The media offered us not only detailed written accounts but live camera coverage of some of the most exciting events of the century.

Again, special interest groups used the media for their own agendas–education must be improved so we could be first in space; expensive technology must be upgraded constantly so we could win the space war. All aspects of life seemed to hinge on our being the victor.

The eighties brought a false sense of national well-being. As an audience, we became complacent and began to accept the wonders of "up close and personal" and first-hand coverage of everything everywhere. We did not stop to ask if what we were seeing had been manipulated. We blindly accepted it. If we saw it on TV, then it must be true.

Unfortunately, that led to the subtle change

we now see in all phases of the media. The facts are no longer a primary issue in coverage. Instead, the questions, "Will it sell?" "Will it bring top ratings?" "Will it serve a particular agenda?" and "How can I manipulate this story to fit my point of view?" were the prime determiners of what was to be covered as top news.

Thus, the media compromised its integrity. They soon discovered that stories of no real importance could be blown all out of proportion, and the public would eat them up. The story did not have to be significant to attract readers and viewers. In fact, the mediamakers soon discovered that the shoddier the merchandise, the more buyers there were. The public bought sex, blood-and-guts violence, pornography, and wild gossip eagerly. They did not seem to care about the facts anymore, either. Thus, there was no deterrent from the public to the lack of integrity presented by the media.

While this is what I have observed happening to the media over the years, I do not think it is an entirely hopeless picture. It is simply a situation that will be remedied when enough people voice their disgust at this downward spiral and demand a change.

You ask me how to cure the problem? Unfortunately, because this generation of mediamakers has been a while in the making, it will take time to create a different type of mediamaker. The one thing we can do today is start being discerning in what we accept from the media; object when we feel there has not been the proper sort of coverage; and withdraw our financial support of those mediamakers who consistently compromise their integrity with sensationalism. If it doesn't sell or rank high in the ratings, rest assured they will discontinue their present approach and try something different.

If they think the public wants the "real news," that is what the media will offer. Let your voice be heard. Don't just sit there and blindly accept what they offer. Demand that the media give you something better.

BUT I'M ONLY ONE

It is easy to think that one person will not make any difference and so do nothing, but many thousands of "ones" can make a tremendous difference. We will take a closer look at Ross Perot later in the book; however, let me state at this point, his United We Stand America is a prime example of the success of this approach. This grass roots organization has attracted many thousands of Americans who want to resume leadership of their country. Unable to function effectively by themselves, they have banded together to create a collective voice that will make a difference.

Don't make the mistake of thinking you are the only person that objects to the direction the mediamakers are going. An indication that the public in general is dissatisfied with the media is the new low of people who watch the major television networks.[15] Viewing has fallen five percent to sixty percent of the viewing audience during prime time. Cable channels are slowly but surely taking their audience from them. Viewers are saying, "I don't like it, so I'm not watching anymore."

Another voice of one is Gary Hart who ran afoul of the media while making a bid for the presidency. Quoting from his memoirs, "The author...had the misfortune to become a pioneer of sorts in a late 20th Century test by the American media of the outer limits of its authority to inquire into the private lives of public figures, if need be by surreptitious surveillance. This book has been written as a brief against those who sought to trivialize the ideal of democratic reform by trivializing the author's life."[16]

As you remember, his ideas on political reform and his efforts to implement them were submerged by the media in tales of his sexual indiscretions. Although it came years later, *The Good Fight* was the result of one man's efforts to undo the mischief wrought by the media.

Others such as Charles J. Givens, financial wizard, have bought space in the newspapers to answer libelous charges that appeared in another arm of the media. After an allegedly libelous article about him appeared in the May 17, 1993, issue of *Newsweek*, his Chief Counsel, David Tedder, took a full page in *USA Today* to answer the charges and to advise the public of the truth about his organization, through which he claims to have helped thousands of people straighten out their financial woes.[17]

BAND TOGETHER FOR ACTION

A group of average Americans have formed the American Family Association, a million-member non-profit group dedicated to standing up against the filth on television. Although the group has been in existence for seventeen years with a good record, they now feel the time has come for the caring American public to force smut off the airwaves and out of the living room. I do not consider myself prudish, but I find I too am upset by the filth being aired today. It far exceeds the bounds of decency, especially for children. You see, you are not alone, and there are at least a million others just like you who have already spoken out for a responsible media.

Groups like these encouraged the founding of World Focus, an organization dedicated to restoring family values and strengthening the moral fiber in America today. In an effort to help families find an alternative to the infidelity, profanity, nudity, racial hatred, alcohol, drugs, sex, and violence found in the media today and provide quality education and entertainment, they published *Manna Magazine*, a resource catalog/magazine that is filled with videos and audio tapes that can be ordered and articles by celebrities who also hold similar values.

Groups representing the older population and minority groups have been formed to insist that all Americans be honestly represented by the media. The older Americans feel that most TV programming presents them in absurd, unflattering, and stereotypical characterizations. The minorities simply want their real lives portrayed–not just the comedy situations. They are also tired of seeing only white America in most programming. They are part of America too, and they feel it is time the media recognized it.[18]

A good friend of mine, who happens to be a young, smart, exuberant African-American, recently told me of his anguish over the media's portrayal of blacks on TV. His perception is that our airwaves are full of deceptive characterizations of young black people. He cited the television show "America's Most Wanted," as typical of the programming. He counted the number of criminals being arrested on a few of the shows. He found that nine out of ten persons arrested were black. He then questioned me, "How will I explain it to my kids when they ask me, Why are all the black people being arrested?"

I ACCUSE

Like a breath of fresh air, however, you have a member of the media censuring the profession occasionally. Suggesting that they take Shirley MacLaine's speech to the American Society of Newspaper Editors seriously, Sarah Vradenburg, commentary editor for *The Akron Beacon Journal* quotes her as saying, "Until the media begins to acknowledge the wellspring of faith that nourishes the heart of America, any who claim to act from love of God will be portrayed as religious fanatics, and people who act nobly, from deep conviction, will continue to be lumped in with bombers, suicidal maniacs, ethnic warriors, and fools."

Ms. Vradenburg also asserts that today much of journalism is an insensitive collection of facts with no framework to shape them into meaning or truth. The media's failure to honestly portray the many positive facets of American life may render the media irrelevant and thus cause them to be written off in future historian's eyes.[19]

LET'S DO IT!

Until the media begins to examine its penchant for sensationalizing the trivial and returns to responsible reporting, the public will continue to be bombarded with trash instead of news and good programming, and we will have to examine with care what we are being fed. Are we falling into the trap of exclaiming, "Would you believe what was the top story today? Wow!" or are we looking beyond the headlines or the breaking story for the real news—the stories that really have an impact on our lives?

Will you then join your voices with those already protesting an irresponsible media and insist on the truth and elimination of trashy programming. If enough of us feel strongly enough to get up from the couch, we can make a difference.

Let's do it!

WORKS CITED

1. Hubler, Shawn and Ford, Andrea. "Amid a Media Crush, Fleiss Pleads Not Guilty." *The Los Angeles Times* 10 August 1993 A1.

2. McGrath, Dan, writer for McClatchy Newspapers. "Madam Heidi is not the only one selling sex." *The Orange County Register* 15 August 1993 Commentary 3.

3. Garment, Suzanne. "Don't Cry for 'Heidigate' Victims—Sex Won't Spoil Success." *The Los Angeles Times* 15 September 1993 M1.

4. Hubler, Shawn and Bates, James. "Heidi's Arrest Is the Talk of Tinseltown." *The Los Angeles Times* 1 August 1993 A1.

5. Fire, Faye and Pristin, Terry. "Heidi Fleiss and the Midsummer Media Madness." *The Los Angeles Times* 14 August 1993 A35.

6. Tabash, Edward. "Stop Jailing Women for 'Their Own Good'." *The Los Angeles Times* August 1993.

7. Shaw, David. "Obsessed With Flash and Trash." *The Los Angeles Times* 16 February 1994 A1.

8. Shaw, David. "Instant Celebrities Are Sometimes Seared by Media Spotlight." *The Los Angeles Times* 16 February 1994 A1.

9. Billiter, Bill. "Stress, Bad Management Cited in Violence." *The Los Angeles Times* 7 May 1993 A38.

10. Nicolos, Michelle and Chow, Robert. "Why post offices are flash points." *The Orange County Register* 7 May 1993 News

11. Albert, J. S. "Postal violence: Cycle of despair turns tragic." *USA Today* 12 May 1993 13A.

12. Personal interviews with military personnel who wish to remain anonymous.

13. Lee, Martin A. & Solomon, Norman. *Unreliable Sources: A Guide to Detecting Bias in News Media* New York: Carol Publishing Group, 1991.

14. The Associated Press. *The Orange County Register* 30 July 1993 News 22.

15. Lee, Martin A. and Solomon, Norman. *Unreliable Sources: A Guide to Detecting Bias in News Media.* New York: Carol Publishing Group, 1991.

16. Personal interviews with military personnel who wish to remain anonymous.

17. Jensen, Elizabeth. "CBS, ABC, NBC Hit a New Low in TV Viewing." *The Wall Street Journal* 20 April 1993.

18. Kirsch, Jonathan. "An Oddly Bloodless Memoir of Gary Hart." *The Los Angeles Times* 26 May 1993 E4.

19. Tedder, David. "So, Here's the Real Story, Janie!" *USA Today* 27 May 1993 5A.

20. DuBrow, Rick. "TV Violence Isn't the Only Issue." *The Los Angeles Times* 31 July 1993 F15.

21. Vradenburg, Sarah. "Largely faithless media invite irrelevancy." *The Orange County Register* 7 May 1993 Metro 9.

Chapter 6

O. J. SIMPSON

Just when you think you've seen and heard it all, something happens to prove the media have only scratched the surface in its use of distortion and violence to sensationalize a story. The event that brought it all home was the never-ending saga of O. J. and Nicole Simpson.

The calvacade criss-crossed the freeways and finally came to a stop in front of a mansion. An estimated 95 million people across the country watched the slow-speed car chase on June 17, 1994, as O. J. Simpson reportedly held a gun to his head threatening to kill himself while his friend, Al Cowlings, drove toward the Simpson home. In the Los Angeles area, no other programming was even offered by the major networks. Along the way, fans cheered the fugitive, video cameras were everywhere snapping pictures of the folk hero suspect as he passed by, and the media went ape in its coverage. Across the nation, there simply was no other news that day. The mile-by-mile chase was captured on film and the public sat entranced for hours watching their television sets as the spectacle unrolled.

Announcers' voices seemed almost disappointed as the so-called chase ended quietly in front of O. J.'s home. Simpson had not killed himself and there were no dramatic attempts to escape. He surrendered quietly after some minutes and was taken away to be booked like any other suspect. KFI-AM, Los Angeles, exhibited the ultimate thirst for sensationalism when it asked its listeners these questions: "Weren't you upset and let down by the lack of a crescendo? How many of you were really hoping for a suicide; for O. J. to blow his head off right on national TV?" What an appalling assumption on their part that viewers would actually want this conclusion to the drama!

However, they were not alone in this type of irresponsible approach. Not willing to sacrifice sensationalism for honesty, *The Los Angeles Times* headlined the story, "Simpson Held After Wild Chase."[1] This, of course, must have brought many a chuckle from those who had witnessed the calvacade's orderly procession across two counties.

Was this the set of one of Hollywood's latest trips into violence? Indirectly, yes. Oliver Stone purchased the rights to use this footage in *Natural Born Killers*, an ambitious film that takes on America's obsession with mass murderers and tabloid TV. However, it occurred in real life right on the freeways of Los Angeles and Orange Counties as O. J. Simpson made his way from Laguna Hills to Brentwood to be arrested for the murder of his wife and her friend, Ron Goldman.

As the calvacade passed the motorists who had been cleared from the freeway lanes to the shoulders, O. J.'s fans cheered him on. Cries of, "Save the Juice," "We love the Juice," "Go O. J.," and "Free O. J.," were heard and notes fluttered as people yelled encouragement to him. There seemed to be no concern on the public's part that two people were dead as the result of a particularly brutal assault. They wanted their hero to know they supported him 100%. He was still their hero.

A FOLK HERO

How did this hero evolve? It started some years before when O.J. Simpson was a college football star. The media had found a perfect success story;

a kid from the wrong part of town who had dabbled in gang activities and then gone on to become one of the most outstanding football players ever. His prowess on the field was legendary, and his engaging smile and winning ways captivated crowds everywhere.

Simpson had a successful pro career with the NFL's Buffalo Bills and then went into sports casting and ultimately acting. The consensus of opinion when he was elected to the University of Southern California's Athletic Hall of Fame in April, 1994, was that here was a man who really deserved the honor, and in fact, the honor may have even been overdue.

The media coverage had allowed the public to think they really knew this man when, of course, they only knew the image the media allowed to be presented. The man himself remained hidden. As one journalist so ably expressed, "We thought we knew him when we didn't know him at all. We just thought we did."[2]

He was a popular guest in the posh spots of Beverly Hills. His beautiful wife, Nicole, added to his image as the "poor boy who had really made it." O. J. was only too happy to acknowledge his fame, sign autographs, and generally make the clientele feel appreciated and welcome. Some people even felt he was the perfect celebrity, the kind who remained approachable.

Fans were not even particularly disturbed when the O. J./Nicole tie began to disintegrate. After all, they were still seen together in what appeared to be normal circumstances, and divorce was not a stranger among celebrities. The children appeared to be a strong link in the couple's relationship.

Even the charges of spousal abuse that Nicole had brought against him in 1989 failed to dampen his fans' spirits. The police and other authorities appeared not to treat it as a particularly serious matter. It was not until the release of the infamous 911 tapes during the pre-trial hearings that the public began to question whether there was another, darker side to this popular man.

A BRUTAL CRIME

Audiences were appalled as the newscasts on June 13, 1994, made the shocking announcement that the brutally slain bodies of Nicole Simpson and her friend, Ron Goldman, had been found in front of her condominium. It appears that only the police seriously considered O. J. Simpson as a possible suspect at that time. In fact, there seems to be evidence that the police efforts concentrated on linking him to the crime to the exclusion of seriously exploring other possibilities. As early as June 15, *The Los Angeles Times* headlines read, "Police Sources Link Evidence to Simpson." According to the article, this evidence was blood, and these sources informed the public that Simpson could be arrested in a matter of days.

GUILTY!

These same police sources also revealed they were focusing on stalking as the motive. The infamous 911 tapes on which Nicole is telling the dispatcher that "He's going nuts!" while O. J. is heard in the background yelling and then kicking the door down were cited as evidence that O. J. stalked his wife with a vengeance, and her murder was the alleged final act.[3] As Nicole Simpson's family began to release additional information that pointed to the conclusion that Simpson was indeed a brutal man who had finally taken spousal abuse too far and had killed his wife, the media began to capitalize on this aspect of the case. It appeared they equated a spousal abuse charge with murder.

The police sources also stated that the DNA tests would prove his guilt. This fact alone disregarded the possibility that the evidence might be disallowed due to its controversial nature. Then, within hours of Simpson's arrest, District Attorney Gil Garcetti went on the air to speculate what the defense strategy would be. It was obvious such grandstanding was for political purposes because of the high profile nature of the case.

THE MOST PUBLICIZED TRIAL

This interlude ushered in what was undoubtedly one of the most publicized and televised pre-trial hearings and trial in history. Beginning with an audience of five million more than watched the 1994 Super Bowl, unprecedented numbers continued to watch each part of the drama unfold. There were even newscasts of people calling in "sick" just to stay home and watch the O. J. saga. Others took personal days so they could glue themselves to the boob tube.

Clearly, people were hooked on the trial. CNN, which aired the trial live, reported that their daytime ratings quadrupled.[4] "NBC Nightly News," "CBS Evening News," and "World News Tonight" on ABC also saw their ratings rise. This increase was attributed to Judge Ito's cutting off trial proceedings early enough to be included in the evening news coverage.[5]

Regular programming was pre-empted as the networks vied for news audiences that often favored CNN. In July, 1994, ABC took the top honors.[6] This blacking out of regular programming did not receive a universally favorable response from area residents. People began to grumble about having only O. J. available to watch. In fact, I had to laugh one evening while I was dining out as I overheard a woman exclaim to her friend, "I'd kill for just one episode of my soaps!"

However, after the trial had ended, a female acquaintance who had faithfully followed the trial every day said this about it. "I don't enjoy the soaps, but I enjoyed the O.J. trial. I learned a lot about how the law works, and I heard a lot that people who saw only the news didn't."

On August 13, 1994, *The Los Angeles Times* announced that the media would not be permitted to see the victims' photos because of the likelihood that they would influence jurors. Judge Lance Ito also took action to limit the coverage of the trial–coverage that has exceeded that of any other case in history.

Ito cited the media's behavior as one of the reasons. "Most of the news media accounts have been factual. However, there are glaring examples of rank rumors, speculation, prurient sensationalism, and outright fabrication that are the result of competitive commercial journalism."[7] He went on to also criticize the news media for the microphones placed so they could eavesdrop on the conversations between Simpson and his lawyer, Robert Shapiro. This, said Ito, violated the sanctity of the client-attorney relationship.

As the hearings continued, Judge Ito found it necessary again to address the false stories being circulated by the media–in particular KNBC-TV. He clearly stated the story of the sock stained with Nicole's blood that was found in O. J.'s bedroom was untrue, unfair, and clearly prejudicial against the defendant. His anger was evident as he threatened to close the press room if the media did not exercise control in the stories they released to the public.

At another point, Judge Ito had to ban two reporters from the courtroom for violating his order against talking during the proceedings. This was in response from notes from two jurors about the news persons' constant whispering.

Normal routine attempts to verify information seem to be ignored. There were no rumors that seemed to need verification. These mistakes in information became part of the public record through repetition. This marked a black day in media integrity. What these erroneous reports did to the ultimate outcome of the trial can only be imagined. However, there is no doubt that they did influence the verdict to some extent.

Ultimately, this knowledge of the falsity of some reports during the trial brings the spotlight of scrutiny on all the news that is reported. Are the "facts" that are being reported to us each day on other subjects just as erroneous? Unfortunately, it seems to be the trend of today–go with any story that seems to be even plausible, and then hope for the best.

As the trial continued, all parties denied being responsible for the leaks that continued to be made to the media. However, no one denies they were an important part of the spin to influence the Grand Jury proceedings. The results of DNA tests, the theory that the murders were the work of a stalker, finding unmelted ice cream near the bodies, Nicole's stopping for ice cream at Ben and Jerry's, and the theory that O. J. was framed by a rogue cop in order to advance his career were all leaked to the press–not disclosed as a result of official proceedings.

Some authorities felt there could be no fair trial because of the overexposure by the media and the conclusions that had been drawn by them. It began with the news conference prior to Simpson's arrest that featured Los Angeles County District Attorney Gil Garcetti and quoted him as saying, "We saw, perhaps, the falling of an American hero."[8] Officials and the media repeatedly drew conclusions as to his guilt. They failed to acknowledge that O. J. was only a prime suspect–he had not been given a trial, and a jury of his peers had not rendered their verdict.

AN UNBIASED JURY?

Selecting a jury was next to impossible. There weren't many people who had not already heard more than they probably wanted to know about the proceedings and had already formed an opinion. This may be one reason why Simpson's attorneys called in defense experts to help in the jury selection. Defense expert Dr. Jo-Ellen Dimitrius stated, "I think it would be very difficult to find twelve people who have not already formed impressions and would be willing to keep an open mind. The amount and quality of publicity that has been brought regarding the trial has created a scenario unprecedented in my career as a consultant."[9] She then went on to say that the selection process would probably be a matter of deselecting people who were adverse to her client.

The publication of Faye Resnick's *Nicole Brown Simpson – The Private Diary of a Life Interrupted* nearly capsized the trial itself. I realize publishers are looking for sales when they publish a work, but it seems to me that the controversial and extremely personal nature of the book indicated it should not have been published until after the jury had returned its verdict. However, I guess dollar signs must have gotten in the way of ethics.

However, in time, twelve jurors and their back-ups were found. Judge Lance Ito was told the jury was racially split and a jury of Simpson's peers. However, as the trial progressed and, one by one, jurors were dismissed, it became evident that a mistrial might have to be declared because there were no longer enough jurors to hear the trial.

The public winced as the details of their off-hours entertainment were revealed and the money being spent for their sequestering was made public. Although many entertainment companies provided videos and movies free of charge to help entertain the jury, these offerings had to be approved by the court.

Defense attorney Robert Shapiro was keenly aware of the power the media wields in these cases. At one point during the preliminary hearings, he was quoted in a magazine article addressed to the Criminal Defense Bar as saying, "You have to be a media hound to win these kinds of high-profile cases,"[10]

The defense released polls that verified the black community was in sympathy with Simpson, and he was compared to Othello and Iago as being caught between the white and black worlds and collapsing under the pressure of trying to carry it off.[11]

During the trial, a *USA Today* CNN/Gallup poll found black and white Americans looked at the criminal justice system very differently. Only 33% of blacks believed the police testify truthfully–down from 52% in 1993. Only 18% were willing to believe police over other witnesses. This was also down from 37% in 1993. Fifty-five percent of the blacks believed Simpson was innocent–most believing Simpson's claim that Mark Fuhrman had framed him.

This last claim is supported by blacks who have been stopped, harassed, and accused by white police officers for no reason. "Based on their experience, African-Americans just don't trust the criminal justice system," according to Ramona Ripston, executive director of the ACLU in Los Angeles. They also feel that the police will lie on the stand to support their claims.[12]

Is this perpetuated by television shows like "Cops," which shows African-Americans being those who are arrested ninety-five percent of the time? From this portrayal, you would think that no whites ever broke the law.

Trying to analyze this polarity between the races, *USA Today* polled their readers. African-American readers answered, "Because of African-Americans' long history of discrimination, they know that justice is not a reality for them," and "We as a race do not see America or its justice system as white Americans see it. We see through the eyes of people who face injustice every day." White readers answered, "Blacks transfer their experiences and their understandable prejudice against the Los Angeles police into this trial. Whites have more faith in the justice system," and, "The answer lies less in a person's race than it does in his individual experiences." Obviously, because of previous experiences, it was impossible for the two groups to view the trial as one entity.[13]

TOO MUCH COVERAGE

It is interesting to note that a Newsweek public opinion poll late in July revealed that 85% of the public interviewed felt there had been too much coverage of the case, and 32% felt that this coverage was biased against Simpson. That there was an overkill of coverage seemed to be borne out by the fact that Simpson rated the cover of *Newsweek* three weeks in a row[14] and the cover of *Time* magazine two weeks.[15] All this before the trial ever began.

Almost all of the coverage assumed Simpson was guilty. Very little consideration was given to other theories or other suspects. At one point, reporters interviewed one another and defended their stand against the accusation they had put Simpson on trial before he was even charged.[16]

From time to time before official information was released, there were reports the weapon was a military trenching tool or a samurai sword, the attacker wore a ski mask (that later turned into a cap that was found at the scene), and that Simpson had killed himself. These reports were subsequently revealed to be false.

Other reports that seemed to have some basis in reality but were distorted by the media included the interview with the owner of the knife store where Simpson allegedly bought the murder weapon. This supposedly fact-filled story was paid for by the tabloids, and no receipt was found for the purchase when the authorities investigated the matter. Then there was the infamous manila envelope, whose contents were the subject of massive speculation. Oh yes, did O. J. actually have $10,000 and a passport in his possession while being pursued in the Bronco? Or were they in Al Cowlings' car? Or were they anywhere?

All of these muddied the entire case. It became almost impossible to sort fiction from reality and understand what really happened, what evidence had actually been gathered, and whether this so-called evidence actually pointed to Simpson as the attacker. As the trial progressed, Americans could tune in at any time of the day and get either a commentary on, a synopsis of, or an instant replay of the trial of the century. Two months into the trial, NBC's "Today" show devoted 28 of 178 segments (168 minutes) to the Simpson case; "Good Morning America" used 21 of 204 segments (126 minutes); while "This Morning" dedicated 14 of 196 segments (73 minutes).

Bookstores reflected the publication of O. J. Simpson's *I Want to Tell You*, Faye Resnick's *The Private Diary of a Life Interrupted*, and Sheila Weller's *Raging Heart* by posting sales in the top ten. All of this before the trial was over and all the evidence was in. Although a new California law prohibits Al Cowlings from publishing his version of the freeway chase until later, he has already given notice that a book will be forthcoming. I am sure Marcia Clark will also enjoy the few million she received for her story.

MEDIA IRRESPONSIBILITY

The media's irresponsibility was evident when all of the early false reports were relayed to the public as official accounts. Even Nicole's therapist violated confidential information when she took to the airwaves to discuss the issue of spousal abuse and Nicole's fear of O. J. At one point, the media even discussed how this case had a much larger meaning–the destruction of the black male role model–which again illustrated how they used a top story to drive a wedge between two ethnic groups instead of trying to bring them together.

At no point did the media attempt to censor what was being broadcast. They offered as much as they could to the public, and it didn't really matter whether it could be verified or not. Each network and station tried to outdo the others with the latest scoop in this unending story.

Geraldo Rivera ran a quarter-page ad in *USA Today* claiming "Rivera Live on CNBC is *the* O.J. Simpson Show." He supported his claims with quotes from three prominent journalists.

The networks spent hours trying to determine whether Simpson was receiving preferential treatment while under arrest. His visitors were carefully monitored by the media, and they issued continuing reports on his daily activities. One became sickened by the incessant tabloid coverage. Every issue of every tabloid had one disgusting account after another of absolute garbage and pure speculation.

Nationwide, lawyers cashed in on their analyses of the proceedings. Even Marcia Clark's alma mater saw an opportunity to sell itself and hired a public relations firm to promote its professors. The media capitalized on these opportunities, and one law professor reported he got from 15 to 25 calls from the media each day.

Even *American Health* found a way to capitalize on the story. Featuring "the former sports caster" on the cover, the inside story, "Why Star Athletes Go Wrong," laments the fact that athletes "bred for physical violence and emotional stagnation" are the major role models for American boys. What a slap in the face for the many admirable role models that our sports scene produces![17]

In a more serious look at the coverage, the *American Journalism Review* chronicled the nation's and the media's obsession with "the passenger in the white Bronco." It discussed how tabloid events are now covered as serious news, and the ratings game plays a major role in deciding what is to be covered as news.[18]

Because of the high publicity given to the remarks of the investigators, lawyers, and judges, the public had already tried Simpson in their own minds. They were presented with evidence that is usually reserved for the trial itself and drew their own conclusions. No matter how carefully the jury was selected, they were probably not presented with much information that had not already been made public. It was probably an extremely difficult task to view already disclosed facts with an unbiased eye.

Every decision that came out of the courtroom was pondered in detail by the media. They speculated as to the reasons behind the decision, second-guessed it, and predicted the implications resulting from it. Nothing was allowed to stand on its own merit. Everything was categorized as harmful or beneficial to the defense or the prosecution. Somehow in this overkill of coverage, the original facts were lost. The fact that two people were brutally murdered was buried in speculation over some action by the key players in the courtroom drama.

At one point during the trial, NBC had to defend itself over charges they rushed to air a story that prompted a famous shouting match between lawyers on the case. This incident pointed to what a media circus the trial became, with the news media speeding to beat everyone else. They allowed no time for circumspection or thought. In the words of Gary Spence, NBC News consultant, "We're all caught up in this disease."[19]

Many mediamakers who are generally respected, such as Larry King, were caught up in capitalizing on the Simpson trial by using a teaser from the trial as a headline, and then having perhaps only a sentence or two about the trial in their commentary. This use of misleading information to capture the public's interest reeks of media distortion at its worst.

The defense team as well as the prosecution team "leaked" tidbits to the media on a regular basis for their use in the future. Many of these were never used in the courtroom, but they had a definite effect in molding media and subsequently public opinion. According to University of Georgia law professor Ron Carlson, "It's more pronounced than in any trial I've ever seen."[20]

Then the media also featured all of the many sub stories that came out of the trial–Marcia Clark's divorce and custody battle, spousal abuse, the racial issue caused by Mark Fuhrman's alleged hatred of blacks, Rosa Lopez's fleeing to her native El Salvador, Kato Kaelin (can you believe at the Radio and Television Correspondents' Associate dinner, people actually stood six deep in line to be photographed with him?[21]), DNA evidence, the parodies of the major players, and dismissed jurors.

The television movie business was not be left out either. Promptly, they made *The Return of Hunter*, which by the network's own admission has similarities to the O. J. Simpson case. Speculation was that NBC's West Coast president, Don Ohlmeyer, used the media to proclaim O.J.'s innocence because they are close friends.[22] Then Fox got into the act by producing a made-for-TV movie, *The O. J. Simpson Story*, which was proclaimed simply a story about his and Nicole's life together and not about his guilt or innocence.[23]

WHAT ARE THE FACTS?

There was no clear motive, no eyewitness, and no murder weapon—yet the media and people all over the world were ready to sentence O. J. to life in prison. Yes, there was the blood and the DNA testing that pointed to him. We also had the bloody glove, ski cap, and alleged bloody sock to contend with.

I do not think the jury was racially motivated (Mark Fuhrman not withstanding). All they needed to acquit O. J. was a reasonable doubt. I speculate that if it were not for the media intervention and craziness, the case would have lasted ninety days, saved the taxpayers millions of dollars, and ended with the same verdict. Even with the "mountain of evidence," there were just too many holes in the prosecution's case.

The only motive that was advanced was that O. J. Simpson abused his wife and finally lost his self-control and murdered her in a fit of uncontrollable jealousy. However, there are many who do not support this theory. No eyewitnesses or murder weapon were found, while the sloppy police work continued to astound citizens around the country. Yet the media still reveled in the probability that O. J. did it.

Even though the jury found him innocent, the media has forgotten we are a nation governed by laws whose citizens are found guilty or not guilty based on those laws. Because of the wrongful death suit brought by the families of the victims, they continue to rehash all of their suppositions–whether they are based on fact or not.

Just think of the kinds of minds O. J. had to buy to defend himself: F. Lee Bailey, Robert Shapiro, Johnnie Cochran, and Alan Dershowitz. Let's assume he did not murder Nicole. "Should the media be allowed to almost force anyone to spend an entire lifetime of earnings just to defend himself?"

PREFERENTIAL TREATMENT?

Much time has been spent on speculating whether any common citizen would have received the same treatment. Obviously, the answer is no. The average citizen would never have been pursued in this way. The many other freeway chases, shoot-outs, and arrests attest otherwise. These people also do not make the headlines for any length of time, and certainly network programming is not pre-empted for the latest on their case.

As in the case of Susan Smith, whose trial for murdering her small children was held during the same time as O. J.'s, there would be public outrage against the suspect; but a public hero does not receive such outrage. The fact that O. J. and Nicole Simpson rank with the celebrities altered everything surrounding the crime. While the media would certainly have sensationalized a similar murder, the people involved made this an example par excellence of the media treatment that can be unleashed. If American legal justice is to be served, this should have been just another murder case to be tried by the California courts. Albeit, there would have been more publicity surrounding it simply because of the fame Simpson had achieved, but the Roman circus that evolved should never have been.

BREAD AND CIRCUS

The possibility remains that the media likened the American public in its mind to that of ancient Rome–give them bread and circus and they are satisfied. The gladiator in this case was, of course, O. J. Simpson, and he had to fight for his life. He was the favorite among the crowd because he was a very popular person, but the lions of the prosecution were waiting to devour him. They intended to crush him if there was the slightest error on his part.

Even though he defeated these lions in the end, the media speculated on the many reasons why he was declared innocent–and none of them included the fact he just might not have committed the crime. Doggedly pursuing him, they continue to keep his life in the spotlight.

THE REALITY GAP

The media may have just seen this as another chance to take a controversial issue, widen the reality gap, and capture an audience that would stay focused on the case until its conclusion. Evidence that this is often the case is coming to light with alarming frequency. In this case, the change in focus from the brutal crime that was committed to the crime's being the result of long-time domestic violence, which is now being declared a national problem, has increased the public's anxiety.

Many family members, friends, and neighbors who possess a volatile personality are now being viewed with suspicion, and children are being examined by medical, social service, and educational personnel with an eye to finding evidence of abuse. Many times, these suspicions simply are not borne out by the facts. Walls are being built in families and among friends by the media's emphasis on domestic violence, and innocent people are being hurt by false accusations.

This change in focus can be likened to the recent studies comparing the reality of life to the amount of risk to which most citizens feel they are subjected. Facts prove that life expectancy is increasing, infant mortality is decreasing, and the death rates from cancer and heart disease are down. However, in a recent poll, 78% of the American interviewed felt they were subjected to more risk today than their parents were. They cite such studies as those that warn of Benzene in Perrier water, Alar on apples, asbestos in buildings, aluminum and zinc as the cause of Alzheimer's disease, and various others that "prove" Chinese, Italian, French, and Mexican food all contribute to heart disease.[24]

ANXIETY ATTACK

The media have widely publicized all of these studies in recent years. Many experts now feel the media is largely to blame for the increased level of anxiety the public is now experiencing. Why? Because the media focuses on and sensationalizes those issues that most frighten their readers and viewers. The case involving O. J. Simpson was a prime example. The media preyed on those in our society who fear domestic violence and exploded those fears because of the murder.

The author of a recent study takes this conclusion one step further. He states, "Media coverage of risk issues is often unbalanced, and that does make reporters responsible for the way people react. Too often, critics say, the media provides not just essential information and legitimate warnings but unwarranted alarms for an increasingly susceptible audience, one willing to see risk in almost everything."[25]

David Ropiek, environmental reporter for WCB-TV in Boston, says, "The most fundamental failing of the media today is in their zeal to have an impact, they are 'seduced' into playing up what is dramatic." As a result, these stories are significantly coloring the public psyche, and the public is now living like "Chicken Littles being told the sky is falling."[26]

HAZARD V. OUTRAGE

Peter Sandman, a risk communication consultant, has determined that hazard and outrage are independent of one another, and the media is in the outrage business. He cites the fact that people with emotional stories to tell about the presumed hazard are usually featured by the media as the basis of a "scientific study," and the worries, fears, and concerns of people will always carry more weight than the disputes and cautions of the experts. In other words, the public is making their decisions on how upset people are about an alleged risk rather than on how likely this risk is to kill you.[27]

The environmental and food additive alarmists are cited for also misleading the public and causing undue concern. However, Bruce Ames, Director of the National Institute of Environmental Health Sciences Center, faults the media for this alarm. He states certain chemicals should be not be banned simply because it is better to be safe than sorry. "It is bad science and bad public policy, and it is bad journalism for the media not to point that out."[28]

CRIME AND DOMESTIC VIOLENCE

Another poll shows that 65% of Americans today base their feelings on crime on media reports, while only 21% base theirs on actual experience. Could the ABC, CBS, and NBC nightly news' recent concentration on crime as a topic be the reason a majority of Americans interviewed shortly after the programs aired said crime was the most important problem facing America today? Many media critics think so.

Is the focus on the O. J. Simpson case one of the reasons so many today feel that domestic violence is such a major problem in American homes? The media has skewed the focus on a high-profile event to bring about a public opinion that may not be supported by the facts. Yes, there is violence in some homes, but is it more than in the past? Or is it simply being featured at this time, so the public will think it is an increasing problem?

Whatever the reason, the fact remains that the media has taken a brutal murder, altered the emphasis, tried the suspect and rendered a verdict, sensationalized the coverage, intruded on the privacy of family members, published all sorts of unfounded information, and speculated wildly on many legal matters, all without serious consideration about what all of this would do not only to the individuals involved but also to the disposition of the case.

A FAIR TRIAL?

I am among those who feel that because of the undue amount of publicity given to the people involved and the case itself, O. J. Simpson did not receive a fair trial. By a fair trial, I mean one in which the facts of the case can be presented dispassionately and without prejudice, and a jury of his peers can be selected and permitted to make its decision. The media ensured that that could not happen.

The disturbing memory of the prejudicial manner in which the media treated a suspected murderer, the horrible memory of the gory details and upsetting graphic displays of the violence surrounding the deaths of those two innocent people, and the callous disregard for their families and the intimate details of their lives will forever be embedded in the darkest corner of my mind.

John Grisham, author of *The Client*, *The Pelican Brief*, and other well-known legal novels as well as a lawyer himself, stated he was repelled by the motion-by-motion coverage of the O. J. Simpson trial. "It's become so absurd. I make a conscious effort every day to avoid it and still it's impossible…I caught myself…hoping the judge would grant a mistrial so it would go away." He finds Court TV truly deplorable. "Banning cameras in the courtroom preserves decorum. It gives almost a level of sanctity where people are expected to behave, where lawyers cannot grandstand for cameras, where judges cannot grandstand and where each word from each witness is not dissected by 'experts'…. The Simpson trial is a perfect example of why cameras do not belong in courtrooms."[29]

Jack Kemp, ex-vice presidential candidate, summed up the thoughts of many of us when he said, "I wish the press would let the case be tried in the courts and not in the media or *USA Today*."

WORKS CITED

1. Newton, Jim, Hubler, Shawn. "Simpson Held After Wild Chase." *The Los Angeles Times* 18 June 1994 A1.

2. Alter, Jonathan. "Television's False Intimacy." *Newsweek* 27 June, 1994: 25.

3. "Police Focus on Stalking Motive in Simpson Case." *The Los Angeles Times* 4 August 1994 A1.

4. Johnson, Peter. "Cable ratings are up, even without O.J. trial." *USA Today* 28 March 1995 3D.

5. Johnson, Peter. "Simpson may be key to 'NBC Nightly News' rise." *USA Today* 15 March 1995 3D.

6. Patsuris, Penelope. "O. J. By the Numbers." *TV Guide* 30 July-5 August 1994: 19.

7 "Media Won't See Victims' Photos in Simpson Case." *The Los Angeles Times* 13 August 1994 A40.

8. Ford, Andrea. "The News Conferences." *The Los Angeles Times* 18 June 1994 A2.

9. "Simpson Defense Expert to Help Pick Jury." *The Los Angeles Times* 11 August 1994 A1.

10. Kaplan, David A. "Three for the Defense." *Newsweek* 11 July 1994: 27.

11. Cose, Ellis. "Caught Between Two Worlds." *Time* 11 July, 1994: 28.

12. Puente, Maria. "Poll: Blacks' confidence in police plummets." *USA Today.* 21 March, 1995 3A.

13. "Voices: Why do whites and blacks look at the O. J. Simpson case so differently?" *USA Today* 24 March 1995 12A.

14. *Newsweek.* 27 June, 1994, 4 July, 1994, and 11 July 1994.

15. *Time* 27 June 1994 and 4 July 1994.

16. Gibbs, Nancy. "End of the Run." *Time* 27 June, 1994: 30.

17. Hainer, Cathy. "Squeezing more out of the Juice chronicle." *USA Today* 20 September, 1994 4D.

18. Ibid.

19. Johnson, Peter. "Did NBC jump the gun in airing O. J. witness?" *USA Today* 20 March 1995 3D.

20. Mauro, Tony. "Tidbits often leaked for future use." *USA Today* 14 March, 1995 4A.

21. Estrich, Susan. "Why's Kato getting all this ink?" *USA Today* 6 April 1995 13A.

22. Bash, Alan. "Hunter movie mixes in a splash of O.J." *USA Today* 27 April 1995 3D.

23. Gable, Donna. "Tuck's defense of Fox O.J. movie." *USA Today* 8 September 1994 3D.

24. Shaw, David. "Headlines and High Anxiety." *The Los Angeles Times* 11 September, 1994 A1.

25. Ibid. A30.

26. Ibid.

27. Ibid.

28. Ibid. A31.

29. Kelly, Katy. "Not-so-trying times for John Grishham." *USA Today.* 17 April, 1995 2D.

Chapter 7

HISTORY AS ENTERTAINMENT

Amid cries of racism and Japan-bashing, the movie *Rising Sun* opened to packed theaters across the nation. This premiered-amid-protests film makes one want to question the reason for the protests. Are they legitimate or are they being staged only to increase viewership–a cheap way of insuring profit?

The special-interest groups that are part of these protests are composed of many people who are quite sincere in their beliefs but have been misled as to why a particular protest should be staged. Are the allegations of these groups valid? Some people expressed concern that the alleged racism shown in the movie, *Rising Sun*, would inflame the feelings of people and hate crimes would increase as a result. Did the movie actually portray anything that could contribute to racial strife? Was the movie actually misrepresented to the protest groups? You be the judge.

In light of the riots in Los Angeles during 1992 and the subsequent airing of hostile feelings between the African-American and Asian communities, it is easy to argue that using Wesley Snipes as the detective was a poor choice. Even though I like Wesley Snipes and think he is a fine actor, I must ask the question, Would many of the charges have been made if Michael Crichton's original character had remained the white person of the novel? What was the reasoning behind Hollywood's choice? Was it a deliberate change in order to have a more controversial plot emerge and thus be able to capitalize on the publicity and demonstrations? This idea is not beyond the realm of possibility, and I think movie makers should learn a real lesson from this incident: a bestseller is best produced with the characters and story line intact.

The media circus to which the public was subjected during the Los Angeles riots made me think of ancient Rome. Gladiators fought one another to the death while crowds looked on. All we had to do was flip on the TV and watch the duel in process. The good guys and the bad guys fought for the streets.

Fire crews were called out to battle the fires that had been set, mobs converged on stores, police set up barricades, and people tried to protect their homes. Would the rescue crews make it to the scene in time? Could they do their jobs and return safely? Would the homeowners save their homes or would the rioters destroy them? With bated breath, people were glued to their sets awaiting the outcome. All of this tragedy was treated as entertainment. Each unfolding drama was presented with an attitude that said, "And here's the next act!" History that is unfolding should not be presented as entertainment. It is news, and if it is serious, it should be presented in that light. No matter how dramatic, it cannot be presented as a diversion if the media is to preserve its integrity. Nor should historical events be used to generate cheap publicity.

How many times have you come out of a movie that received only a small amount of publicity–usually just enough to sketch the plot–and wondered why it hadn't been better advertised? The film was absolutely wonderful! A real sleeper. A case in point is *The Brothers McMullen*, a low budget production that was excellent filmfare. On the other side of the coin, how many times have you come out of a movie that was ballyhooed all over the place and felt a real let-down? It was hardly worth the effort. Why had they spent all that effort and money promoting a dud?

Except in the case of low-budget productions, it is hard to explain why good movies aren't better advertised. If they were, it would be a true public service. Why are bad films highly advertised? I think the reason is obvious. Advertising makes things sell.

In the case of a bad production, the more advertising it receives, the better chance the studio has of recouping their expenses. In too many cases, the studios have used special-interest groups to promote their offerings in order to avoid the cost of advertising by traditional means. Why pay for advertising when headlines don't cost a cent?

The coverage of *Rising Sun* with the accompanying headlines, charges by the Asian community, and four-color photographs, validates the premise that advertising was not needed. Anyone who saw a newspaper knew the movie was playing. There were many in those early audiences who went only because they had heard it was so controversial. I wonder what the box-office would have been had there been only studio advertising to tell the public a new movie was opening?

Other such movies have met similar fates. I remember the racial nonsense that accompanied *White Men Can't Jump*. I thought it was an excellent film, but I felt sad that the real message of the movie had been lost in the hype that was generated by the claims of racial discrimination, etc.

IT'S FREE!

You are laughing at the idea studios would use this type of ploy? In the event you are unaware, advertising by traditional means is expensive. And it is not as effective an audience-getter as controversy. I know a businessman with roots in Hollywood who brags he doesn't need to advertise. He simply makes sure his products receive regular write-ups in industry magazines. As he says, "Why pay for advertising when you can get it for free?"

Now you're saying, "Tony, all this sounds so commercial." It is, and on the darker side, studios are also capitalizing on the biases that already exist. I can think of no other reason for altering a character in a bestseller in the manner in which it was done for *Rising Sun*. Not only were the riots and remaining bad feelings still fresh in people's minds, but during the second trial of the police officers for the Rodney King beating, the media had consistently placed the antipathy between the Asian and the Black communities in the spotlight. Was the studio trying to capitalize on the feelings of their audience? Did they even hope that incidents of violence might arise from the showing as they had when *Colors* and *New Jack City* were first previewed?

Charges of not trying to accommodate the concerns of the Asian community were leveled by the director of UCLA's Asian Studies Center against 20th Century Fox. A USC student claimed she was denied access to a preview of the movie when she used her Asian name while trying to obtain tickets but was able to get them without difficulty when she gave an Anglo name.

The studio allegedly refused to allow a disclaimer at the beginning of the movie that would clearly state the work was fiction, and fears were expressed that the production would escalate the incidence of hate crimes. Detractors of the movie pointed to all the negatives as evidence of one studio's efforts to expand the rift now existing between ethnic groups rather than try to heal it, as the supporters of Warner Brothers claimed had happened when *Falling Down* was released.[1]

In an editorial in *The Los Angeles Times*, Mike Backes, co-writer with Michael Crichton of the screenplay for *Rising Sun*, answered the Media Action Network for Asian Americans' (MANAA) claims that the film inaccurately stereotyped people of Asian Pacific ancestry. After detailing how the Japanese had been portrayed in a range from honest businessmen to opportunistic lawyers, but not as nerdish Asian males, rude Asian foreigners, or villains (all of whom were white American males), he closed with this statement, "*Rising Sun* was never intended...to incite fear, to incite its audience to violence against people of Asian ancestry or condone or encourage racism or prejudice of any sort. It was intended to make Americans aware of the political chicanery that has allowed our foreign trade policies to become the laughingstock of the global marketplace."[2]

Where did MANAA obtain its information that said Asians were portrayed in a different light than they actually were shown in the movie? Did a studio source "leak" this information? Was it a deliberate bit of misinformation to make sure there was a protest staged when the movie was actually released? It is not beyond the realm of possibility to assume this is exactly what happened.

We can draw two conclusions from the *Rising Sun* interchange. Either the Asian community was too sensitive to honest portrayals of their members, or the media deliberately sought an area of conflict upon which they could capitalize. I suspect the truth lies somewhere in between. As human beings, we do react somewhat defensively to anything that places us in less than a favorable light.

Two facts do remain, however: 1) The Japanese corporate community operates in a manner that differs from its traditional American counterpart. How often have you heard the slogan, "Buy American"? Isn't it being heard because American industry is facing lost revenues because the public is buying both imports and products produced here in the United States by foreign based companies? 2) The Asian community was led to believe they were inaccurately portrayed in the movie.

NOBODY'S PERFECT

It seems pretty clear to me that all of these groups have forgotten one thing. All Americans come from somewhere else. Yes, you native Americans, too. I believe you came across the land bridge from Asia. We all have pages in our ethnic history that can never be erased. We can, however, learn important lessons from these mistakes of the past. Unfortunately, making mistakes did not stop with yesterday. Mistakes are still being made by people today. They may be made by people of Anglo, African, Asian, or any other ethnic descent.

The important thing for all of us today is to focus on the issue, determine whether the principle is right or wrong, and then resolve the issue on its merits–not on the background of the people involved. If this were to happen, then the media for its own selfish interests would never again be able to capitalize on a racial issue. To borrow from a well-known phrase, it would be another giant leap for mankind.[3]

Yes, I know all of this is speculation, but we should not be too naive when questioning the motivation used by the media today when making decisions. Too often, ulterior motives become quite evident later on. We have all learned this hard lesson in our personal relationships–there are people who use other people to further their own lives and interests. By the same token, there are unprincipled mediamakers who use interested parties, the audience, and the general public to further their agenda. Interestingly, no one with whom I discussed *Rising Sun* felt the movie was better than the book or the changes in character and story line improved the overall production. Again I ask, What was the motivation?

HOLLYWOOD'S GREATEST TEMPTATION?

Some time back, a movie was released with the provocative title, *The Last Temptation of Christ*. To most of us, we think back to the Biblical account. Now let's see...what was the last temptation? Right? Wrong! The temptation to which this title refers is a fictional one that author Nicholas Kazantzakis has proposed as Christ's final temptation.

The book on which the movie was based came out over thirty years ago and died a quiet death after only a short life. It was not critically acclaimed nor thought of as having theological value. Because it lacked literary or critical merit and was not subjected to an embarrassing avalanche of publicity, it could die with dignity. Not so the movie.

In what appears to be a press campaign to salvage the movie economically, "people" everywhere rose up to protest its showing. Those from the Moral Majority point of view (or so the media claimed) insisted it should never be shown, etc. When their efforts to keep the movie from being circulated failed, Jerry Falwell urged his followers to make "an all out effort to cripple Hollywood."[4] Of course, the offensive would be centered on Universal Pictures, producer of the movie. They were successful to the extent that only 130 theaters of an estimated 130,000 nationwide actually showed the movie.

Yes, I am sure the Christian community was offended by the movie. Maybe it should have been; but in the weeks that followed, crowds attended the movie anyway. Many of those attending were quite candid. "I'm here because I have heard so much about it." Without the focus on the movie because of all the demonstrations against it, I wonder how many people would have even known it was playing? I feel certain there would not have been a large enough attendance to keep the doors open past the first few days.

As it was, with reviews calling it tedious, boring, long and drawn out, the movie was taken off the screens after a relatively short run. Had there been no adverse publicity, those who knew the story would probably have chosen not to attend. Others would have waited for reaction to the film, and then opted for another choice because of the bad reviews. Some people might have gone, not knowing what they were getting into, and quite conceivably would have walked out part-way through the movie because it was so boring.

As it was, only 10-12 million dollars were grossed in sales, while estimates of 16-20 million dollars were made for the cost of the movie. Ken Wales, a veteran Hollywood producer, observed, "The protests probably added some to the box office, or at least made people go see the film sooner."[5] Obviously from this statement, movie makers are aware of the dollar value of demonstrations.

In an effort to determine why the demonstrations were made and who really was responsible for staging them, we have to look at the protests in the light of overall movie making.

Tell me, honestly, do you really think the premise of *The Last Temptation of Christ* is any more offensive to the conscience than *Oh God?* I'm sorry, but even as funny as the movie was, George Burns just did not make it as a Supreme Being. In both cases, according to Christian beliefs, the divine being was degraded.

Another incident relating to *The Last Temptation* occurred in Amherst, Ohio. Protesters of inclusion of this video in the library's collection threatened to defeat a tax levy unless it was removed from the shelves. The library board refused to yield to the pressure and kept the video. The levy passed.

In the confrontation, another title was also protested—*Getting Jesus in the Mood* by Anne Brashler. This particular book is about survivors of abuse. As a result of the publicity about the book, the library had to add eleven more copies to the three on hand to satisfy patrons' requests for the book. The Library Director, Martha Makosky, declared, "A book of literary short stories would not normally have that high a circulation."[6]

This is further evidence that publicity pays big dividends, and it doesn't really matter what is the source of the publicity. I will take this premise one step further; if the publicity does not come as a result of the merit of the work, then mediamakers believe contrived interest is better than no interest at all.

WEST SIDE STORY

Other movies have also been accompanied by protests. One of the most notable is *Colors*, a story of gang life. In this movie, real-life members of rival gangs were used in the casting. When it was released, not only did the NAACP state it should be banned, but the Guardian Angels staged protests outside the home of Dennis Hopper, the director, and co-stars Sean Penn and Robert Duvall.[7]

Of course, all of this was highly publicized by the studio. Not unexpectedly, there were gang skirmishes at the opening. Fortunately, the police department had upped security, so it did not degenerate into a full-blown riot. I imagine most of the country knew this new movie had opened because of the disturbances. However, I would bet the makers of the movie were not prepared for the final outcome—theaters everywhere dropped the film. They did not want to see the opening night's violence night repeated on their property.

I hope this serves as a lesson to producers everywhere; stirring up trouble can backfire and even destroy any hope for profit. It is better to let a production stand on its own merit rather than create controversy, especially when none should exist.

MEDIA WACKOS

Unfortunately, we also have in our midst what I call Media Wackos. They will print anything. It does not have to have even one shred of evidence to support it. We can all recall two such instances that happened a few years ago.

While the whole saga of the Snapple beverage logo was entertaining, it was absolutely ridiculous. Some "know-it-all" journalist circulated an absolutely false story that the K on the Snapple bottle represented the Ku Klux Klan and the ship stood for the slaves brought from Africa. In reality, the K stands for Kosher (it may be drunk by those who observe Jewish dietary law) and the ship is to remind us of the Boston Tea Party (a hallmark of the beginning of American independence and the fight against taxation without representation).

In light of their true meanings and the fact that the KKK is both violently anti-Jewish and anti-black, this story could only fall into the black hole of Media Faux Pas category.

The second such false story also strikes at the heart of the American value system. Proctor and Gamble is still having to combat false stories that have circulated for more than twelve years claiming their logo is a satanic symbol and their company has roots in this belief.

When I inquired about the story at their corporate headquarters, their Consumer Services sent me a packet of information including letters of reference from respected church leaders throughout the United States and reports of legal judgments against those who have continued to perpetrate the lie. The charges were termed "completely ridiculous and false."[8] The history of the logo, which represents the man in the moon overlooking thirteen stars commemorating the original American colonies, was also enclosed.

In the meantime, the Media Wackos had a field day at the expense of respected American corporations and products. I wonder what would happen if newscasters and writers had to document everything they made public? I'd bet we would see a whole lot more truth being disseminated and much less nonsense.

THE REAL STORY IS...

In a little different light, writer Joe McGinniss claimed the stir created by his book, *The Last Brother*, was really not because of the subject matter itself. He stated the furor surrounding his biography of Ted Kennedy was because the Kennedy family is still trying to control history. "If they can make me the issue, then people won't look so closely at Teddy."[9]

Now more than ever, it is important for people to try to discern the reason for a protest and whether it is justified before they blindly follow the direction the crowd seems to be going.

In much the same way, the recent flurry of biographies of prominent people has supposedly revealed intimate secrets about them that were previously unknown. Upon close investigation, these "secrets" do not appear to be true. They were invented by the authors to create a perverse interest in the book and thus increase sales.

In one such example of a lie being created, there is no evidence to prove the charges that Eleanor Roosevelt was not the morally straight-laced personage history made her out to be. Other unflattering portrayals of people who shared the limelight are equally without evidence when they are carefully investigated.

What makes this practice so insidious is that the lies are not restricted to the readership of the book making the accusation. The false stories are picked up by so-called newscasters and talk shows. They are told and retold. Soon they are accepted as truth.

Historian Doris Kearns Goodwin asks, "How else to explain the near-universal acceptance of racy stories about J. Edgar Hoover [that were] in Anthony Summers' biography? The author did not fully document his claim that the former FBI director was a gay cross-dresser who paraded about hotel rooms in skirts and feathers. Yet the tale has been retold in a PBS documentary and is now joked about so often on late-night television shows that it has, for all practical purposes, become gospel."[10]

Filmmakers did not emphasize Tina Turner's triumph over a long period of abuse and her ability to get on with her life in *What's Love Got to Do With It*, but featured her destructive relationship with Ike Turner. In the movie, taken from her best-selling autobiography, *I, Tina*, the producers seemed to think that small portion was what would draw viewers, but there was one important potential viewer who decided to stay away. Tina is quoted as saying, "Why would I want to see Ike Turner beating me up again? If I see the movie, I might just barf all over the place."

In pointing out the discrepancies between the film and her real life, she said, "I've told the real story many times, and people just don't seem to write it." In discussing viewer tastes, she ponders, "For such ugliness to be considered interesting is weird. They wouldn't make a movie on how wonderful my life is now."[11]

Did the highly acclaimed *Jurassic Park* even succumb to this type of cheap publicity? A group of scientists claimed before its release that the movie was anti-science. Dr. Russell Higuchi of Roche Molecular Systems Inc., a leading expert in genetic microbiology, circulated a condemnation of *Jurassic Park* to scientific colleagues.[12]

Since we hardly ever hear of papers that are either pro or con on other types of genetic research, I wonder why the publicity over this one? Could it be that the leak was with an ulterior motive–to boost interest in and ticket sales for the movie? Were they afraid they had only a hit on their hands and not a megahit, so it needed a boost?

Most of the people with whom I have discussed both the book and the movie feel that neither was anti-science, but both were decidedly in favor of science that uses caution when experimenting in areas that have the possibility of results far beyond what has been proven thus far.

One cannot help but also wonder if the upheavals going on in some of the major studios are contributing to the use of less than aboveboard marketing techniques. The dismissals and resignations followed by lawsuits have given us a glimpse of the inner workings of the movie business. Trust me. It's not all sweetness and light. There are some really dark, underhanded machinations occurring.

The assertions by Si Kornblit, head of marketing for Universal, that he had every intention of carrying out his marketing responsibilities for *Jurassic Park* at the time of his termination from the company raises the question, "Did someone hit the panic button because they were afraid with the head honcho gone it wouldn't be a big hit?" Did they decide to make sure of a big box office by employing these additional "advertising techniques"? Quite possibly.

I CANNOT TELL A LIE–BUT I DID

That certain of the media have base motivations for stories that are released, movies that are produced, and books that are written seems to be borne out by Norman Mailer's confession on Mike Wallace's "60 Minutes." During an interview, he confided that a Kennedy-Monroe affair and Kennedy's association with her death were very unlikely. In fact, he also went on to say he did not even believe his own fantasies. He wrote his alleged exposé of their relationship in his 1973 book, *Marilyn*, because "I needed money very badly." Mailer was the first to "expose" the relationship, and the public soon became hooked on the monumental deception. After all, it was such a juicy tidbit about two such famous people!

If one author will admit he wrote what amounts

to lies to make money, what makes us think a whole company of mediamakers will not stage whatever is necessary to increase viewership or readership?

An older colleague of mine once told me of attending a showing of *The Moon is Blue*, which had received the equivalent of an X rating during the '50s. Sitting there in anticipation, along with a theater packed with other people equally in anticipation, they waited to see the scenes that had earned it the rating. Imagine the disappointment when "the" scenes turned out to be the appearance of the heroine in a raincoat–supposedly with nothing underneath. The audience saw only the back of the woman, raincoat and all!

They went home feeling cheated after all of the publicity prior to the showing. They had been led to believe this would be a movie filled with nudity. What a rip-off!

Well, that is exactly what is happening today. Audiences are being ripped off to the tune of millions by authors, producers, and studios that deliberately create controversy over their books, plays, movies, and television shows. They do not really care what it takes to get the audience in or even whether the audience stays for the whole performance. All they want is to hear the cash register ring.

They want to stir interest and thus sales, but unfortunately for the American public, they do not want to do it honestly. Usually they do not want to present an issue that truly is controversial; they would rather create some sort of false hypothesis that makes an accepted truth debatable.

They do not want to expend the effort to create fresh, inviting stories the public will want; they would rather create a publicity stunt to salvage something that should have never been brought to life. They want to steal the integrity from the American media scene.

I say that by maintaining such an attitude and exhibiting such behavior, these mediamakers are undisciplined, unethical, and are deceiving the public. They ought not to be supported. What's the old saying? Get 'em where it hurts–in the pocketbook. Well, stop, look, and listen before you buy. What is being said? Who is saying it? Why is it being said? What do they have to gain? Do I really want to support them by buying the paper, magazine, book, theater or movie ticket? If I do support them, how will I benefit, or will I be hurt in the process? In what way? How will they gain? Do I want to help them?

ENTERTAINMENT AS HISTORY

On a more serious note, I think to the future. Our entertainment scene is going to be viewed as a part of the history of our country. What will be written? Will future generations receive a clear picture of who we were, why we believed as we did, and why we acted as we did? What will they think of the demonstrations at the movies–our entertainment–over charges of racial discrimination or insults to one's beliefs? Will they think we did not know how to separate the serious issues from the make-believe ones? Will they think we were not intelligent enough to resolve our differences through democratic processes?

I am extremely concerned we are painting a very confusing picture for future generations. While we are at the leading edge with legislation to ensure equality for everyone, we are also back in much more primitive times when it comes to expressing our disagreement with ideologies that differ from ours.

Perhaps we can learn from our Native Americans. After an early period of peaceful co-habitation, they were faced with loss of property and personal discrimination. They chose to combat the new settlers in two ways. One group chose to take up arms and "demonstrate" by fighting them. The other group, called the Civilized Tribes, fought them in the courts. I ask you to take a look back into history.

Almost without exception, those who chose the violent path did not achieve their aims. In some cases, entire tribes were wiped out. Those who chose the peaceful, lawful way eventually did achieve much of what they sought. Granted, some of these awards were delayed for too long, but more has been achieved and more will be achieved by lawful pursuit than by violence.

I sincerely hope that the media does not willfully, or even accidentally, paint an incorrect portrait of the America of the 1990s for future generations. I hope the real character of the American people is not masked by the misdirected behavior of a few.

WORKS CITED

1. Dutka, Elaine. "Asian-Americans: Rising Furor Over 'Rising Sun'." *The Los Angeles Times* 28 July 1993 F1.

2. Backes, Mike. "'Sun' Doesn't Perpetuate Stereotypes." *The Los Angeles Times* 7 June 1993 F5.

3. Armstrong, Neil. upon setting foot on the moon for the first time. "That's one small step for a man, one giant leap for mankind." 20 July 1969.

4. Sidev, K. "Last Temptation boycott gets mixed reviews." *Christianity Today* 21 April 1989: 36-37.

5. Ibid 37.

6. Anderson, G. "Temptation tempest threatens levy." *American Libraries* September 1992: 622.

7. "Gangs: will life imitate a movie?" *Newsweek* 25 April 1988: 25.

8. Smith, Anne Jenemann. Public Relations Supervisor, Procter & Gamble Company. 30 December 1992.

9. Donahue, Dierdre. "McGinniss gets hits from all sides." *USA Today* 29 July 1993 2D.

10. Getlin, Josh. "Idol Gossip." *The Los Angeles Times* 24 May 1993 E2.

11. Gunderson, Edna. "Tenacity has everything to do with it." *USA Today* 8 June 1993 A2.

12. Browne, Malcolm W. "Scientists await 'Jurassic Park' with mixed feelings." *The Orange County Register* 19 May 1993 News 12.

13. Citron, Alan and Dutka, Elaine. "Universal Pictures' Real Courtroom Drama." *The Los Angeles Times* 30 July 1993 D5.

Chapter 8

INQUIRING MINDS WANT TO KNOW

"Tell me, Michael, are you a virgin?" Oprah asked in an interview with Michael Jackson at his home. What kind of question is that? Since when is the sexual purity (or not) of a superstar something the general public needs to know about or discuss? Since when did talk show hosts receive a mandate for asking extremely personal questions and expecting to be answered? Since when did exceeding the bounds of good taste become the norm in interviews? Well, it appears, since the proliferation of the talk show.

This phenomenon has gained popularity in the past few years at an incredible rate due, in part, to the insatiable appetite both hosts and audiences seem to have for the minute personal details of someone else's life. The subject matter also has deteriorated to an array of repulsive and degrading lifestyles.

WHAT TO WATCH

Step back in time to 1993 for a moment. Let's suppose your children came home from school at 3 p.m. Your 12-year-old says he doesn't feel well. Would it be all right to just lie down on the couch and watch TV? "Of course," you say. You do not have cable TV, so he has access to only regular programming. What can he watch? Let's see. There is "Beverly Hills, 90210." This show is supposedly for teenagers. Hmmmm. Obviously older teenagers.

Phil Donahue will be discussing religious issues with the audience–which, considering the way Phil badgers people, will undoubtedly turn into a verbal donnybrook. To say nothing of the fact that only tearing down of values will probably occur. Anyway, the subject is not one of consuming interest for most pre-teenagers.

Let's see what the "In The Heat of the Night" offers–sometimes it's OK. Today, it's about three cheerleaders getting killed in a car accident. Real-life, I know, but isn't there anything that would just be pleasant and good to watch? Oprah's going to be discussing the impact of TV violence on kids.

There's always "Chip and Dale" or "Alvin and the Chipmunks." Oh yes, and "People's Court." What a wasteland! You glance through the rest of the late afternoon. Not much better.[1] "Oh well," you say as you grab your jacket. "Why don't I just run down to the corner and pick up some videos for you? I'll be back in a few." You are thinking, "We really are going to have to build up our video collection and maybe add cable. This regular TV programming is for the birds."

Don't think this day was an exception. Actually, it was one of the better days. Let me list some recent talk show programming, and you can decide for yourself. On the same day, you had a choice of:

Donahue - Children conceived after rapes
Oprah - Stepfamily issues
J. Rivers - Dating horror stories
Raphael - Children kidnapped by their birth mothers
Geraldo - Acrimonious divorces

Or let's go to another day:

Donahue - Vengeful first wives
Oprah - Violent teenage girls

J. Rivers	- Love 'em and leave 'em women
Raphael	- People who think they are becoming racists
Geraldo	- Family murder

Or yet another day:

Donahue	- Sex in prison visiting rooms
Oprah	- Interior decorating (interesting...)
J. Rivers	- Futuristic sex
Raphael	- Custodial grandparents sue their children for child support
Geraldo	- Prison visitors raped by guards[2]

While Donahue and Rivers are no longer on the air, there seems to be no shortage of hosts willing to step-in and continue with this "dysfunctional theatre."

Enough? Sorry, but it does not get any better. "48 Hours," in a television special, turned its focus on the lurid talk-show boom. Phil Donahue explained the genre, but the actual issue of how TV exploits people through exhibitionism was avoided.

Remember the class clown who would do absolutely anything for a laugh? Nothing was too embarrassing or too sacred to avoid being targeted? It seems to me that a lot of what we are seeing today on these talk shows are clowns who have become hosts and clowns who have become participants. Together, they are creating some of the most offensive and humiliating hours America has been exposed to on network television.

A perfect example of how current talk shows hosts act was portrayed in the movie *Sleepless in Seattle*. Tom Hanks is speaking with the show psychologist about losing his wife, grieving, and not being able to sleep. At the height of his emotional speech, the talk show host interrupts, "We need to take a commercial break." Frankly, I think we'd all be better off if most of the current hosts took a permanent break.

TELL ALL–OR ELSE!

Members of the media expressed their concern that Michael Jordan had chosen not to comment further on the gambling charges made against him. Even though the article that followed was written half-humorously, half-seriously, the heading read, "Jordan's silence could start disquieting trend." I ask, why is it a disquieting trend when individuals, public figures or Joe A(verage) Citizen, decide they would rather not comment on a situation? This is a free country, isn't it? We do have the right to our own opinions and our own lives lived privately (if we choose), don't we? We are not compelled to answer, are we? The media cannot force us to say anything, can they?

Back to Michael Jordan for a minute. He is perhaps the greatest basketball player of all time–one that transcends racial barriers. My son, a Caucasian, has posters of Michael all over his room and wants to be "just like Michael Jordan." Who cares if Michael gambles? I, for one, do not. Hasn't he done more for the game of basketball than anyone else? Think about all the charity games he plays and the fund-raisers he attends.

In spite of the fact that Jordan had not been accused of doing anything illegal, reports of his gambling filled the air. Concern was expressed that the repetition of the allegations would erode the public's perception of his character. Generally, the endorsement value of a star depends not only on sports skills but an untarnished personal image. I am happy to say that Michael Jordan seems to be a person who is liked and respected in spite of any personal faults instead of because he is Mr. Perfect. I have to agree with Dusty Kidd, a spokesman for Nike Inc., "The number of things you stack up on the positive side of the ledger overwhelm the things written or suggested about him over the last year or two. I think the public perceives him as a great athlete and a person to be admired."[3]

I think the way in which the media speculated on the disappearance and death of Michael's father was absolutely disgraceful. Statements made by Federal investigators fueled the flame. Instead of maintaining silence until the motive was established, statements such as "Federal investigators raised the possibility that James Jordan's business dealings may have something to do with his death," and "Federal authorities refused to say whether the investigation was looking into possible links between James Jordan's death and his son's well-known lavish gambling,"[4] increased speculation among not only the media but the general public as well.

A small question arises at this point. Why is Michael Jordan's gambling well known? Obviously, it is because of Richard Esquinas' book and media hype over his alleged gambling debts. I question whether anyone outside of close followers of Michael's movements would have known he gambles if the media had not escalated it via their ridiculous reporting.

Jesse Jackson, well known for his headline seeking statements, in calling for an investigation of the cremation of Jordan's body said, "It looks to be a part of an organized cover-up and an attempt to destroy evidence."[5] Of course, this may be the truth, but it appears more credence should be given to the statement of South Carolina coroner Tim Brown. "We were left with nobody missing in North Carolina and nobody missing in South Carolina.... It was not done lightly. I hope the family understands why we did what we had to do."[6]

Jackson did not seem to take into consideration that finding an unidentified body (and having no reports of missing persons in the area) and a community hard pressed to find public funds seem to add up to a reasonable course of action that was taken. Jackson's comments seemed to be wild accusations meant to stir up controversy. The media might have served us better in reporting only the facts as they have been uncovered instead of sharing speculations and accusations.

When Michael Jordan decided to leave professional basketball and try his hand at baseball, the media again had a field day at his expense. Instead of simply letting him do his thing, they attached their expectations to his efforts. Thus, he did not measure up because the first day of the season he did not perform as the Superstar.

Michael never said he expected to become a baseball superstar; all he said was that he wanted to play ball and do his best. The media seemed to take a perverse delight in demeaning his efforts. The ultimate insult was the *USA Today*/CNN/Gallup Poll asking whether Jordan should return to the NBA (as if it were the public's decision). When over half of the respondents said yes, the newspaper headlined the poll's results as "Poll: Jordan a gem–on hardwood not the diamond."[7]

I wonder what kind of results they would have had if the question had been, Do you think Michael Jordan should stop playing baseball? Because he is such a great basketball player, nothing made me happier than to see him return to the NBA, but I wouldn't have wanted him to stop playing baseball unless he had satisfied himself that he should quit the game and go back to basketball. Obviously, the need to play baseball was there, or Jordan would not have even tried the sport.

The men and women of the media should have let him have his chance. After all, didn't someone once say, It's better to have tried and failed than never to have tried at all? How many other superstars would even think of exposing themselves to the media's scrutiny by trying a different sport? My hat's off to Jordan for going ahead and giving it a try.

When rumors surfaced he was thinking of returning to basketball, the media cheered him on. He suddenly became the savior of not only basketball, but also of television ratings and advertising.[8] What garbage!

As much as I like and admire Michael Jordan, the success of these industries do not hinge on his returning to basketball. In all honesty, it was a great day for the Chicago Bulls and basketball because he is such a terrific player, but the rest of the world would have survived even if he had not thought of returning to basketball.

As if that weren't enough, when he first returned to the courts, the media was, unkind rather than supportive. For example, after the Bulls lost to the Magic, this comment was made. "Michael Jordan is on the brink of another sport switch. Unless the Chicago Bulls can beat the Orlando Magic twice, the basketball-turned-baseball-turned-basketball star is going to be golfing by next week."[9] With his track record, why should one loss cause a comment such as this to be made?

I could not believe how often the media focused on what Jordan's return to basketball was doing to television ratings—how NBC was capitalizing on his return, how he was now joining the Saturday lineup, how he was changing the course of TV coverage, how TNT was getting ready for Jordanmania, and how he deserved bronze for ratings boost. Then there was the article on how advertisers were cheering the Bulls-Magic NBA matchup.

Why should there be all of this irrelevant trivia about a superstar instead of concentrating on his expertise at his sport, his support of those less fortunate, and how his fans loved to see him back? I ask, Why? Could it be the media is so inward looking, they really can not see the real story for the issues that they think matter?

I am tired of a small group of the media elite trying to discredit those who have made positive contributions to our society. There is an old saying, Nobody's perfect. Well, it holds true for those in the public spotlight as well as the average citizen. Their shortcomings should not be held up as their entire lifestyle and contribution to society.

In the manner that parents tell of their children's misdeeds, discerning what is suitable for others to know and what may hurt the child's future, the media should be just as selective in what they report. Every little thing does not need to be dragged before the public. As the audience has certain things in their past, they really would not want broadcast to the whole world, so do those who are in the public eye. At times, it seems that those who "expose" our heroes do so from a base of jealousy. They seem not to be able to let someone else enjoy success and popularity.

How many faults of the mediamakers are smeared across the front pages? How often are their misdeeds broadcast as the top story on the evening news? Does this mean they are without

fault? Hardly! I contend there is what is probably
an unwritten understanding among those in that
rarefied fraternity that those stories are either ignored or if they must be made public, they are
buried as deeply as possible and given with as few
details as possible. Does this seem like responsible reporting to you–that one segment of our society is singled out as being fair game for bashing
by the media?

The ultimate irresponsible reporting seems to
be James Jordan's funeral. An Associated Press
release stated, "Michael Jordan's much-publicized
life turned very private Sunday as the NBA star
and his family said their good-byes to his slain
father." Oh, Right! The story was accompanied by
a photo of Michael being comforted by his friends
after the funeral. Television coverage was shown
across the nation. Really private! Get real, Associated Press. Privacy, according to Webster, means
"The quality or state of being apart from company
or observation: seclusion: freedom from unauthor-
ized intrusion." Are you trying to tell us that
Michael invited you to the funeral? I don't think
so. You just refused to acknowledge what you did
was an intrusion. You, the media, intruded into a
very private moment.

I must mention at this point that Richard
Esquinas, author of the book claiming Michael
Jordan had extensive gambling debts, is to be
commended for his reaction to the elder Jordan's
death. After praising James Jordan as a fine man,
he commented, "I'm not willing to speculate on
anything to do with his death. The Jordan family
has enough trouble now."[11] Although he may later
theorize about what happened, he respected the
Jordan family at a time of deep sorrow. Take lessons, Associated Press.

Does the media feel they have the right to ask questions about any subject? I would say from the questions posed by newsmen and talk show hosts, they think they hold a sacred trust that entitles them to ask all–know all. Barbara Walters is a good example of someone who asks embarrassing, deeply cutting questions that spark controversy and sometimes even rage–and people stay up at night sitting on the edge of their chairs just waiting for her to do it. If I read history correctly, no one gave anyone in the media this right, it is just a belief they have promulgated.

The narcissistic tell-all atmosphere also seems to be feeding the media negativism we are experiencing. There doesn't seem to be any good news today. What has happened to the concept of the dignity of man? To the concept there were certain things that, though they needed to be addressed, did not need to be brought before a national audience?

As related in *The Media Elite*, former NBC News president Reuven Frank cites instances such as Roger Mudd's request for a Teddy Kennedy imitation from Gary Hart as pointless. Nobody even remembers the answers; they just remember the questions.[12] And I ask, what worthwhile purpose does the question serve? In sharp contrast was the recent tribute paid by Bill Shearer, vice president and general manager of KGFJ, to the late Booker Griffin Jr., a radio talk show host known for his biting criticism of Los Angeles Mayor Tom Bradley. "His long suit and his weak suit was his ability to tell it like it was."[13]

SOAP DOESN'T ALWAYS WASH CLEAN

Of course, you can always turn on the TV set a little earlier in the day and catch the soaps. We have a choice of illicit love, racial bias, violence, alcohol abuse, embezzlement, sex out of control, and threats to expose the past.[14] I do not believe this is a cross-section of life in our country. There are many people who lead productive, normal, responsible lives, and they deserve to be represented by today's media.

While I agree that "Leave It to Beaver" was probably not representative of life during the fifties, how many of you enjoyed more recent programs such as "The Wonder Years" that tugged the strings of memory of your own youth? Frankly, I think it is refreshing to spend a little time reliving a less complicated time in life.

By the same token, I would welcome talk shows that present the good things that are done, people who have made a difference, people who have overcome difficulties to achieve their goals, and people who have refused to let life beat them down–who have chosen to set aside the past and go on with life rather than let it dominate their future. Wouldn't you?

A small ray of light exists in programming that is offered by talk show stations such as KFI-AM in Los Angeles. They feature hosts who take a stand on issues. They are not afraid to present the conservative viewpoint. That people want to hear Rush Limbaugh and others is evidenced by the station's climb up the ratings charts to its current position as No. 4.

When criticized for not offering flaming liberals to offset their present conservative roster, station officials responded, "It's not a matter of ideology; we try to give a common-sense look at problems." Could that be what the public wants to hear? Common sense. I agree with these station officials who ask, "What's wrong with being conservative?" Even the station's liberal Democratic host, Bill Press, says, "KFI has never pressured me to change my views. I believe the station's basic motivation is to live up to its promotional tag of providing "more stimulating talk radio."[15] That, in itself I believe, makes a loud statement as to what constitutes a responsible mediamaker.

If soaps, talk shows, and controversial news programs were eliminated from the airways, would we still watch TV? Yes, of course! Give me a good ball game, a "Cheers" rerun, and the Discovery Channel–that is all I need. This may seem a little idealistic, but most of the junk out there isn't needed; it's just hype, sensationalism, and Nielsen grabbing nonsense.

It is a sad commentary when the May sweeps for ratings are dominated by perverted, violent programs such as "Murder in the Heartland." And what about our illustrious newspapers? Would they sell if they printed only the good news of stories of rescues, humanitarianism, happily married couples, successful young people, etc. Sure they would!

I remember driving with my father down country roads and seeing the metal cylinders people had installed to receive the newspapers. In most cases, there were two cylinders on each property: one for the paper that carried the local news and one for the metropolitan daily of that particular area. In fact, most small towns at that time still had thriving local papers. No, you couldn't read national news in them, but you could find out what was happening in your town. It might be an announcement for the next Bingo game, the local sports recap, the honor roll from the local schools, and of course, news of weddings, engagements, and sad reports of citizens who had passed away.

These stories not only cemented the community, they helped the people see the good that was happening around them.

Think also of the tribute paid at her death to Pat Nixon, wife of the late ex-president Richard Nixon. She was described as a gracious lady–no matter what the circumstances. She never stooped to the level of her husband's opponents; she remained above it all. If she had chosen to "tell all," she could have undoubtedly blown the lid off more than one household. But she chose to let confidences remain just that–as they should be–and let the forces of national justice do their work–as they should. Somewhere we have lost sight of the roles assigned to us, and some think that just because they have the knowledge, they also have the "mandate" to expose others. If wrong has been done, the proper agencies armed with adequate knowledge can bring justice. That is why they exist.

REALITY IS ...

I think another interesting sidelight is the reservation some analysts are holding about childhood flashbacks regarding childhood molestation–a staple on talk shows. These memories, in some cases, are not the reality of what happened but a fabrication that is often innocent.

I remember a friend whose 5-year-old awakened one morning convinced her best friend was dead. She refused to go to school because it would be such a sad place without her friend. Finally, after classes began, the mother called the teacher. No, her daughter's friend had not died. She was, in fact, in class today. Even though the mother persuaded her daughter to accompany her to school, the child would not be convinced her friend was alive. "I know she's dead!" It wasn't until she saw her and touched her, that she believed.

We can only surmise she had a dream so real, she thought it was the truth. What if the facts had not been so easily resolved, would the child have continued to believe her friend was dead?

Even more appalling is the hype and sympathetic position the media takes when a serial killer claims as a defense, "I was molested as a child." The cold-blooded killing of parents by their children is receiving sympathy from the media and other sources now that they are claiming to have been molested as children. Too often recently we have seen these brutal people being painted as mysterious, intelligent demigods.

I greatly admire those people who have overcome mistreatment as children and have gone on to lead productive lives helping those who now find themselves in the types of situation from which they emerged. We need to hear more of these good news success stories.

Do we believe all we hear on these talk shows? Has all that the participants related really happened? Or are they convinced it has because of mistaken memories? Think back to the late Cardinal Joseph Bernardin of Chicago and the sexual abuse charges made by Steven Cook that were headlined throughout the country. Then four months later, Cook withdrew his charges stating that he was no longer sure the memories that had surfaced during hypnosis were "true and accurate."[16] What if Cook had not had the courage to admit he was no longer sure the memories were accurate? Would the public still look on Bernardin as a child abuser because of the media's sensationalization of the charges before the case went to court?

Even more chilling is the case of George Franklin, who was convicted of murder in 1990, after testimony from his daughter that she suddenly remembered many years later of seeing her father murder her friend. After five long years, the verdict was reversed by a federal court judge. This case served as a focal point of the controversial trend in psychiatry, which is dredging up reportedly repressed memories.[17]

Are the people who appear on the talk shows ones who can truly distinguish reality from fantasy? Have they answered an ad seeking people that fit the situation and made up their "juicy" stories? How about the Jerry Springer Show which was caught with an actor in the audience, representing himself as an innocent participant. Or the Yolanda Show, which was airing a segment on scam artists, only to get caught with an actual scam artist on the show. Don't you think the producers should be held accountable? I think these are all questions that must be answered before we can accept everything that is presented as factual. I also lay a charge on the talk show hosts, I believe you are exploiting people for the sake of sensationalism with no regard for honesty or integrity in your reporting or concern for the people involved.

Can the reason for this cavalier treatment of the truth be, "There aren't enough man-bites-dog stories around," as Andy Rooney says? Producers and hosts must scrounge around for something "a little different," and as a result, this spate of quasi-exposés has been unleashed. He says, "There's a shortage of material for television shows because the overwhelming majority of people are nice, law-abiding citizens who aren't movie stars, aren't transsexuals, don't steal, and more than 200 million Americans are not in prison for a murder they didn't commit. They're home watching television."[18]

This brings us to another point. Is this dearth of "real" stories a strong signal for network executives and producers to take another look at their programming and the face of America and produce something worthwhile for us all to watch? It is a sad commentary when my older neighbors say they watch the Nickelodeon channel because they are so tired of the violence and filth on the regular channels today.

LET'S RELAX!

What do the American people prefer to watch? According to the National A. C. Nielsen Ratings,[19] the top three shows at this writing were "Home Improvement," "Roseanne," and "Coach." Clearly, the public wants lighthearted, family style entertainment. Also ranked among the top ten were serious programs including "When No One Will Listen" and "The Last POW?". Hard hitting presentations such as "Prime Time Live" and "20/20" were also listed.

Because America is demonstrating they not only want to be entertained after the day's work, they also want to be informed, I would like to see the media live up to their obligation to make presentations that are completely accurate and to create more shows without violence. I really worry about the effect violent shows could be having on my son. Although we try to monitor what he watches, the stuff is everywhere!

It's sad to realize that even a massive letter writing campaign by the general public failed to sway the decisions made by the television networks to cancel shows that people thoroughly enjoyed. The write-in campaigns to save "Life Goes On,"

"Homefront," "I'll Fly Away," and "Quantum Leap" had no effect on the mediamakers. These were not shows that were simply mindless entertainment. At times, they delivered powerful messages and often were scheduled against impossible-to-beat ratings-getters like "60 Minutes." "Life Goes On" was especially notable for the part it has played in helping the general public understand Down's Syndrome. It appears that so-called soft shows just don't cut the mustard in an era of hard-edged newsmagazines and reality series.[21]

A sad commentary on our times is that the inquiring minds of today apparently do not want to think back to the past unless it is something that has captured its fancy already. When the Fox TV network had a 25th anniversary special on 1968–a momentous year in which both Martin Luther King and Robert Kennedy were assassinated, Vietnamese veterans marched, students rioted on a worldwide basis, the Democratic Presidential Convention was marred by Yippie protests, riots, and strong-arm tactics by the police, flower children abounded, and the Vietnam War truce was signed–only four percent of viewers bothered to watch it.[22]

What we see happening in our country today has strong roots in all of these events...and we are not interested enough to refresh our memories or learn about them if we are among those who were not yet born or old enough to remember. How can we learn from the past if we ignore it?

An encouraging sign is the CBS announcement of its programming schedule. They will continue to emphasize nonviolence and feature a number of programs that, while targeted for a middle-aged viewing audience, will probably be enjoyed by the whole family. Programs such as

"Dr. Quinn, Medicine Woman" and "Touched by an Angel" will continue to appear on the line-up.[23]

Although I am sure there will be some violence, I hope the story plots manage to find a way to solve most of the dilemmas without resorting to violence. It is time to start promoting other methods of finding a solution. It is time to teach the younger ones who will be watching–no matter how the show is tagged–that violence is not the best answer. We are intelligent enough beings to be able to find a better way.

I believe the public also wants more programs that let them relax without being bombarded by someone's "message." There is nothing wrong with much of prime time being used for this purpose. In the same sense that comedy flourished during the depression because people needed a relief valve, comedy is needed today because of the world economic situation and the pressure pot in which we live. If the media is not meeting that need, then they are shirking the responsibility that has been laid on them as keepers of the air waves.

Changes that seem to be occurring within the major networks may also bring hope for the future. NBC has announced that believing the traditional over-the-air broadcasting has a limited future, they are now venturing into cable programming, overseas partnerships, and high-tech ventures. Having dropped from first to third in ratings and plagued by scandals, they are looking to find ways to take advantage of owner GE's high technology base. The dependence on regular network programming will be replaced by programming similar to other cable/entertainment conglomerates.[24]

Andrew Lack, president of NBC News, asserts that news programming will be in news magazine format, but definitely not tabloid in nature.[25] Although Lack is not responsible for the NBC debacle with the fiery truck crashes, it remains to be seen whether his goal can be accomplished.

In France, the suicide of former Prime Minister Pierre Beregovoy was attributed by some to the press. He was deeply wounded by newspaper stories questioning his integrity in receiving an interest-free $190,000 loan from a political crony. The loan was later linked to a $10,0000,000 insider stock trading scandal.

This is in light of the increasingly aggressive French media, which longs to be more independent and adversarial, modeled on the American and British press. Until recently, the French press has placed an individual's privacy above the public's right to know. The French admit they limit freedom of speech and the press in a way that does not exist in the United States.[26] It appears that in its defiance of the limits the political system in France imposes, the press is determined to bring those limits to an end. Here again, the media is trying to determine the course the nation will take instead of reporting on the course the nation is taking.

In the United States, it appears the media are trying to manipulate the course the White House will take in addressing problems that are occurring in other parts of the world. Now whether that manipulation is deliberate or is happening simply because the action appears to be where the media's spotlight is focused, remains to be determined. We sent aid and support to Somalia, but not to untelevised Sudan where thousands died as a result of the horrendous droughts. Bosnia rates coverage, but nothing is mentioned about Angola, where in the words of a respected observer,

"The stench from thousands of corpses slaughtered in its civil war reached up to my helicopter."[27] What about the conflict among the former Soviet provinces in central Asia? Where is the moral outrage against these atrocities? Unaroused. Unaroused because it was not televised.

Even more appalling is the position taken by some TV commentators. They have now switched their outrage to the allies. Of course, this is far from the truth. The Europeans are doing their share in trying to bring peace to these war-torn countries. Unfortunately, only the United States has enough air power to force some kind of truce; but in so doing, it would put an end to the humanitarian efforts now in place that are trying to bring aid to the starving, displaced persons. I have to agree with the analysis of Douglas Hurd, British foreign secretary, "The media are right to anger and horrify us. But anger and horror are not enough as a basis for decisions....Policy cannot be based on a desire to achieve better headlines tomorrow than today."[28]

As indicated by the same spirit of irresponsibility in fulfilling its assigned role, what should be done about the media who present suppositions and accusations as fact? My mind goes immediately to the programs that feature the homeless and world problems such as starvation and AIDS as the fault of the conservative politicians. "They" have not done enough; "they" have hampered efforts to right these problems; "they" have duped the American public into not assuming their position as saviors of the rest of the world. I ask you to look back over the past several administrations. Do you honestly think efforts to right these wrongs ceased while the more conservative Republicans were in power and advanced only when the more liberal Democrats were in the majority? I believe conservatives and liberals alike are concerned about these world issues and have worked to right them and will continue to do so. This concentration of the blame on conservatives is being used by the liberal media executives and producers to discredit the efforts of those with whom they do not agree and to further their own beliefs and objectives.

Ask yourself how mature and honest a media we have that praises Bill Clinton before and immediately following the election as the answer for which our country has been searching, and then in less than 100 days following his inauguration ridicules and criticizes almost everything he does. I say they are pretty fickle and are looking for whatever makes a story. What do you say?

The media seems to have assigned to itself a unique place in our country–the Keeper of Life. Not physical life, but who shall live as a functioning citizen or official in this country. The mediamakers discredit whom they please; they destroy those who do not meet their self-proscribed standards (political or moral); they ridicule whom they choose; they respect no one and no office; and they believe they are the masters of our fate.

MEDIA TURNAROUND

I believe the funeral of Richard Nixon is one of the most blatant media turnarounds that has ever been evidenced. At the time of the Watergate scandal, Nixon was characterized as the perpetrator of the greatest scandal that ever occurred within the presidency. His associates had broken into the Democratic Party headquarters and because he did not immediately disavow their actions, Nixon was immediately implicated.

He approved the steps to divert an FBI investigation because he was afraid their actions in a previous burglary would be uncovered. Inexorably, he was forced to resign the presidency in the face of certain impeachment.

The media painted him in the most disgraceful manner and totally discredited any good that he had accomplished during his years in the Senate and as President. His character was reviled as a two-faced egomaniac with no ethical standards.

However, Nixon determined to rebuild his image, set about writing books on international affairs, touring world capitals, and serving as the unofficial presidential advisor. He became a global elder statesman. To an extent, he accomplished his rehabilitation, as evidenced by the media's reaction to his trip to China.

However, the media coverage of his funeral indicated that he was regarded with great esteem not only by the public but also by the media and the political world. He was hailed as a great citizen and a great statesman to whom the country owed a debt of gratitude.[29]

My question at this point is, Did Richard Nixon's character change in the meantime, or is this again media manipulation? I leave the answer to your judgment.

I also find myself uneasy at the prospect that perhaps this change in the treatment of Nixon is preparation for treating the actions of others in political power as mere indiscretions that the light of history will show were mere specks in the light of their overall political contributions. I do not like to feel that standards do not exist, and that we should not expect our political leaders to set a good example for their constituents.

NO ABDICATION

I, for one, am not willing to abdicate my position as a vital functioning citizen. I believe I still have a say in who will be elected, whether the news I hear is impartial, and whether we are subjected to programming that is just so much garbage. I believe I will have to be active to reverse the trend that has begun, but along with others who care, we can make it happen. I must admit I actually worried about writing this book because my position presented a different viewpoint from most of the media.

Elsewhere in this book, we will examine the ways in which we can alter the media choke hold. We do have a choice. We can surrender without a fight, or we can unite against this octopus that is trying to squeeze the life from all that we hold dear.

WORKS CITED

1. "Wednesday Afternoon." *TV Guide* (July 17-23), 1993): 149-150.

2. "Talk Shows." *USA Today* (Daily listings, 1993).

3. Smith, Martin J. "Is He Now Err Jordan?" *The Orange County Register* 4 June 1993 News 2.

4. "Car seen as key in Jordan slaying." *The Orange County Register* 15 August 1993: News 1.

5. Almond, Elliott and Robbins, Danny. "NBA Superstar Michael Jordan's Father is Slain." *The Los Angeles Times* 14 August 1993 A24.

6. Ibid.

7. Muskat, Carrie. "Poll: Jordan a gem—on hardwood not the diamond." *USA Today* 15 March 1994 1A.

8. Hiestand, Michael. "Jordan's NBS decision affects a lot of people." *USA Today* 14 March 1995. 3C.

9. Ballard, Steve. "Magic Prevail 103-95, lead 3-2." *USA Today* 17 May 1995 1C.

10. "Michael Jordan Family Mourns Loss of Father." *The Los Angeles Times* 16 August 1993 A11.11. Ibid.

12. Lichter, S. Robert, Rothman, Stanley and Lichter, Linda S. *The Media Elite*. New York: Hastings House, 1990.

13. Mitchell, John L. "Booker Griffin Jr.; Black Radio Talk Show Host," *The Los Angeles Times* (8 July 1993).

14. Reichardt, Nancy M. "The Bold and the Pregnant." *The Los Angeles Times* 26 April 1993.

15. Puig, Claudia. "KFI: Turn On, Tune In, Turn Right." *The Los Angeles Times* 20 May 1993 F1.

16. Schmucker, Jane. "Sex suit against cardinal dropped." *USA Today* 1 March 1994 1A.

17. "Repressed-memory verdict reversed." *USA Today*. 5 April 1995 3A.

18. Rooney, Andy. "Fame is the name of TV ratings game." *The Houston Chronicle* 25 April 1993: 6F.

19. June 28-July 4, 1993.

20. Ibid.

21. Du Brow, Rick. "Letter Campaigns Fail to Save Shows." *The Los Angeles Times* 18 May 1993 F11.

22. Ibid.

23. Du Brow, Rick. "CBS Keeps Its Eye on Middle-Aged Viewing Audience." *The Los Angeles Times* 21 May 1993 F1.

24. Lippman, John. "Network Faces Challenges of a New Era." *The Los Angeles Times* 18 April 1993 D1.

25. Hall, Jane. "Seeing the Big Picture at NBC News." *The Los Angeles Times* 14 May 1993 F1.

26. Tempest, Rone. "French Press Role Debated After Suicide." *The Los Angeles Times* 17 May 1993 A4.

27. Griffiths, Eldon. "U.S.'s media hawks are squawking for war." *The Orange County Register* 11 May 1993 Metro 6.

28. Ibid.

29. Gerstenzang, James. "Nixon Gets Hero's Farewell." *The Los Angeles Times*. 28 April 1994 A1."

Chapter 9

TALK SHOW/TABLOID HYSTERIA

Jenny Jones sparked a heated debate on the ethics of the surprise tactics she used on Jonathan Schmitz in her talk show, "The Jenny Jones Show." The segment was about secret admirers and Schmitz was enticed to appear to find out who his secret admirer was. He was stunned when he was introduced to another man who admitted he had a crush on him.

According to Schmitz's testimony, the appearance on the show had "eaten away at him" for three days when he finally shot Scott Amedure after receiving a note from him. Schmitz had thought his admirer would be a woman.

While this segment was not aired publicly, Jones' show has been consistently criticized for focusing on sleazy topics. On-the-air confrontation has soared in talk shows since the polls showed the ratings rise when the "fur flies." However, Columbia University journalism professor Steven Isaacs counters, "What this says is that the media chaos is now total and the sleazification that has been sweeping the land and the media for the last half dozen years produces bizarre events that no one could possibly imagine."[1]

Did Sally Jessy Raphael keep an innocent man in prison? Some viewers feel she did. Others say, "No, she merely presented the facts that provided justice." Let's look at what happened. Supposed memories of sexual abuse were "recovered" by a Charismatic "healer" who had formerly been a comedy actress and law enforcement official. These memories were aired on Raphael's show. The accusations stemming from the memories sent one man to prison and destroyed at least two families. In analyzing the tale of alleged satanic ritual abuse for *The New Yorker* magazine, writer Lawrence Wright claims the media is fixated on such accusations and feeds the frenzy, possibly planting scenarios deep in the minds of people who are unable to differentiate fantasy from memory.

In spite of the plots and characters therapists reportedly recovered that were straight out of a science fiction fantasy, FBI investigators were unable to find a single documented example of the alleged satanic abuse. This story suggests possibly detectives and therapists who interviewed the family in which the abuse was supposed to have taken place unwittingly subjected them to the same sort of "mind control" that destructive cults often use to keep members in line. It is also interesting to note that shortly before making the accusations against her father, one of the daughters had read what is presented as a true story, *Satan's Underground.*

Raphael presented the story of abuse as fact and capitalized on what now appears to be a totally fabricated story that brought untold suffering to an entire community, which may never completely recover from its effects. She featured one of the daughters who claimed to have been abused in the case, one of the purported abusers who felt the talk show offered the only forum available for him to try to reclaim some of his reputation, and an evangelist who was determined to alert the American public to the "epidemic of Satanism" that exists in the country today. Even though the accused's motion to withdraw his guilty plea was pending in the federal courts and the evidence pointed to people who had been subjected to mind-altering techniques, Raphael accepted the accusations as facts that were not to be disputed and the alleged victim as a person worthy of the sympathy of viewers. The show ended with an emotional appeal by the accuser for "people" to believe the victims. Does that make you proud, Sally, feeling as if you have been of service to the public?

Between you and Geraldo Rivera, you would probably run out of things to talk about if you did not use such subjects with so little documentation. Of course, as we mentioned earlier, these are not the only two talk shows on the air; and they are certainly not unique in their choice of subject matter.

Phil Donahue defended this sensationalism with the comment, "If you're going to survive in daytime TV, I'm compelled to remind you that you're competing with semi-naked people rolling around on a water bed in a soap opera. You cannot televise the front page of *The Wall Street Journal* and survive. You just flat can't do it."[3] Maybe therein lies the solution. Because soap operas and talk shows seem to feed on the other's audacity and sensationalism, let's insist on decent programming, and maybe both genres will disappear.

CAN DO...

The Rev. Donald Wildmon, a southern fundamentalist minister who was already known for his protests against movies and TV shows, took out a full-page newspaper ad that featured a form that could be forwarded to ABC as a protest against the TV offering, "NYPD Blue."[4] If you care enough about an issue, it appears you can find a way to make your voice heard. I think we all must start caring enough to be listened to.

FOR GOOD–OR FOR EVIL

Let's take a look at talk shows and tabloid reporting in general to see if we can ascertain any effect–negative or positive–on the values most people esteem today. Almost without exception, day after day, the line-up reads like bad news, worse news, worst news, and the bottom of the cup–the dregs of society who make their statements. Only the people who are talking are not the dregs of society; they are introduced as average citizens with "special" stories to tell. On August 26, 1993, in the Los Angeles area, the Radio Talk Show News consisted of the Reginald Denny beating, Rodney King being picked up for drunk driving, the funeral (music and all) of two firemen who had been killed fighting a brush fire, the death of a Siamese twin following separation surgery, and then finally the conviction of police officers who had beaten a black man. I wanted to yell, Isn't there any good news somewhere? Why do we hear only of the tragedies of the world? Where is the good?

Less than a generation ago, these "special stories" would have been discussed in hushed tones in the privacy of homes. Today, they are still being discussed in the privacy of homes, but the difference is the audience. The audience is not a few family members or close friends; it is the whole world. As a result, people are beginning to think these happenings are the norm, not the exception, and that we have now become a different people.

As a different people, certain individuals are encouraged to pursue endeavors and lifestyles that are in direct conflict with the values they were exposed to as children. The man who becomes angry at his wife and abuses her has been subtly conditioned into believing it's OK because so-and-so talked about also reacting in this way on this talk show or that talk show.

A mom who is at her wits end after a particularly hard day may not even feel guilty when she slaps her kids around. She knows this is the way most of the country acts too, because "they" have told her about it time after time. The teenager who thinks the whole dating scene is a series of one-night stands certainly has found plenty of role models courtesy of our media.

Instead of being appalled by a 12-year-old who had already committed 56 crimes in his short life, the audience of the Montel Williams Show applauded when an audience member said he was a victim. The saying, *Boys will be boys*, used to evoke visions of a pre-teenager involved in some harmless prank-like throwing tires around the flagpole or parking a car inside the school building. Today, we hear that phrase used to describe young men who have sexually abused girls–in one case, a retarded girl. Entirely lost seems to be the Boy Scout image of a helpful little boy. I contend this is a direct result of being consciously and consistently subjected to perverse images. I agree with this thought; the world is a stage, but the play is badly cast.[6]

"The Cristina Show," Mexico's answer to Oprah and Geraldo, has sparked intense public debate since its inception in December, 1992. Calling Cristina a bandit, some Mexican leaders contend it trounces traditional Mexican values and identity. Recognizing that young people are most at risk from watching it, they have been successful in their efforts to move its time slot from 4 p.m. to 11 p.m. Intellectuals and artists say it's trash.

Cristina claims she is bringing modernity and the way people think in big cities to Mexico despite the fact the program grates on a culture where they do not blab everything to the world; where speech is much more formal than it is in the United States, and women are encouraged to hide their intelligence.[7] Whether this "education in cultural differences" will be constructive to Mexico's television industry or will generate the same types of problems that have arisen from the talk shows that now air in our country remains to be seen. We can hope Cristina will learn from her northern counterparts' mistakes. Only time will tell.

I think Arsenio Hall had the right idea. To celebrate the 1,000th episode of his show, he reserved the Hollywood Bowl. There the audience was not subjected to talk, talk, talk, but was treated to music instead. Former show participants such as Madonna, Duran Duran and other notable entertainers belted out favorites in an event that raised $250,000 to benefit the Magic Johnson Foundation for AIDS education and care.[8] What if all talk shows featured "real entertainment" for a worthy cause instead of digging up garbage? Hey! Something good could come from something really bad.

Unfortunately, we all have a spot–usually recognized as desiring bad things–in our psyche that would like be violent or do things we know are not in our best interest. However, most of us have been taught the consequences of following these, as my mother used to call them, "baser instincts." They bring unpleasant things, maybe even punishment, into our lives. We know that for our ultimate good we must overcome these impulses. Most of us do just that; however, an increasing number of younger people are following them instead. With television being cited as the number one reason for the increase in violence in the United States today, the retelling of experiences once thought of as bad or even evil, easily sways a person who does not have a clear sense of right and wrong into doing something to hurt someone else because "everybody is doing it."

Can you believe this? I could only imagine my father's response if I wanted to do something questionable and thought he would say no and said, "But everyone's doing it." Yeah, right! Not in our house.

Fortunately, everyone is not doing it, but the media has so overwhelmed us with this type of programming that even the most right-seeking of us are beginning to feel we are like islands of normalcy in a sea of perverts. I am happy to tell you there are many, many more islands just like you out there. However, we cannot expect a change in what the media presents as life in our country until we start effectively protesting what they portray.

We continue to hear that ratings dictate the need for sex, drugs, and violence. I do not buy this philosophy–nor do any of my friends. The fact that shows such as "Home Improvement," "Coach," "The Cosby Specials," and other so-called light entertainment consistently dominate the field for top watching honors soundly contradicts this claim. You can argue that "Cheers" is for older audiences, but the furor that ensued when the final season was announced is also confirming evidence that drugs and violence are not needed to make a hit. You can even make a case for implied sex–that it attracts a larger audience than steamy see-all, hear-all romps in bed.

Now that Judge Gene Schnelz has ruled that talk shows are not "the media" and therefore not entitled to First Amendment protection in hearing the $25 million lawsuit brought by Scott Amedure's family against Jenny Jones who featured him, perhaps some sanity will return to the subjects that are featured and the manner in which they are aired. I, however, would argue that talk shows are indeed a part of the media.

THE MEDIA AS A COURT OF LAW

That the media seeks sensational subject matter without regard for moral and ethical constraints was all too evident following a murder in northern California. The woman who had walked into an open court and shot the man who allegedly molested her son was termed "The Heroine of the Mother Lode." Montel Williams, Donahue, Oprah, Geraldo, Larry King, scholarly Charles Kuralt, "Good Morning America," and "The Today Show" all clamored for time with her. Movie and TV producers, writers, and agents fought for the rights to her story. One Hollywood producer even termed it a feeding frenzy.[9]

Fortunately, for the American public, interest waned in the light of further evidence of the accused's actual motives for killing the man. However, that does not alter the fact that initially they saw her as a modern day Dirty Harry who could blow away the bad guy and come out the perfect, unblemished avenger. What happened to the American concept of liberty in law whereby a person was considered innocent until proven guilty and entitled to a jury of peers?

We can all understand her outrage on behalf of her son, but nothing in our American way gave her the right to kill in cold blood a man still considered innocent by our courts. As I thought of this case, I was reminded of something that happened shortly before. A school custodian was accused of rape by a young girl. The man in question seemed to fit all the evidence and was even positively identified by the girl. Even though he protested his innocence, he was arrested and jailed.

He was identified by name in the media. Needless to say, his family was subjected to all sorts of abuse as a result. Fortunately for him, his family continued to believe in his innocence and sought to have it proved. Some thirty days after his arrest, DNA tests proved conclusively he could not have been the rapist. He was immediately released.[10]

In the meantime, the media had a field day at his expense. Just like the Mother Lode Heroine, it appears the media had already brought its own verdict before he was tried.

You also have to ask questions such as, Was the newspaper justified in heading an article about the death of an infant that had previously been hospitalized for seizures, "Father's shaking allegedly kills baby"?[11] This question is asked in light of the information contained in the article that medical personnel immediately accused the man of having shaken the infant too hard, and that was the reason the baby suffered bleeding in the brain and subsequently died. Both parents of the child denied the allegations from the outset.

While the medical personnel's explanation may be the truth, at the time of the accusations, no irrefutable evidence or confession of guilt had been offered. In addition, there was no explanation for the previous seizures, which had occurred before the father came to live with the mother and her parents. I find such assumptions disquieting, don't you?

While doing research for this book, an even more alarming event occurred. The conviction of Michael Jackson for child molestation by the press while he was out of the country on tour and before he even had a chance to make a statement. This man was declared guilty by the media before any charges were filed, almost as soon as the allegations were made. From the time the police started investigating his homes, newscasters, mainline newspapers, and scandal sheets told audiences how Michael had done this and had done that. It did not seem to matter to them that he was not there to defend himself or even ask officials why they were searching his property. They had a really big story; Michael Jackson was actually a truly depraved person who molested children.

I was so disgusted by this whole affair that as I tried to write about it, I am sure you can feel my anger seeping out of these pages. I will try to contrast the Michael Jackson we all know to the media's portrayal of his character. First of all, I doubt if many other stars today are as generous to the children of America as Michael Jackson. His work with the Make-a-Wish Foundation, Camp Good Times for child-victims of cancer, opening his fantasyland estate Neverland to terminally ill children, sending relief to the war-torn Balkan countries, providing counseling, drug prevention programs, and healthcare for inner city children, and aiding many individual families who simply needed help have shown us his caring nature. If anyone in our country today deserves the title, Friend of the Children, I think it is Michael Jackson—quirks and all.

To have the type of unfounded allegations made about him accepted as the truth by the media and disseminated to every living room in America should have been a criminal offense.

Early reports indicated Jackson was the subject of an investigation by the LAPD as a result of charges made after an extortion attempt had gone awry. In spite of police assertions about their concern that the investigation be done with absolute fairness to everyone involved, KNBC-TV aired reports claiming Jackson had abused a child at his home.[12]

The media tracked leads that would identify the child who claimed he had been abused, while the Los Angeles Country Inter-Agency Council on Child Abuse and Neglect advised caution, saying, "It is premature to attach much credibility to this yet. Celebrities are vulnerable to extortion. I have seen many allegations made against high-profile entertainers that were not substantiated."[13] Since we did not hear of these allegations from our news people, we can only conclude these individuals were much more fortunate than Michael Jackson that the media didn't get wind of their stories. In Jackson's case, the information came from an unnamed police source with knowledge of the case who betrayed confidential matters and went public.

As substantiation for the caution of not believing all allegations of child abuse, recently released statistics indicate 40% of all divorce cases have charges of child abuse filed against at least one of the partners. The charges are filed to increase the settlement rights of the accuser, but 90% of these claims prove to be false. When you translate those percentages into numbers of individuals, a large portion of our populace is accused every year of child abuse, but 90 out of every 100 people accused are actually innocent. Makes you wonder why any credence was given to the charges against Michael Jackson in the first place–considering they came to light during the continuation of a long, messy divorce.

Mainstream news media stooped to the

tabloid level in their coverage. I thought the *New York Post's* headline, "Peter Pan or Pervert?"[14] was absolutely revolting. Less than a week after the allegations broke, Michael Jackson was being treated as if he were guilty of all charges. The media's "right to know" does not include speculating in public about his relationship with minor children. Not only did the media declare Michael guilty in their own paper court, they branded the child for life. In the same sense that these charges will be with Jackson for the rest of his life, they will also be with the thirteen-year-old boy. He will always be known as the child who said Michael Jackson did.... I wonder how these mediamakers can sleep at night?

Articles began to appear in so-called legitimate, mainline publications advising parents how to deal with the stories of Michael Jackson's abuse of minors. The more conservative ones featured articles on how to deal with the alleged charges of molesting children.

The die was cast, however. The stigma of betraying his friends, the children, by mistreating them was firmly attached to Michael's person. The tabloids, both written and verbal, shared with their audiences the details of the supposed sexual encounters, which in turn forced parents to ask for professional advice on what they should tell their own youngsters about this abuse.

Suddenly, Jackson's emphasis on children's toys, his shopping sprees in toy stores, his Neverland estate and subsequent Peter Pan image were viewed in a grotesque light. His desire to live the childhood he had been denied was suspect. The media now portrayed him as a perverted pedophile who used these devices to lure innocent children into his clutches.

Could it be the media was venting its own envy over Michael's' being able to bring a Disney ambiance to his life that they could not bring to theirs? Not many of us have the ability to create such a wonderland.

One of the most unfair aspects of this travesty of responsible reporting was the conclusion most mediamakers drew. Even if Jackson were found innocent, the allegations will be remembered, and he will never again be regarded as harmlessly "different" or an innocent child-man.

"They" said he molested the children, he abused them, and he betrayed their confidence as their friend, so Michael must always be regarded with suspicion and as someone with whom children may not be safe. The motivation for all of his generosity will now be suspect. His image has been shattered into a million pieces by the unproved allegations that were headlined by those news persons who did not care about the truth–all they wanted was a bigger, more juicy story than their competitors had.

The question of media ethics was discussed in a recent newspaper article. No one questioned the use of Michael Jackson's name as the accused. The issue seemed to be over whether the accuser's name should be published. Pardon me, but with charges this serious, no coverage should be given until formal charges have been filed in the courts. The media has no right to subject anyone to trial by gossip. The right of the accused to a fair trial has not been repealed!

In this same article, the authors asked, "Since no charges have been filed and the police investigation is incomplete, should news organizations have reported the investigation, knowing the shadow it would cast across Jackson's career?"

Unfortunately, that question appeared to be irrelevant to the newsmen who responded. Their main concern was whether they should make the boy's name public. The publishing of his obscured picture and the description of his parents were debated. Editor Tonnie Katz's opinion seemed to sum up the general opinion:"...We do not reveal the name of alleged sexual abuse victims, regardless of their age. We feel the identities of such people, particularly if they are children, should be protected except in extraordinary cases, and this is not one of them."[15]

I think we need to change our perspective here. Wasn't Michael Jackson a victim too? Only if he had been charged and convicted would he have become the victimizer. Just because he was an adult did not make him open to published accusations. He should have had the same rights as the so-called victim until guilt was determined. Since there were charges of extortion, I think this precaution was especially applicable in his case.

Both district attorneys who had been conducting separate investigations in Los Angeles and Santa Barbara counties announced they did not have enough evidence to charge Jackson with a single crime, and so were calling off the investigation. Even though both indicated they believed him guilty and had others who claimed to have been molested by him, they were unable to produce a single person who would testify.

Santa Barbara County DA Thomas Sneddon continued to refer to the alleged additional accusers as victims, which was tantamount to saying that Jackson was guilty of those crimes. What a cheap shot![16]

This seemed to make the original reason of extortion submitted for the accusation more plausible. The boy's parents simply wanted to cash in on the charges, not subject them to the scrutiny of a criminal court proceeding.

When Jackson's short-lived marriage to Priscilla Presley disintegrated, the child-molestation charges again surfaced in the press. Some tabloids featured articles claiming that his marriage had been a sham, and that he had used a wife as a coverup for his perverted behavior.

On "ABC World News Tonight," Peter Jennings asked the question, "Even though it's legal to air charges, should the media? How extensively, and who, if anyone, determines if these accusations ever make the light of day?" As he pointed out, the media's zest for scandal involving public figures had emphasized the ease with which one person can accuse another and become an item that appears everywhere.

In citing several cases (including Michael Jackson's), he noted the one thing they all had in common—the charges were not proven, but were serious enough to threaten to ruin the reputations of the accused.

Jennings stated that we all love gossip and the days when the media repressed stories about famous personages are over. The rules of the game have changed. What are the new rules? Richard Kaplan, Editor of *The Star*, stated, "We would not have run the story on Michael Jackson if there had not been a serious charge leveled at him in a court of law. For every story we publish, there are 10 or 15 we don't." Media critic Ken Auletta countered with pointing out how much of the press went crazy over this story. They lost their sense of proportion and began treating the allegations as fact.

Cited as a role model for handling such charges, *The New York Times* deliberately downplayed Gennifer Flowers' adultery charges against Bill Clinton. Max Frankel, editor, said that they knew of the allegations but did not think them of major importance; they printed three minor paragraphs that said a suit had been brought and the figure named denied it.

Jennings pointed out that the day was long past, however, when a handful of media giants decided what would or would not be seen. Even if the network news media decided not to air a story, a few minutes later one of the tabloids would break the story. As Frankel expressed it, "We're all reduced to the standards of the lowest common denominator. Some scandal sheet somewhere can light the match and a prairie fire quickly spreads across the country."

Jerry Naughman, former Editor of *The New York Post*, commented he did not know how to be fair about this other than the old journalistic rule of letting it all get out there; and letting the public decide what was right or wrong. Jeff Greenfield, of ABC News, then asked a very pertinent question, Where does this leave victims such as Ray Donovan, former Cabinet member who received a not guilty verdict on the charges leveled against him? Donovan, after pointing out that the press had ruined his reputation by their assumption of his guilt, had asked, "To which office do I now go to get my reputation back?" His answer was, Out in the cold.[17]

In confirmation of this change in the basic rules by which the media operates, Bill Woestendiek, director of the School of Journalism at USC, states, "[Newspapers] used to compete fiercely. But we didn't cross the line anywhere near like they are today. Good editors wouldn't let you cross that line." Robert Sims, news director of KNX-AM radio, declared, "I think people are less inclined to hold off on what they know is a juicy story." Mark Hoffman, vice president of news for KNBC-TV (the station that originally broke the Jackson story), defended his position by saying his station decided to break the story only after its accuracy was confirmed.[18]

I ask you, what accuracy? Was it accuracy when the only facts they had at that point were: 1) the police were conducting an investigation; 2) Michael Jackson was out of the country; and 3) the investigation was as the result of a failed extortion plot and the subsequent charges that were filed? The additional information he claimed he had came from unnamed sources, and this information may or may not have proven to be true when it was thoroughly investigated?

I think the whole situation at this point fell into the realm of gossip following unproved charges made by someone whose parents were conceivably trying to take revenge on a megastar who would not yield to their demands for money. Again, our irresponsible media proved its propensity for taking something sensational, injecting a well-known personality, convening their own court, and pronouncing judgment–making or breaking the person in the process.

Then when Michael Jackson made a reputed $11 million settlement with the teenager who accused him, the media continued to debate his fate. Knowing full well that they had destroyed his image forever by their pre-determination that Jackson was guilty, not one mediamaker seemed to listen to Michael as he continued to maintain his innocence. They did not want to believe that he simply had been hurt deeply by the experience and wanted peace and his privacy back–at any price.[19]

The media wanted the public to understand that settling out of court was an open admission of his guilt (not true). They insisted that because he was famous and had money, he could abuse children and get away with it (again, not true).

A few weeks after the settlement was announced, his sister Janet was interviewed. When asked if he was guilty, she confirmed her unqualified belief in his innocence, stating, "He's completely innocent. I would give my left arm, my foot to prove he's innocent." She mentioned how she had stopped listening to the news because they were just sensationalizing everything and lying about things, and how it hurt to have friends turn against you for money. Then she made a very astute observation, "Now it's kinda died down.... It's always someone."[20]

Supported by leaders of the West Coast Region of the NAACP, Michael also was critical of the media coverage. "I am particularly upset by the handling of this...matter by the incredible, terrible mass media. At every opportunity, the media has dissected and manipulated these allegations to reach their own conclusions," Michael charged. Then he asked the public to "wait and hear the truth before you label or condemn me. Don't treat me like a criminal because I am innocent."[21]

Who gained from all of this? Talk shows. They now had a new, timely topic for discussion–*Men Who Have Been Falsely Accused of Sexual Crimes.* Tune in tomorrow and the next day, and the next, for the in-depth interviews. Then after that, we can have a whole series on *Children Who Falsely Accuse Adults of Sexual Crimes.*

Then when that subject is worn out, we could move on to *People Who Fail to Extort Money and Resort to Tales of Sexual Deviance as Revenge.* Now, we're ready for *Wives of Men Who Have Been Falsely Accused of Sexual Crimes.* The list is endless. How many ways can you vary the same subject to inundate the public with cheap, sensational, shoddy stories? I just hope we don't find out.

Frankly, I'd like to see a talk show on *Talk Show Hosts Who Lost Their Jobs Because of Their Disregard for the Truth.* Although the topic is one we would all like to hear discussed, networks would probably be hard put to find anyone to participate because show hosts just don't lose their jobs over that issue.

Who will lose? Certainly Michael Jackson will lose the most. His reputation has already suffered a major blow and will probably be seriously compromised even more. There is already evidence that his popularity is waning. The aura of the accusations seems to have left him under a permanent cloud.

Then, as a probable side-effect of the damage to Michael, the beneficiaries of Michael Jackson's generosity will lose. All of the wonderful things he has done for others were as a result of the money he made entertaining us. Should this campaign to discredit him succeed, those who need help the most may be deprived of many of the good things he has been able to give to them.

Does our media stop to think of those they may hurt when they act in such an irresponsible manner? A resounding, No, I don't think so. They do not care who gets trampled in the process. All they want is to have the top story out there. Does that story have to be true? No. Does that story have to be confirmed? No. Does that story have to conform to ethical standards? No. All it has to do is generate bucks.

I CANNOT TELL A LIE

I said to my wife, "Let's go pick up a few groceries." While we waited at the check-out stand, we scanned the tabloids offered for sale. There was the latest scandal about the royals, gossip about Loni Anderson and Burt Reynolds, a story on the monster that attacked a fishing vessel in the Great Lakes, finding Satan's skull, and other highly unlikely events. The number of cases won recently against these purveyors of yellow journalism by celebrities makes you wonder if anything they print is the truth. If it isn't, why are they still in print? Can it be that the public's appetite for the violent, the gory, the unbelievable, the perverted, and the scandalous insures their continued good health?

Let's look at what these scandal sheets have in the way of stories. The week Michael Jackson was smeared across front pages everywhere, *The National Enquirer* featured stories about "Michael Jackson Child Abuse Scandal–World Exclusive," "Accuser, 13, Tells All: Boy's full horrifying story (3-page special report) and the shocking details behind police investigation," and "Loni's New Lover–Handsome lawyer who's helping her forget Burt." We were treated to a glamour shot of Loni. Unfortunately, the man she's supposed to be interested in rated only a mug shot.

The feature photo was Michael Jackson in one of the ugliest grimaces he could surely have mustered. Needless to say, this was not the Michael Jackson we saw in videos, movies, and news shots–even on the go from one place to another. I would guess the photo was a still shot captured from a musical performance–hardly representative of the man himself.

Not to be outdone, *The Star* showed us a two-thirds page photo of Michael and "the boy" who reportedly made the accusations. The headline was "Angry Dad's Court Plea, Keep Michael Jackson Away From My Boy," while the caption reads, "Jackson with boy who's in middle of sex-scandal storm. STAR is withholding his identity. His face has been obscured by a computer technique."

In order not to single out Jackson, there were also headlines about how "Burt Lied About Loni on TV–voice expert," "After His Fling, How wife keeps Bryant Gumbel on short leash," "Kiss the Bride! Sexy Kim Basinger's barefoot wedding on the beach," and "Raymond Burr's Gallant Last Days: Dying star hosts farewell dinners for friends."

I do not have to explain here that the Jackson headlines were pure speculation at this point. On to the inside of *The Star*. Let's see, we found out on page two that Mel Gibson was accused of being a boozer, but there was hope. He took his family along with him on location to rescue him.

Juicy tidbits on Fergie filled the next page. Then we turned the page to find an article full of speculation about the late David Janssen's death many years ago.[22] After so long, you would think they could leave him alone! But no, they speculated that his death was not due a heart attack, which was given as the official cause, but as the result of a bacchanalian orgy. I find it extremely hard to believe that the police department of a major city investigating the death of a well-known actor was going to ignore anything. As evidence, we found that Janssen's first wife was now writing a tell-all-about biography of him and a rehash of what were supposed to be details of his personal life, which had been evidently in total disarray. What we really had was a scandal sheet that wanted to capitalize on the release of Harrison Ford's movie based on Janssen's old TV series.

After wading through pages of "all the things you were never supposed to know" about other celebrities, I came across a two-page spread filled with pictures of Kim Basinger's dream wedding. At last! Good news. As I read, a sense of unease began to grip me. Even in such a happy moment, Kim was not immune. Tucked away in the middle of the article was the revelation of all the precautions she took to keep it a private event.[23] But did that stop this tabloid from crashing it? Of course not, the public had a right to know. The persons involved had no rights.

How did *The National Enquirer* treat this week in history? They too found a way to take advantage of the movie, *The Fugitive*. Instead of focusing on Janssen, they turned their sights on one of the movie's stars, Tommy Lee Jones. I learned he had had a rotten home life. Just how rotten it was was detailed in two and a half columns, while Tommy Lee's high school and college scholarships were summarized in two brief paragraphs–and this included Vice President Al Gore's analysis of his former roommate.

Jones' present life was told in four paragraphs, three of which were a rehash of his former life. What a missed opportunity! Instead of an inspiring story of triumph over terrible odds, readers were consigned to wade through all the dirt. Do you agree that was no way to present the news?

Kim and Alec didn't escape *The Enquirer* either. If I read only this article, I would not know it was to have been a private wedding. I did note, however, that comments came from either "inside sources" or a "pal of the couple." That didn't explain how the tabloid got the pictures for the illustrations, however.

Many of the stories in both tabloids featured

the same famous people. There were articles on Kelsey Grammer's divorce and the bizarre charges he made against his wife. With his new television series screening, reader interest was already insured.

I also found myself wondering if the respected Raymond Burr wouldn't have preferred to go without the publicity. Why shouldn't he have entertained his friends? Most people who know they have only a short time to live do choose to say good-bye in one way or another, but why must his good-byes have been subjected to such a morbid spotlight?

The headlines told us that "Kiefer Sutherland toils on convict road gang." As I read this article, I found it was not quite that way. He was among those who are doing community service as a result of a DUI conviction. A drive along Los Angeles freeways any week-end will reveal hundreds of other such persons working with road crews.

I believe it is unfair to term them convicts because the word itself implies someone who is serving a long prison sentence. These roadside workers are people who have broken a law but are not such a menace to society they must be locked away. But the absolute truth would not make such a good headline, would it?

It is encouraging when a star occasionally brings a case against such a paper and wins it. We can only hope more stars have the courage to do so. If the public's confidence in the veracity of these tabloids is shaken, it may be that readership will fall off to such an extent that to publish them will no longer be profitable. I am convinced circulation would continue to remain at a high level if these periodicals changed their approach to a truthful one with no sensationalism. After all, the

American public does like to read about their celebrities–and sometimes, truth is stranger than fiction.

Even more respected periodicals such as *TV Guide* evidently are not too careful in reporting their "facts" as evidenced by Nancy McKeon's complaint about their description of her relationship with Michael J. Fox. The magazine quoted her as saying, "It's fair to say it was my first and most important love affair." Says Nancy, "I don't think I've ever used the term 'love affair'. It's not how I speak...I take exception to people trivializing something in my life."[24]

Danielle Steel filed a lawsuit over a planned biography of her by Lorenzo Benet and Vickie Bane who wrote an article for *People* magazine describing Steel's marriage to two ex-convicts.[25] If only the facts were presented, would Steel even have a basis for the suit?

More well known, of course, is the lawsuit of psychoanalyst Jeffrey Masson against Janet Malcolm and *The New Yorker* magazine. After a series of interviews following Masson's discharge from his position because he held renegade views on Sigmund Freud, Malcolm wrote two highly uncomplimentary stories about him portraying him as an egomaniacal sex fiend.

Masson charged that Malcolm had invented five quotations and described certain events in error to enrich a devastating portrait of him.[26] When Malcolm could produce only one of the quotes from the tapes of her interviews, the jury found libel. *The New Yorker* was absolved of blame by concluding Malcolm worked as an independent contractor, not as an employee, when she wrote her articles about Masson. Because the jury was deadlocked on the question of damages, a mistrial was declared.[27]

On the other side of the coin, you have those who would sue the media for reporting the facts. Randy Kraft, a convicted serial killer of possibly as many as sixty-five people, brought a libel suit against the publishers of a book detailing his crime spree. The killer, who is now awaiting execution on death row at San Quentin, claimed it damaged his reputation, cast him as a sick, twisted man without moral values, exposed him to hatred, contempt, and ridicule, and destroyed his chances for future employment.

I think few of us would argue that the portrait was probably pretty accurate and to be honest, what chances does a man on death row have for future employment on this earth? I think Warner Books is justified in objecting to the nearly $25,000 it spent to defend itself in the suit that was dismissed by the courts.[28]

YEAH! AND WHO SAYS?

Sensationalism is not the only vice of the media; disrespect is rampant. Citizens of our country are being inculcated with the idea that there is no person, no office, or no institution that merits respect. It's all right to "put down" anything you want.

I venture to say the current rash of so-called humor at the expense of our President is causing us to judge the office of president harshly. When the White House is compared to a jail and a President who helped direct our nation on a positive course of action is characterized by the comment, "Anybody can grow up to be President, and Ronald Reagan proved it,"[29] a very derogatory picture of the office is painted. I suppose the article was written to be funny, but I fail to see the humor in something that shows so much disrespect.

Another indication of disrespect surfaced within the industry itself. Hal Fishman, KTLA anchorman, threatened to quit over a slanderous statement made by another station employee on the "Morning News" The station's bad-boy entertainment reporter Sam Rubin had stated that Fishman once "wore a skirt for a co-anchor job in Spokane" as a part of a bit in which he compared Fishman to Dustin Hoffman, who portrayed a woman in *Tootsie*.

Who can argue with Fishman when he stated, "I don't think that making an outrageous, preposterous slander about someone whose success is based on credibility and honesty is at all funny.... To say someone engages in aberrational behavior, I don't think that is a joke." He went on to say he had never held a job in Spokane and was not a cross-dresser.

I think Rubin's dismissal of the incident shows his shallowness. "Since the incident, Mr. Fishman's 'News at 10' remains the No. 1 news show in its time slot. The viewing public has gotten over it." And what makes him think so? Who did he poll? If you are like me, whenever you see Rubin or hear his name, you will remember the tasteless attack on a respected member of the media.

This lack of respect by the media was illustrated in yet another way. Residents of Hermosa Beach, California, filed a suit against the city to block filming of the series "90210." Even though the producers had obtained the necessary city permits, residents complained of mistreatment by the film crews whose behavior was likened to an invasion by an army who preempted their rights to the neighborhood. When residents were criticized by the industry for not thinking globally or of Southern California, where life is fueled by the

[film] industry, a former broadcaster offered these words of wisdom, "Hollywood, we understand you have other location problems but this is the core of the issue. Don't use global, economic or symbolic rationalizations to cloud the issue, and don't blame us for your behavior. Take a lesson from Bill Cosby's crew–use courtesy and common sense. Folks will go out of their way to help you and encourage you to come back to the neighborhood. It really is that simple. Oh, and wouldn't that stop runaway production, improve local economies and reinforce the 'cachet of California'?"

Another obvious signal of disrespect was evidenced by Connie Chung in her now-famous interview with Kathleen Gingrich, mother of Newt Gingrich. She violated one of the first rules of responsible reporting, betraying a confidence. Ms. Gingrich had told her confidentially that her son thought "Hillary Clinton was a bitch," but Connie was so hungry for a sensational tidbit that she broadcast the opinion nationwide. I was infuriated at not only Connie's disrespect but also at her willingness to "make news" at the expense of an elderly woman.

REMEMBER, YOU HEARD IT HERE

When KCBS in Los Angeles decided to fire its news director, it was amid accusations of sensationalism and staff rebellion. One has only to think back to news reports accompanied by urgent, doom-impending tones as the words were spoken. Televised footage that was later criticized as inappropriate for live coverage and stories of the seamier side of life in Los Angeles seemed to bear this out.

However, in an editorial, John Lippman, the former news director, defended "Action News." The ratings for the program were their highest in 10 years. This was attributed to the fact that the program addressed topics important to viewers.[30]

I wonder. In the light of current findings of the addictive power of violence, were viewers attracted to that newscast simply because that was where the violent action was? It was where they could relive murders, robberies, rapes, car chases, and other crimes? It was vicarious satisfaction of their need for a violence fix?

In an analysis of his years broadcasting the news, Jerry Dunphy asserted, "You can do quality when you are dedicated to doing good journalism.... When your dictum is ratings, things begin to disintegrate just a bit from the purity of the news that we knew [in the 60s]." When asked if it was the heated competition that has diluted the news product, he replied, "I'm sad to say it, but it has skewed the judgment of everyone from management down to the news departments."

He also indicated there was an overemphasis on crime, sensational blood-and-guts stories, and replacing regular programming with interminable repeats of minor happenings.[31] I concur with his assessment, "There is just too much ado about nothing."

Concern is being expressed in some quarters by the changes in network news coverage. Instead of the narrator of a story being there up close and personal, too often the newsperson is simply narrating from his or her city office a video report that has come in from some distant point.

Analysts are concerned that because of the distance between the reporter and the story, it is more difficult to examine the issues insightfully, and shallow reporting will result.[32] It leads one to wonder, will any 'real' news remain, or will we have only a choice of pabulum or cherries jubilee?

One has to ask if irresponsible reporting has caused the media to wreak vengeance on itself. Were the debacles staged by the press during the Bork and Thomas nominations to the Supreme Court responsible for the announcement that there would be a secret session during the hearings for nominee Ruth Bader Ginsburg?

Would more responsible reporting have averted this decision? I think so. The sensational and biased reporting techniques used so muddied the actual hearings that well meaning committee personnel felt it was necessary to limit access by the press and the public. I find myself resenting any limitation on my formerly permitted freedom to know that was caused by an irresponsible few.

We also now find that the Justice Department has barred the press from federal arrest and search raids because of the poor judgment shown by news crews in tipping off the Branch Davidians that a raid was imminent.[33] While we must agree with those who say the Justice Department showed poor judgment in making this information available to the media, we must also conclude the press showed even poorer judgment in tattling to the cult.

What if the media had acted responsibly in letting the Justice Department do its thing without trying to generate headlines from it? Could a national tragedy have been averted?

With the challenges to sources of information and legal challenges on how the information was obtained and whether a news outlet committed an invasion of privacy to convince employees to break confidentiality agreements, it appears the old rules of First Amendment protection have changed. The press may no longer be able to run rampant with their reporting.

Chills went down my spine when I heard President Clinton blast radio talk show hosts as "promoters of paranoia" and "loud and angry voices in America" that were somehow linked to the tragedy in Oklahoma City. He then called for more "discipline" in relation to freedom of speech. I shudder when I think of where that "discipline" may lead.

I find myself extremely concerned that the excesses we see in the media today can possibly lead to censorship, ostensibly for our own good. The idea that censorship must be imposed in a country that is built on freedom of the press as a basic right of its people is totally abhorrent to me–and I think to all freedom loving people anywhere. We cannot let a few destroy what so many have labored for so many years to create. We cannot let the efforts of Thomas Jefferson, James Franklin, and Peter Zenger be destroyed by irresponsibility. We must protect these rights and strive to restrain those who would see them destroyed.

WORKS CITED

1. Johnson, Peter. "Guest's death leaves talk show world abuzz." *USA Today* 13 March 1995 3D.

2. Wright, Lawrence. "Remembering Satan—Part I." *The New Yorker* 17 May, 1993 60-81. "Remembering Satan—Part II." *The New Yorker* 24 May 1993: 54-76.

3. Smith, Liz. "Donahue on the Defensive." *The Los Angeles Times* 2 June 1993 F4.

4. "Morning Report." *The Los Angeles Times* 2 June 1993 F4.

5. Parsons, Dana. "For Skewed Look at Adult Life, Turn on TV Talk Show." *The Los Angeles Times* 14 May 1993 B12.

6. Ibid.

7. Miller, Marjorie. "Cristina's Controversy." *The Los Angeles Times* 25 May 1993 H4.

8. Graham, Jefferson. "Arsenio's night of 1,000 shows." *USA Today* 14 May 1993 3D.

9. Arax, Mark. "Luster Fades for Killer of Molester." *The Los Angeles Times* 18 May 1993 A3, A21.

10. Weber, Tracy. "Custodian Cleared of Charges." *The Orange County Register* 24 April 1993 News 16.

11. Kelly, Erin. "Father's shaking allegedly kills baby." *The Orange County Register* 8 April 1993 B1.

12. Merl, Jane and Hubler, Shawn. "Michael Jackson Is Subject of Investigation by LAPD." *The Los Angeles Times* 24 August 1993 A3.

13. Tilton-Durfee, Deanne in an article by Wallace, Amy and Nazario, Sonia. "Probe of Jackson Linked to Abuse Case." *The Los Angeles Times* 25 August 1993 A12.

14. Rosenberg, Howard. "Forget the Facts—We Want the Story!" *The Los Angeles Times* 27 August 1993.

15. Smith, Martin J. and Hodgins, Paul. "Case poses ethical dilemmas for media." *The Orange County Register* 27 August 1993 News 19.

16. Wickham, DeWayne. "A Cheap shot at Michael Jackson." *USA Today* 26 September 1994 11A.

17. ABC World News Tonight, mid-December 1993.

18. Ibid.

19. della Cava, Marco R., Thomas, Karen and Daniels, Charlene. "A mixed message if Jackson settles." *USA Today* 25 January 1994 D1.

20. Gundersen, Edna. "Standing by big brother and parents." *USA Today* 18 February 1994 1D.

21. "Jackson: Singer Denies Molesting 13-Year-Old." *The Los Angeles Times* 23 December 1993 A1.

22. *Star* 7 September, 1993 6-7.

23. Ibid 36-37.

24. "McKeon differs on facts of love life." *USA Today* 10 May 1993 D2.

25. "People." *The Orange County Register* 29 July 1993 News 2.

26. Warren, Jenifer. "Libel Trial Is Spicy Stew of Law, Freud, Sex." *The Los Angeles Times* 14 May 1993 A3.

27. Warren, Jenifer. "Mistrial Ends New Yorker Libel Case." *The Los Angeles Times* 4 June 1993 A3.

28. Horn, John. "Libel suit filed by killer dismissed." *The Orange County Register* 15 May 1993 News 4.

29. Morrison, Patt. "The Unfriendly Confines." *The Los Angeles Times Magazine* 1 August 1993 6.

30. Lippman, John. "Action News Reflects a Changing City." *The Los Angeles Times* 17 May 1993 F5.

31. Weinstein, Steve. "Sensationalized News Should Be Passe." *The Los Angeles Times* 5 June 1993 F1.

32. Rosenberg, Howard. "Newscasts: What Isn't in Picture." *The Los Angeles Times* 4 June 1993 F1.

33. Everbach, Tracy. "Siege prompts new media policy." *The Dallas Morning News* 7 May 1993 26 A

Chapter 10

THE CLINTON CAMPAIGN

Nowhere in recent years has the fickle nature of the media been more in evidence than in their treatment of Bill Clinton—the fair-haired wonder who was elected the youngest president in the history of the United States. You may say you're not surprised. After all, look at the reasons why he was elected in the first place.

Why was he elected? It wasn't so much for a positive reason as it was for a negative one. It wasn't that the American people wanted to see Clinton run the country; they just did not want to see Bush back in the White House for another term.

In a graduate class called Values and Decision Making, I wrote a research paper titled, "Why the American People Chose Bill Clinton." As part of my research, I surveyed my family, friends, colleagues, and some of my associates who said they had voted for Clinton, and this is what they revealed. Most felt that a major shift in governmental philosophy was needed.

Not only were they voting against Bush, they saw Al Gore as a reason to vote for Clinton. I think this probably represents a major flaw in understanding how our executive system works because, short of Clinton's death, Gore has not played, nor will he play, a major role in decision-making. Also entering into the reasons was the resemblance to JFK that Clinton bears. Did the media project this strategically placed image?

Most voters had become dissatisfied with the direction life in the United States was taking. The social security system seemed to be failing, spending for healthcare and military needs was out of hand, there was social unrest, the educational system needed revamping, the national debt had reached over $350 billion, minority rights were not being honored, tensions overseas were increasing, and the planet seemed doomed ecologically. The government was not listening, and most felt they were being taxed far beyond their means. People seemed less interested in evaluating statistics than they were in simply changing things.

SLICK WILLIE

More personable than the other candidates, Bill Clinton seemed to provide what the nation valued: affection, respect, change, individuality, skill, understanding, power and influence, goods and services, well-being and responsibility. He appeared to have "pulled himself up by his bootstraps," and seemed to be just like "the boy next door." What a winning combination! We eventually saw this president play the saxophone on Arsenio Hall's program and dance the jitterbug donned in white socks, penny loafers, and an Ivy League sweater.

The media did its part in continuing to keep this image in front of the American public. Most often, Clinton was portrayed in the rosy light of being the answer to all our problems. Literally, he was the fair-haired boy who would set things straight in a world that had gone topsy-turvy. *The Boston Globe* stated in a feature article, "Bill Clinton was elected president after convincing voters that government could accomplish far more than it had during the Reagan and Bush years."[1]

The debates among the candidates clearly brought out his boyish good looks. He benefited from the good angle of the camera as opposed to

Ross Perot, who was consistently featured from a bad angle. Anything that could have detracted from Clinton's shining image was censored. The other candidates were not so lucky. The public saw them as they were–warts and all.

Bill Moyers was asked if Clinton's use of television was as revolutionary as Kennedy's was. He answered, "Kennedy used it well for that time, but Clinton is the first candidate who knows how rich the medium is in its variety of expressions. Although he's no great orator, he's the most natural politician I've seen since Kennedy."[2]

ABC News Special Correspondent Cokie Roberts said the Clinton team was incredible at creating the most media-hip presidency ever. "Not only did they go over our heads to town meetings and talk shows, but their TV pictures were gorgeous. The triumphant entry into Washington was something the likes of which you've never seen."[3]

While Bush and Perot had to defend the positions they had taken on political and corporate leadership, Clinton was not asked to explain his mediocre governorship of Arkansas. Instead, he was portrayed as the great rescuer of a state that prior to his election had wallowed in illiteracy and poverty.

I was interested in the evaluation of a man who had lived near Little Rock during his governorship. He maintained Clinton was not highly regarded while he was governor, and most residents of Arkansas felt by and large he had not done much of anything of a positive nature for the state.

Yet the media did not seem to feel that his tenure as governor was a basis on which to judge the type of president he might be. They just kept asserting that he was what our country needed; whereas Bush had led our country to the brink of economic disaster, and Perot was considered a corporate dictator who undoubtedly would be the same type of president–an unthinkable concept in a nation that governs itself.

The November elections came. Clinton was elected by 43% of the American people–not even a majority let alone a popular mandate. Even though more people voted in this election than had in any other, not even half of the voters thought he was the best choice. At that, he still received more than twice the number of electoral votes that Bush did. It was obvious the public wanted a change.

THEN, THE BANANA PEEL

However, the media's enchantment with the new president was short-lived. Within the magic first 100 days, Clinton's halo became tarnished and with only 36% of the public approving his performance, articles questioning his ability to function well as president were common throughout the United States.

Time magazine's cover on June 7, 1993, showed a very small picture of Bill Clinton and very large type proclaiming him "The Incredible Shrinking President."[4]

Never before in history had a president been so characterized. The article described his presidency to date as "beset since its inception by miscalculations and self-inflicted wounds," and included a reference to his "balmy" decision to have his hair trimmed while blocking take-offs of other aircraft at Los Angeles' busy International Airport and accusations of cronyism in staffing the White House Travel Office.[5] The same article also claimed a top aide had stated publicly what the public had been saying in private, "Under Clinton, the U. S. was retreating from leadership in the world."

Not to be outdone, *Newsweek* featured a pensive Bill Clinton on the cover and the question, "What's Wrong?" in large type. Beneath the large headline was the statement, "Ugh! A Mess in the White House."[6] Clearly, Clinton had fallen from grace in the eyes of the media.

Dan Rather, Connie Chung, Tom Brokow, George Will, and other top news personalities agreed the Clinton communications machine, so carefully honed during the election, had begun to fall apart almost overnight. The new Administration felt they could continue to perpetuate the kind of television manipulation they had perfected during the campaign. Some news persons saw Clinton as being overtly obvious that he was out to show everyone he had mastered the TV medium instead of using it to his advantage without drawing attention to the fact, thus making his manipulations a story instead of a strategy.

That he had greatly benefited from replacing George Stephanopopoulos with David Gergen was generally acknowledged by everyone. Gergen, who had previously guided Ronald Reagan, tried to get Clinton to emulate some of the TV style of Reagan, whose use of TV was widely recognized as masterful. Stephanopopoulos and Gergen became a very powerful team and were quite successful in obtaining the headlines they wanted to see about the President. When asked if he felt they were experts at manipulating coverage, Dan Rather answered, "Damn right."[7]

A poll taken by CNN/*Time* showed that in February 67% of Americans felt Clinton was a strong and decisive leader, but by May, only 38% still felt the same way. Their perception of his concern for the average American fell from 79% to 64%. Compared to Jimmy Carter who had also made the same campaign promise to "Make Americans feel good about themselves again," only 32% said he had made a good start compared to 60% who felt Carter had done so when polled in May, 1977.

Did the public think he could deal effectively with Congress? 41% said no while only 23% said yes.[8] Ross Perot even stated he would not consider giving Clinton a job anywhere above middle management.

PRESS, GO HOME!

That Clinton had no experience with the Washington scene was apparent and evidently rubbed the media the wrong way. He even banned reporters from areas of the White House where they had previously been welcome. The media quickly seized every opportunity to paint him as the country bumpkin who was woefully inept at his job. I'm not going to argue he did some pretty dumb things, but the media showed absolutely no mercy or sympathy during his first steps as a baby president.

I think this emphasizes their role as the ones on whom you cannot rely to present an unbiased account of events. Had they been sincere supporters of him as president, I don't think they would have sensationalized the fumbles he made to such a great extent. I believe this simply shows their desire for a really good story supersedes their concern for the truth. A president can do anything as long as it is within their prescribed boundaries and they will support him, but if he strays away from them, the media is unmerciful.

Clinton had displayed his ineptitude and lack of Washington savvy by his choice of advisers, doling out positions of favoritism to friends, placing his need for a trim above the transportation needs of a major airport, and making inappropriate choices for appointees. He became the "new boy in class" in the eyes of the press. Because he did not fit into their clique, they chose to make fun of him and ridicule his unwise decisions.

Please understand I am not defending any of these actions on Clinton's part, I am simply stating that this is what I see as having happened to turn the press from being ardent supporters of the President-elect to being derisive detractors of the newly elected President. Bill Clinton simply did not fit in with the crowd.

In true underdog fashion, Clinton seized the opportunity to blame his political troubles on the media. While admitting errors in judgment, he expressed his anger over the media's blowing "stupid little things" out of proportion. He accused the media of giving the defeat of his economic stimulus package fifty times the press coverage the approval of his budget outline received.

He also claimed they were neglecting the "real issues." I wonder if the tower personnel at LAX or the hundreds of persons waiting for over an hour to take off felt his haircut was just a stupid little thing that should have been unworthy of media notice? Defending the media, Larry Sabato, a University of Virginia professor and media critic, said, "The press is a useful target, sometimes even a deserving target. But it's substance, not coverage that's causing [the President] problems."[9]

THERE IS NO BILL CLINTON

Headlines such as "Confidence in Clinton Is Slipping Among Many Business Leaders,"[10] "President loses a big perk,"[11] "Clinton the Snake-Oil Salesman Is Not the President He Said He Would Be,"[12] "Is the problem really Clinton?"[13] "For

Clinton, a blunder storm,"[14] "Bill Clinton's Excellent Adventure: How a President Can Promise One Thing and Deliver Something Else,"[15] "Clinton presidency lacks discipline and a sense of priorities,"[16] and "A president's principles: 'There is no Bill Clinton'"[17] mirrored what the media across the nation was saying. Bill Clinton's honeymoon with the press was definitely over.

By and large, the support given to him by the media during his campaign for the presidency had disappeared. In its place were ridicule and criticism. Even newspapers that tried to continue their support showed signs of buckling under the barrage of questionable issues and mistakes that characterized the early Clinton Administration. An article meant to support the President was headlined, "Clinton's 100 days: Key domestic initiatives are still taking shape," and began, "Bill Clinton promised a laser show but has produced a fireworks display."[18] While they were not willing to say Clinton did not keep his campaign promises in so many words, the meaning was there. He had said one thing before the election and done another following it. The Limbaugh letter, albeit extremely right-wing, even published a full page report called "Lies, Lies, and More Lies" (a compilation of direct quotations and promises made by Clinton and eventually broken).

The biggest problem that faced the Clinton Administration became not to prove the substance of his ideas but to prove that he and his staff were not incompetent.[19] The media held the White House staff in contempt, and nothing could be more deadly to someone in the political arena than that. What it means is that no matter what he does and no matter what he says, the media will look for the flaw in it, the ridiculous aspect that could be interpreted into it, and then try to convince their readers and listeners there is no way this person is deserving of the office. The ideas and proposals will not be analyzed for content or effect on our country; they will be infused with Clinton's personality to such an extent, the issue at hand will go unnoticed.

Gene Sperling, one of Clinton's top economic policy advisors, argued the budget was the most honest ever, and called the President the smartest, most dedicated president ever. He then berated reporters about their duty to portray the Clinton budget as much better than past budgets.[20] It seemed to me that such an attitude created an atmosphere of distrust and animosity. I am sure the press had a clearly defined sense of duty, and to be told by an outsider to report an event in a given light was an affront to their dignity. Although I have no proof of this, I venture to say this type of performance caused them to start looking for any weaknesses in the budget and find areas where it was not better than the budgets of the past.

Many reporters were saying the key to Clinton's success with the media would be whether he maintained an adequate level of accessibility and whether they would come to feel they could trust what he and his aides said.

ABC correspondent Britt Hume summed it up this way, "The administration tends to try to spin everything and simply sell, sell, sell. It's too early to say for sure, but they've shown a tendency to stray toward a credibility gap more than once."[21]

Others had such comments as, "Those of us who covered Clinton in New Hampshire...came away with some questions about his frankness, but not about his indomitability or political acumen." "Comparatively few Americans ever intended to elect a president who was a captive of the left wing of the Democratic Party. They haven't changed their minds." "DIAGNOSIS: Apparent and inexplicable infection by the George Bush syndrome, characterized by acute trouble with the vision thing and atrophy of the skills that, under better conditions, enabled patient to be elected." "[Clinton] lacks the commanding presence that lends weight to the words and actions of great leaders.... His presidency stands on shaky ground."[22] Almost universally, Clinton has clearly lost the support of the media. As one writer put it, "Everybody seemed to be on Clinton's case."[23]

That so much contempt and hostility should be generated so quickly between two camps that once had a mutual admiration society flourishing caused much speculation. Some wondered if Clinton's confidence that he could explain his way out of anything was the basis. Others felt White House public relations with the press was abysmal. Yet others thought Clinton's lack of accountability for his actions was the root. Whatever the cause, Clinton now faced a larger problem than most of the political ones he had to battle–how to get back into the good graces of the media.

Every possible angle of Clinton's latest faux pas was explored. The celebrated $200 hair trim on the runway spawned articles that explored how many other things $200 would buy (including how many haircuts at a standard barber shop); why the hair stylist had no last name but did have a personal publicist; how much it cost the airlines to sit there and wait; how Clinton blew his "regular guy" image with that one; and was it evidence he was out of touch with the American people? I don't have to tell you that having a target who was Public Figure #1 made the media's creative juices flow with reckless abandon.

WHERE WAS BILL?

Memorial Day, of course, revived memories of one of the key issues in the 1992 campaign–that of Clinton's avoidance of the draft and his definite anti-military position during the Vietnam war. As he spoke before a crowd gathered at the Vietnam Memorial, he was jeered by many. Rarely in history has a President received such a reaction at a public gathering.

Clinton had bitterly opposed the war, and the veterans just as bitterly remembered it with taunts of "Where was Bill?" and "Coward." Of course, the media featured this as further evidence of the lack of support Clinton had throughout the United States. One writer even described his approval ratings as being in freefall.[24]

Even the Japanese press was not as kind as it once had been during Clinton's visit. There were jokes about his 22,000 yen ($200) haircut and his decline in popularity. One newspaper even asserted, "Without the support of Hillary Clinton, Bill Clinton would have never become president."[25] When you stop to consider that the culture in which males are dominant was the source of this comment, the statement says a mouthful.

In an editorial decrying Clinton's apparent dumping of the African-Americans who had broadly supported him, the writer described our ship of state as being commanded by Captain Marshmallow.[26] Another editorial stated flatly, "Clinton's main problem is Clinton. He lies."[27] He was characterized as "Having a Rodney Dangerfield problem. He just doesn't get any respect. He has a character problem...and so is unable to assume the bully pulpit as moral leader like most presidents do."[28]

Often the nickname of Slick Willie was used

instead of his real name when his policies or actions were described. It is unfortunate, but I venture to say few people in our country had any doubt to whom the media was referring. Respect was definitely absent from the characterization. Another editorial commenting on Slick Willie's performance said, "I only wish there was a better example of presidential integrity for kids in civics classes around the country to watch. There is no Bill Clinton. That is, he has no principles that he will stick to when the going gets rough. His great passion is to be popular. I suppose you could call that a principle. If so, that's the only one he has."[29]

Increasingly, the media questioned Clinton's motives and his methods. They pointed to his willingness to find scapegoats whenever he did not measure up. They also insisted the public increasingly disliked Clinton's image–the bitten lip, the theatrical silences, the practiced righteous replies, and more importantly his policies that he hoped would bring higher taxes and social change.[30]

It was obvious that unless they could change the image the American people were forming of the President, he was in real trouble and without support from the populace. What should the Administration do to change the direction of the perception of Bill Clinton?

A DAY IN THE LIFE...

When NBC and the President were teamed on "A Day at the White House" in an effort for the troubled network and the equally-troubled Clinton to polish their images following the credibility gap both had demonstrated during the past few months, reviewers of the program were not kind. One reviewer in describing a photo session of an exchange between Tom Brokaw and Bill Clinton said, "It was a photo opportunity deluxe, and this handsome, graying people's servant hoped to use it to improve his image and create public sympathy and admiration. And use it he did. He looked sincere...confident...resolute...sharp...strong... thoughtful...wise...relaxed, yet firm...humble, yet determined. Above all he looked presidential. And Clinton didn't look bad, either."[31]

They were described as schmoozing together, and the dialog was ridiculed. On and on the review went, putting down not only Brokaw's performance, but the President himself. Even though I know such a program was made for propaganda reasons, I think the reviews simply reflected the media's attitude that the President could do no right, and sarcasm and derision were chosen as the tools to again attack his person.

Frankly, even though the performances may not have rated Oscars, here was an effort to show the American people what their president does for a living. I rate that a top story because we pay his salary.

Although critical of Clinton's first 100 days in office, the evaluation by *The New York Times* was a breath of fresh air compared to most other newspapers. The emphasis was not on Clinton as a person, but on the issues and the discharge of his duties as President.

Although his personality was analyzed, it was done so in contrast to the traits of other presidents. Why the public could expect a different approach to the same problem was explained. Political theorist scholars analyzed what had happened and why. A detailed article on Clinton's own analysis of his performance was included. I appreciated this detailed, honest evaluation of Clinton's leadership. Chalk one up for Arthur

Sulzberger, Jr., publisher of *The Times*–good, straightforward journalism; that is what the media is supposed to transmit.

Of course, there were those mediamakers who felt this score keeping of Clinton's presidential performance was trivializing both government and journalism. They cited the flaps over unimportant events as evidence the media was acting as time-keeper, umpire, and judge in determining who "won" this week instead of simply reporting the facts and letting the public decide their merits.

They also accused the Administration of evaluating their decisions in light of their reception by the press, thus hollowing politics into a game of perception—not the reality of action and consequences. Serious journalism became a joke as scandals were manufactured from a speck of dust, and the media stood back as the results of its foisting its perception on the American people became evident with their regard of him as a bumbling clown wallowing in the hopeless mess government had become.[32]

DESIGNING WOMAN?

Undoubtedly part of the reason the media was so out of sorts with Clinton was Harry Thomason's unfortunate remark while trying to explain away his interference in the travel office, "The Clinton people don't like the press."[33] This is hardly the kind of remark to endear the Administration to the media.

Linda Bloodworth-Thomason further escalated the feud by saying, "The Washington press corps practices central casting in every administration. There has always got to be a Lady Macbeth, a big fool relative, an unscrupulous businessman and sleazy immoral people from Hollywood. In Harry's and my case, they've decided to assign us the last two categories."[34]

In interviews on ABC's "Good Morning America" and CNN's "Larry King Live," they complained of their "scurrilous" treatment by the press following the White House travel office scandal. They contradicted specific personal insults they claimed to have received from the press.

I would also object to some of the characterizations, but I was brought up short when they insisted they were not Hollywood producers but decent Arkansans. It seems to me that while they certainly can claim Arkansas as their home state, they really cannot deny their occupations. It is interesting to note that one senior White House aide was quoted as saying to the press, "Harry and Linda appearing on television is not what I'd call a smart move. They should be keeping quiet and getting out of the way. I really don't understand why we keep doing this sort of stuff."[35]

Obviously, with this type of comment, they realized the Administration was responsible for part of the bad press and should have tried to minimize it instead of adding to it. Sometimes, keeping quiet says a thousand words.

The Administration also evidently failed to come to grips with the realization that though Bill Clinton was elected President, that did not mean he had the approval and support of even the 43% who voted for him. Instead, it meant those 43% definitely did not approve of either of the other candidates.

Instead of seeking to reassure public credulity following the Gennifer Flowers and draft board controversies, Clinton embarked on a campaign of breaking campaign promises right and left. Soon, he was seen as a master of glibness and evasion.

My opinion is that it is too bad for the American people that losing a vote of confidence does not force a national election immediately. Instead, we must endure the remainder of the term until the prescribed four years has passed–even if we immediately see we've made a mistake.

HILLARY OF ARK

Why the press did not question Hillary Rodham Clinton's role in the government is something many Americans wondered. She outranked the Cabinet and functioned without portfolio.

In what was probably one of the most blatant examples of nepotism, Bill Clinton appointed his wife as chief of the health care task force. During the time of transition between the election and the inauguration, the president-to-be had made it plain she was to be his primary advisor. As a first step, she moved her office to one near the Oval Office. I wonder how many Americans knew they were electing a co-presidency team when they voted for Clinton?

A friend of mine summed it up, "Had I voted for Clinton, I would be thinking 'I've been robbed' right now. I wasn't even given a choice about Hillary, and I certainly never remember Bill saying anything like, 'Well, you know I won't be making any decision without the little woman's OK.' I want my money back!" Personally, I don't question her intelligence or ability. I just found it odd that while the media was "crucifying" her husband, they were "sanctifying" her.

At least, the press had the integrity to question JFK's appointment of his brother Robert Kennedy as Attorney General. The propriety of appointing a relative to a high office in the administration was debated. Finally, the media came to the conclusion that nothing illegal had been done and that while some felt there were others who were more qualified than Robert Kennedy, he was at least qualified for the job. Many of the media, however, still maintained that JFK had shown poor judgment in choosing a relative for the job.

I believe in Clinton's case, the media was remiss in its responsibility by not questioning such actions taken by the Administration. Please understand it is not that I feel Hillary was unqualified to assist, it is simply that our form of government is not designed to function in this manner. I was absolutely shocked at the President's response when the first health care task force meetings behind closed doors were questioned by a member of the press who read from the rules book how such meetings were to be held–they were to be open to the public. Obviously annoyed, Clinton shot back, "We have important things to do here. We can't let [everyone] have a say in them. There isn't time." A chill ran down my spine. In his mind, the legality of an issue was subordinate to its place on the agenda. Bill, I hate to tell you, but that is not the American way; it is the way a dictatorship functions.

Some Washington observers described Hillary as "the Eleanor Roosevelt of her generation." However, presidential scholar Stephen Hess of the Brookings Institute believed that comparison was wrong. "This is a case where the president has appointed–anointed–his wife to be the designer of that...program which is most crucial and important to the success of his administration. For various reasons, he can't make her an official of this government. In everything but name, she is a Cabinet minister without portfolio."[37] I believe that issue was among those the media should have been questioning.

They should also have questioned why the Administration functioned in a manner that was clearly outside the provisions made by our laws. Why should it have been permitted to do so? What was the motivation for such actions? Instead, it appeared the President was following the same agenda they had and, therefore, not subject to question in those areas. Their only duty was to support him. If you closely examine what happened, you will see not the issues, but the person of Bill Clinton, was being attacked. He was open for ridicule and derision, but for the most part, the path he was taking our country down was not questioned.

NOW, WHERE TO?

I would also venture to say that the reason Hillary was not being questioned was that the media recognized Bill and Hillary were in sync. They both agreed on quotas for women and minorities in all appointed positions, supported federally funded abortions, homosexuals in the military, women in combat positions, enlarged medical care, reduced scientific research, and increased taxation. Irwin Stelzer in "Commentary" asserted, "Billary is not a two-headed horse, trying to move Left and Right either simultaneously or alternately, depending on whether the president or his wife has the whip hand. They're both wielding the whip, driving the horse as far left as we'll let it go. It really doesn't make any difference which one is in the saddle."[38]

At the risk of sounding like a doomsayer, I wonder if the only question the media had on the direction this two-some was taking us was, Do we really need to go through the motions and expense of an election when we have the perfect duo to take our country where we need to go?

We all realize the media used Dan Quayle to their best advantage. He was portrayed as always having his foot in his mouth and woefully ignorant. Remember the "potatoe" incident? His comments about Murphy Brown were used again and again as evidence of how out of touch the Administration was with the American people and how they couldn't really relate to the "common" people. Quayle's actual comment was, "Bearing babies irresponsibly is wrong. Failing to support children one has fathered is wrong. It doesn't help matters when prime-time TV has Murphy Brown—a character who supposedly epitomizes today's intelligent. highly paid, professional woman—mocking the importance of fathers by bearing a child alone and calling it just another lifestyle choice." As it turned out, he wasn't so far off after all, but, of course, we didn't know that until after the election.

While I personally believe children benefit from having two parents, I realize there are many one-parent homes that have children who are doing well. It is just a fact of life today that not all marriages make it, and sometimes there are children involved. Quayle simply was making the same analogy to raising children alone that has been drawn about violence on television. Prime-time programs serve as role models, and a model that is advocating something less than ideal fails to create an image that should be followed. However, because it is a role model, many people seek to follow the example that has been set even though it is flawed.

William Galston, President Clinton's domestic adviser, now says, "The data suggest that the best anti-poverty program for America's children is a stable, intact family."[39] That certainly was not new information that had come to light since the election. I think Robert Rector, senior policy analyst for the Heritage Foundation, hit the nail on the head when he commented, "Everyone agreed with Quayle all along, but Quayle was just such a punching bag, I don't think he could say apple pie is good without getting roasted."[40]

Again, the media failed to serve the public by focusing on the individual and ridiculing the person rather than dealing with the issue. As a result, Clinton scored another hit because the liberal media made fun of the incumbents.

I fault the media also in not making public the figures that proved the economy had begun to turn around during the presidential campaign. Instead, they headlined Clinton's accusations that the economy was still wallowing in recession.

Less than a month after the elections, reports were published that the recovery was gaining strength and the economic outlook was indeed brightening. These predictions were based on October figures. In addition, worker productivity made its largest gain in two decades during 1992, and orders for U.S. factory goods soared to a record high.

I have this very uneasy feeling in the pit of my stomach the media deliberately withheld news of this trend from the public until after Clinton was assured of being in office. The media even buried the impact the Gulf War had on the deficit. Had the truth been presented and Clinton's lack of integrity unveiled before the elections, would the American people have been so eager to change in his direction?

Because Clinton is the consummate politician, he had undoubtedly observed that this strategy worked for FDR and could conceivably work again. FDR certainly should take credit for most of the economic strides that helped the American people out of the depression, but history would suggest that Herbert Hoover had already started some of the programs for which FDR received the credit.

FDR was elected because he had convinced the public he was the one who held the answer to their problems in his hands. I often wonder, as stated so eloquently in the movie *The American President*, "If we had television 60 years ago, would the American people have elected a man in a wheelchair?" Like FDR, all Clinton had to do was convince the electorate Bush would continue to let us flounder in a sagging economy while he had the answers that would turn the tide. The media assisted him ably in his efforts. They simply did not tell us the economy was improving. Bush had found an answer or two himself. Instead, they let the people continue to believe, "It's the economy, stupid!" and Clinton was elected. A survey by the Times Mirror Center for People and the Press showed that 43% of the people they polled said the press was unfair to Bill Clinton.[41] 51% thought the media was being fair. Most felt that Clinton had brought his own problems on himself. He simply had not done a very good job.

When the midterm elections resulted in a Republican majority in Congress, they did not "win a majority" or receive a "mandate for change" as the Democrats had done previously. According to the media, they "seized power" and staged a "shock capture of both houses." Clearly, the media carefully chooses its words in describing liberal views as opposed to more conservative ones.

Compare the media's terminology when describing the Democrats gaining control of any branch of government. They "put an end to gridlock." However, when the GOP manages to do the same, it becomes the "end of the two-party system."

It is interesting to note that *Newsweek* stated, "Bill Clinton promised an administration that 'looks like America,' but America last week chose a Congress that looked and sounded like Rush Limbaugh...largely white and male." When you look at the facts, however, a different picture emerges. Congress has always had a majority of white males—even when it was controlled by the Democrats. Interestingly enough, the present Congress has an improved minority and white representation over previous ones.[42]

In fact, for the first time, a woman chaired the powerful Labor and Human Resources Committee. I wonder if the fact that Nancy Kassebaum is a Republican has anything to do with the media's ignoring this accomplishment. If she had been a Democrat, you can bet she would have been on the covers of magazines and her achievement would have been hailed as Woman of the Year.

Hillary's involvement with the Whitewater scandal has been carefully played down. In fact, you would think this was just another small-town petty theft trial instead of a multi-million dollar swindle. The media has carefully briefly and favorably reported on her testimony, carefully not putting her in an unfavorable light. This hardly seems fair to the rest of the populace, does it?

Clinton, himself, is barely mentioned, and as far as the media is concerned, he bears no guilt in the dealings. If somebody has to get the axe in this affair, the media clearly is on Bill's side.

In Fornigate, Clinton was not censured by the media at all. Instead, the alleged victim, Paula

Jones, was hammered in sixty-seven percent of the stories about the affair, and the state trooper who came forward to corroborate her account received bad press seventy-seven percent of the time.

I believe this irresponsible reporting is not because the media likes Clinton so much; it is because the Republicans are now in control of Congress and have hopes of recapturing the presidency, and that would not further the liberal cause, which is the media's agenda.

I had to laugh at the truth of the following quotation. "The good news for Clinton is that the public trusts the press even less than it trusts him. Imagine the trouble he'd be in if Whitewater and Fornigate became an obsession for somebody the public really trusts—like Oprah or Barney."[43]

More seriously, I do not necessarily think the press has been unfair to Bill Clinton, but I do feel they have picked the wrong things to emphasize. I think his performance in itself bears close scrutiny and that is what the media should be exposing in detail to its audience. In my opinion, the press has been grossly unfair to the American people rather than to the President. They most probably withheld vital information both before and after the election that could have altered our knowledge of what is really happening in our country. By withholding it, they failed to serve the people. They shirked their primary responsibility and they encouraged and helped initiate an agenda with which many Americans do not agree. I say leave Bill, the person, alone. Focus on his agenda and his policies. If you disagree with Clinton's politics, do something about it.

As you watch the news and programming, ask yourself this question, "Is the media focusing on the issue or on the person?" Then answer that question. Then ask yourself, "Where should the focus have been?" If there is disagreement between your two answers, ask yourself, "Why?"

WORKS CITED

1. Kranish, Michael and Putzel, Michael. "After rocky start, Clinton to renew focus." *The Boston Sunday Globe* 25 April 1993 1.

2. Dreifus, Claudia. "Prince of PBS." *Modern Maturity* October-November 1993: 84.

3. Miller, Ron, Knight-Ridder Newspapers. "Bill Clinton learns steps in dance with media." *The Orange County Register* 30 July 1993 Show 46.

4. *Time* 7 June 1993 Cover.

5. Duffy, Michael. "That Sinking Feeling." *Time* 7 June 1993 23.

6. *Newsweek* 7 June 1993 Cover.

7. Miller, Ron, Knight-Ridder Newspapers. "Bill Clinton learns steps in dance with media." *The Orange County Register* 30 July 1993 Show 44.

8. *Newsweek* 7 June 1993 25

9. Nichols, Bill. "Clinton's ire zeroes in on familiar target: The press." *USA Today* 28 May 1993 8A.

10. Nasar, Sylvia. "Confidence in Clinton is Slipping Among Many Business Leaders." *The New York Times* 9 May 1993 1.

11. Wolf, Richard and Welch, William M. "President loses a big perk." *USA Today* 27 May 1993 13A.

12. Thomas, Cal. "Clinton the Snake-Oil Salesman Is Not the President He Said He Would Be." *The Salt Lake Tribune* 2 May 1993.

13. Snow, Tony. "Is the problem really Clinton?" *USA Today* 3 June 1993 13A.

14. Benedetto, Richard. "For Clinton, a blunder storm." *USA Today* 7 June 1993 6A.

15. Phillips, Kevin. "Bill Clinton's Excellent Adventure." *The Los Angeles Times* 2 May 1993 M1.

16. Blonston, Gary. "Clinton presidency lacks discipline and a sense of priorities." *The Orange County Register* 16 May 1993 News 22.

17. Hentoff, Nat. "A president's principles: 'There is no Bill Clinton'." *The Orange County Register* 6 June 1993 Commentary 1.

18. Hines, Cragg. "Clinton's 100 days." *The Houston Chronicle* 25 April 1993 1A.

19. Rosenstiel, Thomas B. "To Media, White House Staff Has Become a Joke." *The Los Angeles Times* 28 May 1993 A10.

20. Hilzenrath, David S. and Mufson, Steven. "Keeper of the Flame." *The Washington Post* 9 May 1993 H4.

21. Phillips, Leslie. "President, media stay at arm's length." *USA Today* 26 April 1993 4A.

22. "Opinionline." *USA Today* 24 May 1993 13A.

23. Boyd, Robert S. "Billboard: Clinton's Runs, Hits & Errors." *Salt Lake Tribune* 2 May 1993 A8.

24. Nichols, Bill. "Visit sparks jeers, cheers for president." *USA Today* 1 June 1993 2A.

25. The *Daily Mainichi Newspaper* as reported by Hearst Newspapers. "Japanese avid for stories about U.S. first family." *The Orange County Register* 7 July 1993 News 3.

26. Reynolds, Barbara. "Guinier's supporters could mutiny on Clinton's ship." *USA Today* 11 June 1993 13A.

27. Samuelson, Robert J. "The Politics of Overpromise." *The Los Angeles Times* 10 June 1993.

28. Buchanan, Patrick J. "Clinton risks being Carterized." *The Orange County Register* 29 April 1993 Metro 9.

29. Hentoff, Nat. "A president's principles: There is no Bill Clinton." *The Orange County Register* 6 June 1993 Commentary 1.

30. Snow, Tony. "Is the problem really Clinton? *USA Today* 3 June 1993 13A.

31. Rosenberg, Howard. "Bill & Tom's Obsequious Adventures." *The Los Angeles Times* 10 May 1993 B11.

32. Rosen, Jay. "Down With the Weekly Box Score." *The Los Angeles Times* 8 June 1993 B11.

33. Geyer, Georgie Ann. "Saints Alive!" *The Orange County Register* 30 May 1993 Commentary 1.

34. Johnson, Peter. "Bloodworth-Thomason, on the record in D.C." *USA Today* 25 May 1993.

35. Richter, Paul. "Thomasons Decry Being Cast as Villains." *The Los Angeles Times* 27 May 1993 A20.

36. Limbaugh, Rush. "Lies, Lies." House Republican Conference and Press Reports. 1993.

37. McDonald, Greg. "A very public player." *The Houston Chronicle* 25 April 1993 18A.

38. Fields, Suzanne. "Bill, Hillary are wedded to radical change." *The Orange County Register* 6 May 1993 Commentary 4.

39. Durkin, Miriam, Knight-Ridder Newspapers. "Officials rethink family issues and admit Quayle had a point." *The Orange County Register* 7 May 1993 Accent 5.

40. Ibid.

41. Rosenstiel, Thomas B. "43% Surveyed Say Press Is Unfair to Clinton." *The Los Angeles Times* 10 June 1993 A27.

42. Urschel, Joe. "On media scoreboards, don't Republicans count?" *USA Today* 18 November, 1994 13A.

43. Snow, Tony. "Uneven coverage of Clinton by media." *USA Today* 24 October 1994 13A.

Chapter 11

ROSS PEROT

Who is Ross Perot, that enigmatic personage who appeared on the 1992 American political scene with such force? His ability to arouse strong emotional responses in people has been labeled both an asset and a liability. Said one Texan, "You either love him and give him wholehearted support, or you hate his guts." There are not many today who can evoke such a clear-cut reaction. Most of those in politics have half-hearted support from those who are in favor of their agenda and lukewarm resistance from those who oppose it.

RELEASE OUR POWs!

Let's take a closer look at Ross Perot, the person, and the principles he espouses. Although a phenomenally successful businessman, the founder and owner of Dallas-based Electronic Data Systems first came to the attention of the public with his efforts to help POWs in Vietnam in 1969. A graduate of Annapolis, he remembered his classmates who had given their lives in this conflict, and his heart went out to those still being held prisoner, perhaps never to return home again. He led a campaign to publicize the plight of those still held captive. Even after an attempt on his life, he did not abandon those prisoners who needed his help.

He even chartered a jet and tried to fly dinner into Hanoi for the prisoners. This gesture was rejected by the North Vietnamese government, but it generated invaluable publicity for his cause. The American people saw a knight in shining armor who still cared about those our government had seemingly forgotten, and they rallied behind Perot. As the grassroots campaign throughout the United States blossomed, treatment of the prisoners did indeed improve. Mail and packages began to get through to them, names were released, and as the prisoners heard of the efforts on their behalf, their morale was boosted enormously.

WINGS OF EAGLES[1]

He next came into the public eye with his daring rescue of two EDS employees who were being held as prisoners in an Iranian jail. His willingness to risk his life for those who worked for him stirred the deep feelings most American hold that you look after your own–those for whom you are responsible. His sense of personal responsibility would not let him abandon them to whatever whim the revolutionary Iranian government decided to visit on the prisoners.

After failing to muster assistance from governmental sources and being aware his employees were in extreme danger if they remained in prison, he personally organized and trained a group of EDS employees to rescue them. The rescue involved hiring an ex-Green Beret officer to turn volunteers from EDS into a crack commando team. The fact that they did successfully rescue the two prisoners without incurring any casualties attests to their readiness.

Perot, himself, made the dangerous trip into the country to personally oversee the effort. When it became necessary for him to supervise from Turkey, he willingly handed over the Iranian operation to Bull Simons, an ex-Green Beret. Supporters point out that this ability to enlist top people and then resist the urge to micromanage them is an invaluable asset to any politician. If a politician can surround himself or herself with a cadre of people who are knowledgeable in their fields then the government will function as it should.

After the flurry caused by the rescue died away, Perot did not receive much national attention until the 1992 national elections, although he had fought a few other small battles–trying to save Wall Street, taking on General Motors, and reforming both the Texas drug laws and the educational system. Then he turned to the political scene, accompanied by national television coverage, much hoopla, and his assurance to "fix it."

WHOSE FACE?

His detractors like to point out that there are several faces of H. Ross Perot. There is the face he wanted presented to the public, the face his associates saw, the face the media created, and the face that the public finally saw and rejected.

His supporters insist this is not the case. They contend there are only two faces of H. Ross Perot; one is the real Ross Perot while the other is the face that the media and those who fear his honest and open approach have created; and this second face bears no resemblance to the real person.

Even though the election with its charges and counter charges is long over, it still is not clear why a fifth of the voters chose Perot as their candidate of choice. Many say it was because they chose to vote against one of the other candidates. Others insist it was because he offered alternatives and solutions that no other candidate did. They voted for Ross Perot for two reasons: 1) they wanted to send a clear signal to then-President Bush that they were not pleased with his administration; and 2) they appreciated Perot's no-nonsense approach to business. People also believed he would eliminate government bureaucracy.

What is clear as a result of the election is that there is a ground swell of American citizens who are saying, "We are tired of the same old political trivia being offered election after election. We want a change–and we want this change to be for the better."

I CAN DO IT!

Does Ross Perot offer this kind of change? By some measure, there is no doubt that he does. He is full of answers and optimistic in his assessment of what he can do for the country. He projects a can-do spirit with enthusiasm. He points out the shortcomings of the government while promising solutions to the problems that beset our country. He has great appeal among the middle-class who are overwhelmed by taxes, regulations, and out-of-pocket costs for necessities such as child care and long-term health care. They see his can-do attitude and individualism as the answer to increased government intervention into their lives.

Clouding this portrait, however, is the Ross Perot that emerged during the campaign. This Ross Perot seemed to fear opposition and defeat and so withdrew rather than face them. The intense media scrutiny appeared to have cowed him completely. Some point out that this withdrawal simply was evidence of his thin-skinned, paranoid side that is so easily offended and his do-it-my-way-or-no-way attitude. Could it be Perot was sick and tired of the media's control of the election and constant effort to put him down? His past record would lead one to believe he was not afraid of anything— and he certainly has not appeared to be since that time. His withdrawal from the 1992 election is ultimately what "killed" him in the 1996 election.

IF THE PEOPLE WANT ME...

No one can deny his flair for the spectacular when he announced his 1992 candidacy on the "Larry King Live" television show. Not even his family knew before they heard the broadcast. The first part of his campaign was speedy and spontaneous, and the workers were fresh and invigorated. It was like nothing the public had seen on the political scene for too many years.

Then his announcement that he would no longer be a candidate not only blasted the hopes of those who saw in Perot a different type of candidate–one who could change things–but completely shattered the image of the positive go-getter that had been projected during the first part of the campaign. His volunteers felt betrayed and shamed that Perot, in reality, appeared to be a quitter who couldn't stand the heat. To restore the confidence of his backers would be a major endeavor for Ross Perot.

He proved that he could not only restore their confidence, he could become the most successful third-party candidate since Teddy Roosevelt. While this may be small consolation to those who felt that had he not withdrawn from the presidential race, he might have actually won the election, or at least thrown it into the House of Representatives, it is no small accomplishment. An accomplishment that was achieved through an active appeal directly to the public.

Although the media was quiet on the issue and there has not been much publicity, Ross Perot quietly formed a third party. This third party opposed both Bill Clinton and Bob Dole and hoped to capture the presidency. The Dole/Kemp ticket is the one that undoubtedly caused Perot trouble.

PEROT'S USE OF THE MEDIA

Although he was criticized by his detractors for spending his private funds for television time, I think most of the people admired this ability and applauded it because it pointed to his being a self-made man. Actually, he received huge chunks of free television time.[2] Talk shows welcomed him, and he was a frequent guest on cable television. He was able to bypass the evaluations offered by major network commentators and appeal directly to the public.

As he was interviewed or offered the opportunity to air his views, no one interpreted them for the listeners. They were free to form their own opinions based on what they had heard.

Some analysts feel this is a shortcoming of today's media coverage; however, others say it offers a freedom greatly needed to let the public hear the truth and draw their own conclusions. As a concerned citizen, I was glad for the opportunity to hear a candidate's views presented directly to me without the filter of a commentator's interpretation and opinion. It allowed me to see the person, warts and all, and decide for myself whether I thought him worthy of my vote or whether one of the other candidates should receive it. It must have worked for Perot because people voted for him.

UNITED WE STAND

Not having to spend money for television coverage let Ross Perot add to the funds of his **United We Stand America**, which in turn kept his campaign going. One critic saw it this way, "The grass roots of Mr. Perot's campaign are heavily watered by Mr. Perot himself."[3] Others felt that although these contributions strengthened the dependency of the organization on Perot's support, they kept Perot himself from becoming in debt to anyone else for his successes. Therefore, he could indeed be the people's advocate because he "owed" no one.

His critics continued to blast Perot as being the candidate without solutions. After having listened to his campaign and read his United We Stand, I disagree strongly. I feel he does offer solutions. However, I must concede they are solutions the liberal element of our country does not see as answers. They require sacrifice on the part of the people, a rugged individualistic approach to solving the major problems that exist today, and encourage the private business and industrial sectors rather than increasing government support and subsidies for international competitors. These solutions lessen the influence the government has in individual lives, and this is anathema to the liberals, of course.

AN OUTSIDER'S VIEW

Perot offered a solution to the gridlock that enveloped the country both politically and economically. He was an "outsider." He was not a professional politician; he was a businessman who had spent his life solving problems. He could relate to the common man who also was not a politician and who in most cases was much less successful financially than Perot but definitely, within his or her circles, a problem solver. Mr. or Ms. Everyday Person looked on Perot as the one who could bring relief from the increasing governmental intrusion and blundering because he was free to come in and "clean house" and many Americans felt that was exactly what was needed.

MEDIA PARANOIA

As Ross Perot's original campaign for the Presidency continued to flourish, it became evident the media was becoming more and more apprehensive at his effortless success in reaching the voting public directly. After all, in their own eyes, they had become the new political party.[4] He was bypassing their channel to the people–the channel of interpretation. Obviously, Perot was lessening their influence with mainline America. He was going to the people directly!

Of even more danger to the media was Perot's freedom to take his campaign against the establishment (including the media) directly to the people.[5] They would have no chance to alter it or soften its blows. They would have no opportunity to be judgmental in what was presented to the public. The media would not have their usual opportunity to assess a candidate, determine whether in their opinion he was suitable and successful, and then present his carefully edited remarks to the audience. Perot's remarks would stand as he delivered them.

Unfortunately for Ross Perot, the media decided he was not temperamentally fit to be president, and so emphasized that opinion in commentary after commentary during his 1992 campaign. They voiced reservations about his alleged paranoia and dangerously unbalanced emotional state. I believe these allegations simply reaffirmed the media's own paranoia at losing its illegitimate hold as a screen through which all candidates must be filtered and their unbalanced view that increased government control is the answer to all of America's problems.

I wonder what kind of an election we could have if the only news of elections that was permitted was the actual, unfiltered and unedited remarks each candidate made while campaigning; if the media were constrained from offering their opinions as news; and if the American people could make a choice dependent only upon their own evaluation of what they had personally seen and heard?

I'm sure we would hear cries of, "But we have freedom of speech!" from the media. But isn't that what we see happening too often today? The "other voice" is being denied freedom of speech. They are only being offered an edited, filtered voice that emanates from the established media. I am delighted to see that the American electorate had a chance during this particular election to make a choice based on criteria that included unfiltered public appearances.

AMERICA, HOW DO YOU FEEL?

Since the last election, Ross Perot has not faded from the American scene. He has continued to bring **United We Stand America** to the attention of the public. Its Mission Statement, "We the people of United We Stand America, recognizing that our republic was founded as a government of the people, unite to restore the integrity of our economic and political systems. We commit ourselves to organize, to educate, to participate in the political process, and to hold our public servants accountable. We shall rebuild our country, renew its economic, moral and social strength, and return the sovereignty of America to her people," has touched the heart strings of countless Americans.

His national television polls of how the public feels on certain issues evoked a strong response. Overwhelmingly, the people liked these programs, wanted more of this type of programming, and wanted **United We Stand America** to continue as an organization. Obviously, the public was saying they desired a change toward more traditional values. They were not offended by his assertions that the person in the mirror is responsible for the mess we are in and responsible for providing the solutions. His solution is admittedly simplistic. All we have to do is reform our government, rebuild our country, stop spending our children's money, and pay off our debts.

NO NAFTA

Ross Perot continued his pro-America stance quite emphatically with his opposition to the North American Free Trade Agreement (NAFTA). Buying time on television to expose what he considered its dangers and drawbacks, he was even able to debate the issue with Vice President Gore. Unfortunately, this debate was akin to the infamous Nixon-Kennedy debate. Remember, if you listened on the radio, Nixon won; however, the handsome, charismatic JFK won hands-down on television.

Now that NAFTA is a few years old, we will eventually see if Perot's predictions will come true and Americans will lose jobs as industry starts using a cheaper labor force.

One thing I personally know is that many of my friends in the trucking industry are voicing concern for the safety of American road users because Mexican truck drivers are not required to have the knowledge base and road skills that

American drivers must have to obtain their commercial driver's licenses. They feel that passage of NAFTA will unleash an avalanche of unskilled drivers who will present constant danger to American drivers. The other point of their concern is the damage that will occur to the infrastructure of our highway system by the traffic of trucking fleets that do not meet U.S. standards for weight or safety regulations.

Perot, of course, has his own version of NAFTA that he says will work and will protect American jobs as well. First of all, we must not violate national sovereignty nor the legal rights of U.S. citizens; jobs and wages for both American and Mexican workers must be increased; health standards must remain high; and the agreement must be enforceable.

It is interesting to see that even though the present NAFTA agreement has already presented many of the problems Perot foresaw, his alternate proposal has not received more attention. Can it be because it is the type of agreement we should have had in the first place?

THE PEOPLE'S ADVOCATE

No matter what the outcome for both Perot's political and trade proposals, I believe he will remain on the scene as what he perceives to be the People's Advocate, telling people to wake up and take back their country. It belongs to them. I do not believe Perot will be able to remain silent as the battle ensues for the path our country will take.

I believe that Ross Perot appealed to the American people because he espouses beliefs that they, too, hold. Americans do not want to become just another number in the system or another cog in the socialistic machine that lumbers through the life of the country. They believe they are worthwhile in their own right, are valuable as individuals, and have a right to work out their own solutions to the problems that exist by using methods that encourage free enterprise, entrepeneurship, and the traditional American way of life. I would personally back him if I could get an audience with him.

Perot was and is like a breath of fresh air. He is not evasive about his beliefs and what he would like to see happen in our country, Although he has had to constantly battle media prejudice and lies about him both during the 1992 campaign and since that time, he stands for truth in media. Americans everywhere who were tired of being lied to by the media responded. They too wanted the truth. The citizenry appreciated his forthrightness and the role model he presented as an honest and candid person.

As concerned citizens, we must also realize when the media is worried about a candidate, they resort to jokes about his or her appearance. In Perot's case, it was his ears. Did we ever hear anything about Clinton's appearance? Oh yes, we heard the constant comparison, "He's just like JFK." In both cases, these comments were meant to sway the public's opinion of a candidate on the basis of looks rather than performance and goals.

A DIFFERENT KIND OF ROLE MODEL

I believe Ross Perot gives us all something to emulate in our lives–being able to negotiate honestly and openly. This example is too often lacking on the political scene. I believe that not only should we learn from his personal example, but we also have much to learn about the qualities for which we should look in a candidate.

I was rather taken aback when I realized following the 1992 election that I was not as well informed about either of the major candidates as I should have been. I had made far too many assumptions. I suspect that I was not alone in this position. I hope all of us will learn from this experience and become more informed voters who really try to know those for whom they will be voting.

Ross Perot has made a profound impact on America not in just being a different kind of candidate but in organizing the public in a way similar to no other to try to reform the political system and change the direction the country is headed. Following his First National Referendum, the Gordon S. Black Corporation polled the public. Commenting on the 20 percent of respondents who said they planned to join United We Stand America, he said, "It appears that more than 20 million adults heard or watched Mr. Perot's broadcast.... If anywhere near the 20% join United We Stand America, it will have succeeded in creating the largest citizens' organization in the history of the United States. An organization with 20 million or more adults will be larger than the entire labor movement in the United States, and it will have the potential to be the most influential organization ever."[6]

Now that's what I call an accomplishment!

WORKS CITED

1. Follett, Ken. *On Wings of Eagles* (The story of the heroic rescue mission of his employees by H. Ross Perot) New York: Signet/Penguin, 1983.

2. Ceaser, James, Busch, Andrew. *Upside Down and Inside Out* Lanham, MD: Rowman and Littlefield, 1993. 106.

3. Noah, Tim. "Perot Waters His Grass Roots Heavily," *The Wall Street Journal* 30 September 1992. A18.

4. Barber, James as cited in Ceaser, James and Busch, Andrew. *Upside Down and Inside Out* Lanham, MD: Rowman and Littlefield, 1993 114.

5. Ibid. 115.

6. Ibid. 158.

Chapter 12

GROSS INJUSTICE

Reginald Denny, Rodney King, Laurence Powell, Stacy Koon, Damian Williams, Ted Briseno, and the Denny's Restaurant chain all evoke images of racial injustice in our minds. Some are victims; some are perpetrators. All have been featured by the media, we cannot escape it today. There are those who suffer from it; those who would capitalize on it; and those who simply seem to be caught in the backlash that surrounds us all. If a certain group does not like a movie, a story or an article in the newspaper, too often we find it labeled as another instance of racial injustice.

Let's take a look at how the issue of racial injustice has been affected by the media's treatment of it. Did the media in any way contribute to the Los Angeles riots? I believe that it did–at least indirectly. Why do I say this? I remember passing through my family room the fateful afternoon the riots began. The television set was on. I caught a glimpse of a man-woman news team. They were debating whether the events unfolding at the corner of Florence and Normandie should continue to air. Did they have an obligation to their audience or were they showing something that should be accompanied by editorial comment later? Naturally, that exchange caught my attention. The station then flashed back to the beating of Reginald Denny then in progress.

WE ARE SUSPENDING NORMAL PROGRAMMING...

Coverage of the events there and throughout South-Central Los Angeles continued until the riots were brought under control. Too often it was done with a sensational, racial injustice-provoking approach. At the time, I wondered what effect this coverage was having on those who were rioting. Did it escalate the events? Did the participants get a thrill from seeing themselves on television? Did their actions fuel the violence evidenced as others began to attack the neighboring areas? Did the coverage add an "everybody's doing it" atmosphere that beckoned viewers to join the rioters—people that would not have done so had the media been silent or treated the situation in a different manner?

There is no question the media must assume some responsibility for the spread of the violence. They certainly did not start it, but neither did they work to stem it. Let's take a look at how they covered it.

First of all, the media was everywhere. Audiences were "treated" to eyewitness accounts of mobs looting and burning stores, beating anyone who happened to get in their way, and crowds grossly out of control. We were also constantly reminded of the lack of police protection or intervention. In fact, several instances of alleged police retreat were recounted. It was almost as if the media was saying, "Go ahead. Riot! No one is going to stop you."

WHO'S RODNEY KING?

The riots have been universally blamed on the acquittal of the police officers in the beating of Rodney King. With 20/20 hindsight, I wonder who first made that claim? Was it the media, with an eye toward sensationalism? Perhaps, if the first "temper tantrum" had not been accompanied by the news that the riots had begun, the outcome might have been different. You ask why I feel this way? I think back to an interview later with one of the rioters. The newsperson asked him if he was rioting because of the Rodney King verdict. His reply was, "Who's Rodney King?"

I abhor what the police did to King–nobody should be subjected to that kind of treatment, but I must ask the question, Throughout the days after the video of King's beating was first shown and before the verdict was handed down, did the media make an effort to present open forums of the whole issue of alleged police brutality in light of almost overwhelming odds against them in certain metropolitan areas? No; instead, they latched onto the police brutality aspect of the situation because "it made news," never once considering what the final outcome might be if they did not offer a more balanced view of the arrest and an attempt to provide a peaceful solution to the problems that existed.

More headlines could be generated if they focused on police brutality, so the media turned Rodney King into a hero. He was portrayed as a helpless victim, not as the person he really is– someone who has run afoul of the law on many occasions and was alleged by the police to have been under the influence of drugs at the time. While police brutality was evident in this case, there was no balance of cases offered in which the police had suffered as a result of not being forcible enough when trying to arrest a suspect. No counter statistics were offered on the number of officers that had been wounded or killed because they stopped a lawbreaker in good faith who turned out to be someone who would rather kill than surrender.

Instead, we had a "black and white" picture of the bad guys beating some poor helpless victim.

Only this time, the good guy wore black. Would you invite Rodney King over for dinner or allow your children to befriend him? Please realize these comments have absolutely nothing to do with race.

Yes, you can argue that past years of racial injustice warranted this interpretation, but here again, we cannot judge an issue except as it stands today. We cannot tweak the facts to make a point. We must examine them honestly in the cold, hard light of truth.

I am extremely concerned about the role the media will play in solving the racial issues that plague our society today. When I read an editorial about the racial problems in the United States and find such statements as, "The root of our racial divide is not the question of multicultural education so much as the issue of forced assimilation. Any minorities willing to accept a narrow version of America's history or its continuing discrimination will find broad acceptance," and "Those who don't will become targets in our race war."[1] I cannot believe these comments sow the seeds of peace.

A GREAT ROLE MODEL

To blame a bad attitude that erupts into violence on existing economic conditions is to deny a victory to those who have chosen to rise above the difficulties. Someone I really admire is Les Brown, a motivational speaker and author of *Live Your Dreams*. Not only did he come from a minority group, he was one of twins who were abandoned by their father at the age of three weeks. Raised by a single parent, he was regarded as educably retarded as a child but chose not to let all this stand in his way. He pursued the upward path and became the man behind five award-winning specials for PBS.[2]

How many other men can say the same? Ask yourself the unsettling question, Even though he is an excellent role model, how often is Les Brown featured as part of the answer to racial unrest and alleged injustice? I hope his outstanding specials are evidence he is finally getting the recognition and spotlight he so deserves.

THE MEDIA ARMY

For those of you who have never heard of him, Sir Eldon Griffiths is a former member of the British House of Commons, currently director of the Center for International Business at Chapman University, and the President of the Orange County World Affairs Council.

He writes of returning from Russia the day after the verdict was handed down following the second trial of the officers for the Rodney King beating. His disgust with the media is evident in his commentary of the lead stories. He describes the media army's reaction to the rumor the judge was about to make an announcement, "Eight TV helicopters–more than there are in the entire Bosnian air force–within minutes took to the sky. Hundreds of reporters grabbed their gas masks (!), pulled on their flak jackets (!), and raced to prearranged 'observation posts' scattered around south-central L.A." And then as quiet prevailed in Los Angeles, "The media showed signs of frustration, even disappointment that L.A. didn't explode. Editors, waiting for hard news of battles, violence, casualties, don't want [this quiet] to happen."

In conducting a post-mortem, he felt the media should have answered three charges: 1) The media exalted an alleged robber, drunk, and speedster into something approaching a cult hero, who will, as a result of the coverage, receive millions for his troubles; 2) LA has been portrayed as a "sink of mass hysteria where the drop of a camera shutter turns [citizens] into an angry mob;" and 3) The media used a great lack of perspective in depriving Californians of other important news around the world.

To support this last charge, he details important (to the future of our country) trials in Brazil, Italy, and Russia and a recent survey that found 38% of adults and 53% per high school students did not connect the Holocaust with Nazism or Adolf Hitler. Let me add that the same survey showed 22% of adults and 20% of high school students were not even convinced it had happened![3]

He closed by asking where the media circus will move to for its next saga. The Amy Fisher/Joey Buttafuco saga in New York?[4] Well, what do you know, that's exactly where they went.

Another outsider looking in voiced his concern over the casting aside of the importance of due process for a desired outcome. He stated, "The tenor as well as the aims of our legal system have been changing. Politicians, including their legal appointees such as the attorney general of the United States of America, are focused not on process but on result. The country is in danger of becoming a semi-civilized lynch mob."

He continued, "Too many leaders treated the event as a contest where they were awaiting a desired result, and never mind the process. After the first trial resulted in what most people felt was a bad verdict, this was not written off as the cost of trusting due process of law. Instead a new trial was demanded, even though by the tradition of our legal system this came very close to being double jeopardy."[5]

AND THE VERDICT IS . . .

Unfortunately, we did not hear many of our commentators echoing these same sentiments. Rather they expressed concern prior to the verdict about what would happen if...and afterward commented on whether the verdict was a fair one and how a riot was avoided because the "right" verdict was handed down. In the process, news persons did not seem concerned that Rodney King was still a free man who had not been prosecuted for drunk driving, resisting arrest, or violating his parole. I wonder if their lack of concern about the process by which the verdict was reached could be attributed to their sympathy with the liberal political viewpoint and its agenda?

After the verdict in the second trial of the officers was handed down, newspaper articles contained sentiments such as, "What might the verdicts provoke? I'm thinking how crazy it's going to get,' a 27-year-old college student said, wide-eyed, describing an anxiety that has spread over much of Los Angeles like a sulfur smog,"[6] "Guarded Calm Follows Verdict in King Case," "The city is spared the nightmare that some had feared,"[7] "The verdict: peace in L.A.,"[8] "Wise, Just King Verdict Demonstrates Americans' Capacity to Right Wrongs,"[9] and "A federal jury convicted two police officers Saturday of violating the civil rights of black motorist Rodney King in his video-taped beating, bringing peace to a city where an earlier trial led to the nation's worst rioting in decades."[10] Paper after paper carried the sentiment that "no morning had carried more dread." Implied in almost every account was the fear that was supposed to permeate the entire populace of the LA basin-if any verdict but guilty was brought down, there was going to be another riot.

Very little was mentioned about the feeling within the affected community that things were under control, and that another riot simply was not going to happen. There were thousands of African-American, Asian, Hispanic, and white people who did not riot the first time and certainly had no intention of rioting if another one broke out. The media seemed to also ignore the fact that Koreans have owned businesses there for years without incident or altercation.

Sad to say, broader concerns such as those expressed by former Chief of LA Police Daryl Gates that the officers had been subjected to double jeopardy[11] and the statement by Ira Salzman, lawyer for Stacey Koon, "Justice is not a circus. Stacey Koon is not some sacrificial animal to be cast aside for peace in Los Angeles,"[12] were buried deep in the papers. Even Koon's comments that he felt no responsibility for the riots but that King should feel guilty[13] were not widely disseminated.

I was equally concerned about the articles that appeared prior to the sentencing that purportedly calculated what a fair sentence would be, thus setting the stage for dissatisfaction when sentencing occurred. Because these estimates were reported to be from federal government sources, it was implied should the judge decide on any other sentences, he would most certainly be remiss in his responsibility.

In most cases, the estimates were higher than the actual sentences. It was almost as though the media was setting the scene for a riot because they were disappointed the last one failed. Is this twisted mind-set what we are really seeing today in many of our news releases? I certainly hope not, but I am beginning to wonder.

Why does the media expect trouble from the

black community if a preconceived verdict is not reached and yet does not expect trouble from the white community when a desired verdict is not reached? Why is it they did not even consider the white community might be incensed if the men who beat Reginald Denny were not convicted? Is it because such sentiments would be dismissed by the public and, therefore, not newsworthy? Are white people really less likely to riot? Is the press interested only in firing up minority special interest groups? Why are only the black people portrayed as rioters or potential rioters? Is it the media is only interested in hype that will clearly sell newspapers?

Some commentators even voiced apprehension that if the Denny attackers were found guilty, it would incite the black community to another riot. I found it very disconcerting that this type of concern was being expressed by the media. It was almost as though we were being held hostage. This observation is in light of the fact that Denny was a completely innocent person who happened to be in the wrong place at the wrong time; whereas King was a known lawbreaker. These threats were made that if preconceived determinations of guilt were not confirmed by our judicial system, riots would occur.

One paper featured an article discussing this possibility in an article headlined, "The Rodney King trial is over, and worries about riots are shelved pending the Reginald Denny trial."[14] Where are the mediamakers who are responding to these threats by trying to bring understanding and healing to a hurting city? Again, let me make it clear that no one should ever be subjected to the type of "animal beating" both Reginald Denny and Rodney King experienced, but how will we ever realize racial harmony if the media continues to drive a liberal wedge between us all?

SEE DICK RUN

Their treatment of both cases emits an attitude resembling that of a teacher who sees a student in the class misbehaving. Instead of censuring that person, the teacher calls for the rest of the class to watch the misbehavior. I do not have to tell you where that will lead. That's right. We have someone going totally out of control because there are no limits. Why don't we see violent acts reported as such?

Webster defines a crowd as "a great body of people;" whereas, a mob is a "large or disorderly crowd, especially one bent on riotous or destructive action." I do not believe the Los Angeles riots were so much a result of civil unrest as they were a mob out of control and without restraint that was being encouraged by a "watch Johnny misbehave" attitude.

Of the over seven hundred persons convicted of looting in the year following the riots, over sixty percent had been arrested before, and half of those had prior felony convictions. Their reasons for stealing were varied: "C'mon man. I just wanted some free stuff like everyone else," "I only wanted to make a sandwich," "I didn't loot this gun [AK-47]. I just bought it from a 'smoker' [riot arsonist]," and "Me, my brother, another big Samoan, and a black guy all went down there. It was the big Samoan's idea to get a radio."

Prosecutors voiced concern that media coverage had drawn out the criminal element, "This is something they cannot watch on TV without getting up and participating."[15] In an evaluation of the Long Beach man who had stolen two car stereos, his probation officer wrote, "He was not angered by the Rodney King decision, nor did he feel troubled by any prejudice or sense of oppression. The defendant simply was an opportunistic parasite."[16]

While an occasional article such as the one quoted here presented the facts about the riot as they were then emerging, the media in general continued to blame the white community for the conditions that led to the riot and the trial for lighting the fuse. I ask you, If the police officers had been black, would the beating have been any more acceptable? Absolutely not!

In an effort to place responsibility on another segment of society, articles appeared that blamed Hollywood for not supplying the industry-wide rebuilding efforts that many envisioned. The authors of these articles certainly lost sight of the aid that the film community did provide. I am sure this accounting is not complete, but it is generally known that Michael Jackson alone gave $1.25 million to provide services to inner city children, Barbara Streisand donated $100,000, Garth Brooks raised $1 million in concerts to be combined with another $1 million from the United Way, and many executives joined the Rebuild LA Task Force. Continuing efforts now total well into the millions. That seems to me to be a pretty sizable chunk toward fixing something they did not break.

However, critics say that what concerns them is the large amount the entertainment industry takes specifically out of the African-American community compared to the small amount they are willing to invest into rebuilding it.[17] I wonder if in giving these critics a forum, the media is confusing giving people in the inner city opportunities in the entertainment industry with actually taking income away from it. I fail to see why anyone should pay for giving others an opportunity for making good in our country.

More than a year after the riots, area newspapers ran series after series about the riots and pontificated about the reasons for them. I have yet to read one article putting forth the view that people without legal restraints simply seized an excuse to rob, beat, steal, and kill. Stop to think about it. If the true target of the unrest had been the white community (because of the white policemen involved in the trial) would there have been people of other ethnic groups who were victims? The media appears to have refused to accept that premise. They chose instead to point the finger at those outside the affected community.

The U. S. Civil Rights Commission held hearings on the riots. The media dutifully reported the charges they would investigate. Among those allegations were that news broadcasts showed bias during the riots with wholesale indictments of minorities as being no more than looters.[18] Yes, there was a lot shown on the rioters, but if I remember correctly, they were simply termed rioters or looters. I do not believe they were ethnically identified. It was, of course, impossible not to determine certain ethnic groups simply because we saw faces. In defense of the media, I must also say I do not remember minorities being characterized, they were simply looters.

Please do not misunderstand my comments here. I disagree with the media when they constantly show only blacks or Hispanics in a bad light, but I also agree things have really gone wrong in the inner city. However, I do not believe that excuses violent behavior on anyone's part any more than taking welfare instead of working excuses the person who simply does not want to make the effort.

It has not been so long ago that these parts of our community were a good place to live and raise families. You did not drive by and see bars on the windows. You were not advised to lock all car doors before driving through or to never walk alone there. I think the real question is, What happened here? Why did life go sour? I am afraid those are the questions that are not being addressed by the media, and I ask, Why not?

In an analysis of an article that had appeared in *The New York Times*,[19] Thomas Sowell examined the issue of racial injustice. The article had blamed all of America for youth crime in the ghetto, using such phrases as "alarming rise in violence is due to American values," and ghetto youths are criminals because of their "American upbringing." Speaking from his own experience, he pointed out that most black youths do not grow up to be criminals and that blaming crime on society rather on the criminals condemns law-abiding inner-city residents to hide behind their locked doors at night.

Delving deeper into the issue, Sowell asserted this constant hate-America talk is a part of the mind-set that has led to the destruction of both moral values and law enforcement over the past thirty years. The year Earl Warren became Chief Justice of the United States (1953), our country experienced the lowest homicide rate in four decades. Following his Court's judicial revolution in the criminal justice system, the rate shot up until in 1991, it was double what it had been in 1953.

According to Sowell, the policy of implementing expensive social programs that supposedly dealt with the root causes of crime, reduced law enforcement, and the policy of intellectuals making excuses for criminals that was started by Warren, continued by Ramsey Clark during the 1960s, and espoused today by Janet Reno, did not take into consideration the issue of personal responsibility for one's actions.

Even the statistics showed that these programs have not lowered the crime rate but, in fact, were in effect during a time when it soared to new heights. As he pointed out, "It will never occur to [the liberals] to blame themselves. Liberals are often wrong but never in doubt." Citing thirty years of experience in the failure of the liberal policies and the blacks who must live in fear in the inner city, he then asked the disturbing question, "Is the well-being of black people less important than scoring ideological points or denouncing America?"

Supporting this position is author Stanley Fish, who states, "Discrimination is not a deviant practice, but simply the practice everyone is always and already engaged in."[20] He continues by asserting a course of social action ought to be measured, not by an appeal to some abstract principle, such as justice or fairness, but by the consequences that are expected to follow the said action.

PLACING THE BLAME

Again, the media seemed to be following another agenda that precluded questioning in that direction. In a ten-page section of the *Los Angeles Times*, "Understanding the Riots Part 5: The Path to Recovery," the lead story accused "us" of not seeing, or wanting to see, the children of the inner city. It continued with the indictments: seeing and not rescuing these children corrupted our most basic instincts, and it was our fault the legislators of the '60s made them soft with their "guilt money."

We were completely wrong when we pointed out the abuses of the welfare system while our retired populace demanded more. The author further asserted, "Things do not 'work' with the poor because "we" do not want them to work. Because of racism." He even claimed that "when we look at a lonely [and he says] trapped child in the ghetto, we see the lurking brute the jury saw in Rodney King [who was] surrounded by dozens of armed men who could not feel safe till the 50th–or 500th–blow was dealt out."[21]

I don't know when I've read something so inflammatory. For anyone—black or white—who read this article, the desire to cooperate in rebuilding the city and the relationships within it was firmly squelched. What kind of a responsible mediamaker could pen such a diatribe?

Unfortunately, this was not an isolated article. Most of the section was filled with the viewpoint that *we* are to blame for the riots! We did not do enough for the people in South Central LA. We must support this and support that out of taxpayers' money so they can have special programs that will give them an edge in rebuilding.

The conservatives were blamed for promoting the viewpoint that poverty programs cause poverty. We were told we should restore the minimum wage to a level that guaranteed a minimally decent living.[22] I cannot believe this statement comes at a time when the minimum wage is at its highest level! I must agree, however, with the proposal that instead of a welfare system, a public works program should be initiated.

Another article claimed South Central LA as black territory. They were only "clearing the land" for rebuilding when they burned store after store. Rioting was presented as being acceptable from that viewpoint. Why did they take out mostly Korean stores? Because they were only revolting against another visiting merchant class who made money from conducting business there but chose to live elsewhere. [23]

In another article, the verdicts in the Latasha Harlins and Rodney King cases were termed "in your face" for their kin. Then-President Bush's statement to "prosecute every last looter" was termed a perverse and counterproductive law-and-order reflex.

Let me state I have the utmost sympathy for anyone who lives in that type of environment and is trying to make a better life. I know it is extremely difficult, but I cannot understand the reasoning that says anarchy is OK just because where you live is less than ideal.

One article proposed among other things: 1) City and county authorities should call off the dogs of war and abandon their vindictive prosecution of petty offenders; 2) The misconduct of the Police Department must be investigated; and 3) The LAPD's unwinnable war on gangs must be abandoned.

Hogwash! This is a country established on a foundation of law and order and the rights of individuals. What rights could individuals have if these proposals were actually implemented?

The more rational observations and proposals by Roger Wilkins, Jack Kemp, and Antonia Hernandez were tucked away well into the section. Even Jesse Jackson, whose proposals were somewhat more radical did not rate a spot before page 7. If you were willing to wade through all the extremely liberal, almost seditious proposals, the voice of reason was given a chance to speak its piece, but it was placed in a position where it would hardly be noticed.

YOU CAN DO IT TOO!

How much better it would have been to have presented mature, workable solutions to what everybody acknowledged was a problem, or to have filled those pages with stories of those who have already begun the rebuilding process? The *Denver Post* took such an approach. On the cover page of their *USA Weekend Supplement*, a picture of workers from Los Angeles laboring together to rebuild their neighborhoods was featured. Inside were stories about people who made a difference in their community's lives. Along with these stories were cash awards for their neighborhoods. The outstanding group, who received $1,000 for their B.O.N.D. (Beautify Our Neighborhood District), was from the Harvard Heights neighborhood just north of the riot-torn part of Los Angeles. Quoted as saying, "Making any kind of difference here is tough,"[25] a "rainbow" of fifty people periodically cleans and spruces up the area.

One of the oldest participants, 73-year-old Joe Henderson said, "A lot of people who have moved in don't have too much pride in the community. I think this did a lot of good as far as showing that we care about our neighborhood."[26] Carter Curtiss, LA police liaison for the area, said of the effort, "They definitely helped organize the community. Other folks on the block joined in just because they were out there. Hard as we try, the police can't be everywhere. People have to take charge of their neighborhoods and help solve their own problems."[27]

In another instance, an article told of a graduate of the Los Angeles Police Academy who wanted to be assigned to the neighborhood where he grew up–South Central Los Angeles.[28] This man could be featured as a role model for youngsters today who think there is no way out. He grew up where they live and found a way to be a productive member of society.

The stories of how the food scene in Koreatown survived the riots and prospers today and how certain members of the Korean community were rebuilding their businesses and relationships with their black and Hispanic customers[30] would also be excellent motivation for those whose businesses were damaged or destroyed by the riots and must be rebuilt.

Carole Little is an example of one such company that rebuilt following $11 million in riot damage. Sales of the women's apparel manufacturer have increased from $200 million in 1992 to over $275 million today. They are now faced with the need to expand.[31]

I found the story of Donna Simon who was shot during the riots particularly sad and yet inspiring. The singer and dancer had gone to the aid of a young man being attacked by a woman with a crowbar. Companions of the woman shot Ms. Simon. A native of the riot area, she said she still cannot believe how incredibly stupid some of her friends were to loot last year. After months in the hospital and undergoing therapy, she resumed her career.[32] There is a lot to be said for the positive effects of sharing a "Can Do!" philosophy.

That not all of the residents of the area felt the verdict in the trial of the officers was fair was evidenced by more than $100,000 that poured in from a grass roots campaign to help the families of the officers. Asked why he contributed to the fund, the owner of a company that distributes sailboat parts said, "I think there are a great number of thinking people who do not have a means of expression for the rage they feel inside over this political baloney which the Rodney King case has been from the very beginning."

The owner of a beauty shop replied, "I just felt very bad for the officers because that they were doing their job."[33] Yes, the officers were doing their job, but the issue was they stepped out of bounds. They got caught up in the moment, became enraged, and did something they will always regret. There is no way I can condone what they did.

THE MEDIA GRADES ITSELF

How does the media feel about itself as a result of the trials? In spite of promises to remain restrained in their reporting of the verdict, they were criticized for their dramatic treatment of it.[34] Others felt the media behaved well. Reporters were live in front of police headquarters instead of hovering over the scene in helicopters, and the language and tone of voice remained calm. [35]

In a survey conducted by the Times Mirror Corporation, one out of two persons indicated they followed the story closely. However, twenty-six percent felt the press was excessive in its coverage. Fifty-six percent said they felt the press contributed to the riots following the first trial because the coverage encouraged people to go and join the rioting. Fifty-four percent thought the coverage of the second trial was fair; while thirty-four percent viewed it as biased.[36]

Randy Jordan, publisher of *Black Orange*, an African-American magazine, stated, "The media hyped this thing like it was a boxing match. Not a day went by when there wasn't some type of promotion on the radio, television or newspaper that count-downed the days until the big match. It was sickening."[37] Even the movie studios were forced to worry over potential violence related to the King trial and rethink marketing for *Bound by Honor* and *Boiling Point*.[38]

It was apparent the media was hoping the trial would continue to generate increased revenues as evidenced by their more than generous offers and payments to trial participants for interviews. Amateur cameraman George Holliday was the first to profit from the incident. He was paid $500 for the video. Stacey Koon received a reputed $10,000 for an exclusive interview with "A Current Affair," and Ted Briseno received $25,000 for an appearance on "Donahue."

Although the dollar amount was not announced, the jury foreman, known only as Bob, was paid for an appearance on "Inside Edition." Another juror refused an interview with a leading newspaper because he could be paid for his remarks by other sources. Although Holliday's lawsuit against every major network was dismissed, he received a handsome payment from Spike Lee for the video's use in *Malcolm X*. Others prominent in the proceedings either agreed to write their memoirs or negotiated with major publishers to do so.[39] It was obvious the media did not intend to let the incident be forgotten.

"There's big money to be made in being shameless and baring one's sins to the world," revealed Brian Stonehill, director of media-studies at Pomona College. "The market teaches us that discretion and silence are not as highly paid as exposure and confession." Harland Brown, attorney for Ted Briseno, made the chilling observation, "It's easy to pontificate, but in the real world, you've got to buy your groceries. They don't give you credit for doing free television or having your life destroyed by publicity."[40] Therefore, I must ask, Was it prudent for the media to pay these knucklehead cops anything?

It would also appear that the four L.A. police-men were not the only ones who had their lives destroyed by publicity. Did the foreknowledge by members of the media of the impending raid by BATF agents on the Branch Davidian compound in Waco, Texas and the media circus that followed have anything to do with the ultimate outcome that left those who remained in the compound dead? Let's look at how the media in general handled the coverage and how the liberal element of the media, with its disregard of the freedom Americans have to worship as they please, may have contrib-uted to the gross injustice done to the followers of David Koresh.

THE HOLOCAUST?

During the long siege, the public was con-stantly bombarded with the details of their Branch Davidians' "different" lifestyle. Many questions were raised about whether their obviously differ-ent religious beliefs figured in the charges against them in the first place. Were they also victims of injustice–not racial this time, but religious?

It is an accepted fact the media informed those at the compound that agents of the Bureau of Alcohol, Tobacco and Firearms were going to make a raid,[42] and reports on the stand-off were often the top story of the day. Constantly in the fore-front of these reports were the fears that those in the compound would commit mass suicide as the cult members had done in Jonestown. Bizarre as-pects of their religious lifestyle were featured day after day. Suspicion of their beliefs and the rea-sons for their not surrendering were constantly injected into the reports.

The public was kept apprised of the latest speculation about the group and David Koresh himself, who was portrayed as not just the leader but a Manson-type psychopath who used physical abuse, manipulation, and sexual domination to rule his followers. Detailed descriptions of their lives and the alleged firearms cache were often featured.

Day after day, if any new comment from Koresh was forthcoming, the media grabbed it and ran. The nation knew it by the time of the next broadcast or edition of the paper. That the story was an audience-getter was proven when his 58-minute radio address simulcast on television became the ratings hit in the Dallas-Ft. Worth viewing area.[43] When it seemed the public was losing interest, new twists were added to the story. Further details were revealed, and more speculation offered about the group. Even after the fiery end, day after day we saw feature stories about those who died. Daily newspapers became tabloids.

The same day Koresh made his broadcast, David Overton, Channel 5 (Dallas/Ft. Worth) news director, complained of the way the media was being manhandled. According to him, they were given misinformation by federal officials. Twice they were told that 20 children had been released on a school bus. Both times this information was incorrect. The federal sources later denied saying it. Overton said, "They're just playing this game, and it's totally unnecessary. I think they're doing an abysmal job."[44]

The federal agents justified their animosity toward the media with the excuse the media blew the ATF's cover. I suppose that was the reason they also used one of their armored fighting vehicles to flatten a reporter's car that got in the way.[45] One of the ATF's agents who was wounded in the initial attack almost immediately filed suit against the *Waco Tribune Herald* for disclosing to the cult a raid was imminent. I wonder where the paper got their information?

A MEDIA FEEDING FRENZY?

It was obvious the media thought this was a major breaking story. Within twenty-four hours of the time it was apparent there was going to be a stand-off, over 40 satellite trucks and 500 reporters, photographers, producers, and technicians had converged on the spot. There was worldwide interest. Crews from as far away as Japan had come. They didn't just come and stay in motels to hear the news. They pitched tents, laid utility lines, moved into motor homes, slept in their cars, rented generators, heaters, and TV sets. They leased whatever property they could in the area. They literally established their own city complete with trash pickup and delivery service. They interviewed residents, haunted the bars, and even paid for information and silence from participants until the show aired.[46] Would David Koresh have had the same drive to continue with the siege if apparent interest had died following his initial radio broadcast?

In his column in *The New York Times*, "Critic's Notebook," Walter Goodman compares the drama that unfolded at Waco with a television production. He discussed how it had turned into a sendup of all the G-Men series of the past, how the FBI spokesman spent a lot of time in front of the cameras, Koresh emerged as the central figure and almost demanded a spectacular climax to the production. This was fulfilled in the fiery end.

When the cause of the fire was questioned, federal representatives categorically stated that the cult killed themselves. After all, "What sort of ending would it have been, what sort of climax for his followers and for all those who had been following his story if he had led the true believers shuffling out into the handcuffs of the nonbelievers and the eye of the television camera? His cosmic pretensions required either a shoot-out while the cameras were turning or, better still by the standards of television special effects, an apocalypse of his own creation."

Then Goodman asked the horrifying question, "Hadn't the expectation–even (can it be?) hope–of some such spectacle been in viewers' minds for weeks?"[47] Were they waiting for their violence fix? Could the tragic end have been averted if Koresh had thought no one was watching (and indeed no one was because the stand-off was *not* being televised)?

SUFFER THE LITTLE CHILDREN?

Many of us found it disturbing that reports early on indicated the children that had been released were said by psychologists to have had a stable, loving homelife–albeit strange to most of us–and showed no signs of abuse. Then, in contradiction, as the day for the final assault approached, Attorney General Janet Reno suddenly became concerned about lack of sanitary facilities and child abuse. Her order to attack the compound is said to have come as a result of these concerns.[48] The rest is history.

Reports that were released indicated the children had been abused. Psychiatrists testified there was not only sexual abuse, but the children were also beaten. Yet the lawyer for the cult claimed he saw no evidence of this on his visits. So-called cult awareness experts said child abuse is always the pattern of these groups.

The newspapers also carried stories almost

daily of therapists who instilled false memories of sexual abuse into patients and how many children learn to believe they have memories of incidents that never happened. One disillusioned former member even alleged he suspected Koresh was interested in the human sacrifice of children. It appeared that by not questioning why there were contradictory reports, many mediamakers rushed to the side of the federal government, supported their claims that the children had to be rescued, and thus sanctioned this extension of federal power.

Too many questions still remain unanswered to say anyone knows the truth. Who set the fire? Did they commit suicide? Did they abuse their children? Did Koresh really promise to come out and bring his followers with him several times prior to the final blaze? The answers that emerged depend on the media airing them.

It seems we live in an age when you choose a side and then find support for your position. You do not look for the truth with cold, scientific precision. One widely circulated statement disseminated as fact, but in reality was one man's opinion, was this, "Oh, My God, they're killing themselves," made by FBI agent Bob Ricks. News broadcasts and newspapers repeated the comment in the context there was irrefutable evidence of such a claim.

At the same time headlines were proclaiming "Mass Suicide," former members were saying, "No, there were no plans for mass suicide." Federal officials have to date failed to produce the agents who supposedly heard the Davidians say, "The fires are lit."

In what I felt was wildly speculative reporting, one article indicated that tests had not yet determined whether there was any truth to the early FBI reports that some children were killed by lethal injection.[49] That, in my opinion, is a possibility that never should have been aired outside a forensics lab. I question the authenticity of the detailed description of expressions on the children's faces given in some articles. If the bodies were so badly burned it was going to be difficult to identify them, would a recognizable expression still remain, or was this another cheap attempt to "make" a story?

Today, we still see articles about how to deal with extremist groups. I must ask if the media is fueling the fires of distrust of something they do not understand with this sort of reporting. We are told there are other cults as potentially dangerous "out there" by Webb Hubbell, Assistant Attorney General, and he says the question is how to handle them.[50] Several other groups were cited, and the article concluded with the observation that until the government learns how to deal with these people, it is a tragedy that could occur again.

What I see in these articles is anticipation of the next confrontation. The reader is being subtly urged to look for it. After all, it sells newspapers. Even an article describing conditions as the forensic experts found them in the compound ended with the sentence, "CNN plans extended live coverage of today's congressional hearings."[51]

JUST THE FACTS, PLEASE

Each rumor or detail that came from the investigation was treated as truth. Many of these speculations were later proved to be totally unfounded, and yet the media continued to feature them as fact. Even after a survivor had said the fires were started accidentally by a lantern that was knocked over, the media continued to report the fires were set by the group. I cannot help wondering why. Had they convened their own court and determined the survivor was lying, or were the claims of mass suicide simply better headlines?

As the investigation continued, the media painted the group as wildly fanatic and armed to the teeth with illegal weapons. They completely ignored statements by the cultists who managed to escape, neighbors and townspeople who knew some of the group, as well as the existing laws that govern the possession and use of firearms in Texas. Whether or not they agreed with the laws and lifestyle was not the issue. The issue was whether the cult lived in actual defiance of the laws. I am not condoning cults, but the media needs to report only the facts, not their speculations.

Another question that must be answered is the one of child abuse. I love children and have complete contempt for those who harm them. I cannot deny that innocent children lost their lives as a result of what happened in Waco, but whose fault it was has not yet been proven. As the multitude of lawsuits now pending may bring forth additional facts, I think the media did an absolute disservice to the American public by its unbridled speculation as to the cause of the final blaze and actual conditions within the compound.

What I saw was a group of people following what cannot be denied was a compelling leader who caused them to exchange what we call normal lives out in the world for one away from it all. I don't know about you, but there have been times when I've wanted a simpler life; and while I chose not to make that choice, I cannot fault those who do. I also see a very definite suspicion of those who want to be different. In the past, we have seen it toward such larger groups such as the Amish, who in the past have had to fight the government for the right to educate their children as they saw fit, and the Mormons. Smaller, more dissident groups seem to have generated even more distrust today.

Many people pointed to Koresh's Messianic delusion as evidence he had brainwashed his group into doing his bidding. I think it only proved they all desperately wanted someone to lead them and tell them what to do. Unfortunately, they chose a bad role model.

The question of whether Koresh actually taught his followers methods of suicide, etc. is still open to question. It has not been proved these allegations were valid, but our media seemed to accept each accusation as fact. David Koresh may have been a "wacko," but he should never have died in Waco.

THE UNTOUCHABLES?

The controversy surrounding the legality of the first attack against the compound seems to have been put to rest by the media. I'm not sure whether it was the philosophy of *might makes right* or what, but the BATF was declared innocent. In the days prior to the final effort against the compound, an occasional journalist was still questioning the legitimacy of the action itself, and to my knowledge, these questions have yet to be answered. Yes, I know the federal agents were reinstated, but that in itself does not answer the original charges.

In an article by a senior columnist, several unwarranted and high-handed attacks by this agency were cited. In December, a resident of Tulsa, Oklahoma, came home to find his house thoroughly trashed, his gun safe broken into and guns strewn everywhere. As he looked at the wreckage, the utility companies stopped by to tell him they had been ordered to discontinue service. Then he found a note that said, "Nothing Found–ATF." The ATF refused to repair or pay for the damages. When the homeowner tried to get a copy of the affidavit supporting the search warrant to determine if there was probable cause, he was not able to because the affidavit had been sealed.

Previously, in Orange County, California, a couple had their apartment broken into and ransacked in a pre-dawn raid. Supposedly, the BATF had been tipped off that gang members occupied the apartment. As it turned out, they had, but several months previously. Again the BATF assumed no responsibility for the damage or for an apology. In light of these types of actions by the BATF, why wasn't the media asking, Was the original attack at Waco justified, and should the standoff have been continued?[52]

Again, the media remained silent about the way previous charges against the cult, and in particular David Koresh, were handled in a peaceful way. What made this charge any different? There had been no violence in 1988 when gunfire broke out between Koresh and George Roden reportedly for control of the cult. Koresh surrendered peacefully and was eventually released and his firearms returned.

Previous allegations of child abuse had been investigated by Texas authorities and found to be groundless. Authorities had not been restricted in their access to the compound to investigate the charges. What now warranted a full scale attack when the charges were only of Koresh's allegedly failing to pay excise taxes so he could assemble automatic weapons (not the possession of such) and his immoral lifestyle?

I abhor the loss of life in the first raid, but my original question as to who was responsible still has not been answered. Unfortunately, it probably never will be. The media so obscured what should have been the real questions by their coverage, the truth will not, in all likelihood, emerge, nor will there be pressure for it to because the majority of the media stopped asking these questions.[53]

No wonder the public was confused by the picture of life in the compound. A writer for Knight-Ridder Newspapers described life for the children in the compound as consisting of Bible studies that featured spankings for mistakes and very simple, often not nutritious, meals. Their only recreation was playing in the fields on good days. Often they were confined, beaten, and abused. No toys, Nintendo, Happy Meals, Barney, Santa Claus, tooth fairy, birthday cards, or Little League.[54]

In contrast, life was described as Spartan but filled by loving affection by authorities to whom the children were released in late February. Did the media later take its stand only to support the Federal claims, which many questioned? Janet Reno's obsession with so-called child abuse cases was clearly demonstrated during her term as prosecutor in Dade County, Florida.[55] Perhaps the media should have questioned her previous performances instead of blindly supporting her actions in the Waco case.

IS BIG BROTHER WATCHING YOU?

Concern the Federal Government is flexing its muscle in trying to control certain religious persuasions has been voiced. With the avowed Liberal stance of the media and its support of more Federal control over our lives, could their willingness to support the federal actions without question be to further the Liberal agenda?

Some religious groups urged the federal government to refrain from using its investigation into the Waco tragedy as a means to define a valid religion. Unfortunately, these concerns did not receive the headlines that the support of federal actions received. Instead, they were buried in a quiet article in the "Religion" section of the newspaper.[56]

No matter whether you attend church or not, I am sure you question what business the Federal Government has in trying to establish what is or what is not a valid religion. Our Constitution guarantees its citizens freedom of religion the same as it guarantees freedom of the press. Why isn't a responsible press questioning whether indeed the Federal Government is overstepping its bounds?

With almost twenty different religious organizations from most of the major denominations voicing this concern, there must be some grounds for it. I believe a responsible press should be questioning the government's role.

Additional questions arise, such as why the compound was described as filthy with garbage and human feces after the fire when previous visits by other persons including child welfare personnel did not report any such conditions. This filth was given by the Federal government as the reason the compound was bulldozed even before the investigation was complete. At the risk of sounding suspicious, it seems like a good way to get rid of the evidence.

It seems to me that if the media were to analyze its own news releases, they too would question many of these actions. Again, I am prompted to ask, Is this a deliberate attempt on the part of the media to present a story that will support the liberal agenda?

Tony Cooper, a law enforcement consultant who teaches terrorism, negotiation and conflict resolution at the University of Texas at Dallas expressed his concern over federal agents who shadow fringe groups that have a penchant for amassing private arsenals. "I see the formation of a curious crusading mentality among certain law enforcement agencies to stamp out what they see as a threat to government generally. It's an exaggerated concern that they are facing a nationwide conspiracy that somehow this will get out of control unless it is stamped out at a very early stage." [57]

In supporting and apparently helping to cover up the actions of the federal officials who appeared to be overstepping the authority given to them by the Constitution, the media abdicated its responsibility to the people of America–their obligation to be truthful in telling us what is happening.

The media as a whole seemed to ignore the issue of religious freedom. Residents of the compound were called brain-washed fanatics who in some way really deserved the fate that befell them. However, we did find a few probing writers who analyzed the situation. One writer made the caustic observation, "Even though our constitution guarantees freedom of religion and the right to bear arms, those rights apply only to white mainstream Protestants who go deer hunting once a year."[58] Letters to the editor often compared the stand-off to the persecution of the Jews during the Holocaust.[59]

However, two journalists probed more deeply into governmental attitudes in the case. The first, Cal Thomas, drew what he called "disturbing conclusions." He was concerned about the growing antipathy of federal officials toward anything they regard as religious, whether bizarre or traditional.

He asserted the government placed religion in a different category from problems involving ethnic groups. He cited the Los Angeles riots and prison uprisings as examples. The same forces, fatigue and frustration, were evident there, but no precipitous action was taken. He then recounted governmental dealings with anything that could be termed, "fundamentalist," "sect," or "cult": specifically a Michigan mother who was arrested and charged with truancy for home schooling her child; the National Endowment for the Arts subsidizing anti-religious and even blasphemous works; and a rabbi who was forbidden by the Supreme Court to mention the name of God at a public school graduation ceremony. He then quoted *The Wall Street Journal*, "The enemies and critics of the Enlightenment, the Age of Reason, will say we are getting what we deserve for happily accepting that God was dead. They warned us about removing organized faith from the center of active ideas, indeed ridiculing it. Now we see that the religious urge is strong enough that in many confused lives, healthy faith is supplanted by much weird behavior, such as the Koresh cult."[60] Thomas then warned that until our government learns to respect and support the simple faith and traditional values, they may be increasingly forced to deal with aberrants.[61]

The second, Mary Z. Stange, associate professor at Skidmore College, described the action at Waco as something that could happen only in our country. According to the civil dogma we hold, religious wars are fought on foreign soil and the state's intervention against a religious group (religious oppression) happens only elsewhere. In the United States, when federal forces attack a religious group, "It is for their own good and the public benefit."

She too questioned the media's lauding the federal agents for their restraint in holding their fire and the publicized FBI comments that the women and children died because the mothers lacked "maternal instinct." I found myself shuddering when I read her final comment, "What we don't like or understand, we call crazy. We make it a subject of jokes. Sometimes, we kill it."[62]

TERROR IN THE MIDWEST

Citizens across the country were shocked when news of a terrorist bombing in the Midwest was broadcast. Those things simply do not happen in the heart of our country. Yes, it did happen in New York City at the World Trade Center. This happened in the heartland of America.

The bombing of the Federal building in Oklahoma City was unthinkable. The media immediately began to release stories about the possible suspects. At the beginning, Muslim extremists were suspected. Unfortunately for those who had immigrated from that part of the world, life was pretty unbearable for a few days until it was ascertained the extremists were not to blame.

Then federal agents issued a statement they were sure the bombing was connected to the Waco holocaust, which had occurred (almost to the day) two years previously. They even intimated the day care center had been targeted as revenge for the children who died in the Branch Davidian compound. Survivors of the ill-fated cult raid claimed there could be no connection.

The media seized the information about the possible link, drew their own conclusions why there would be a leak and "treated" the public to a recap of this tragic event. We saw again the terrible final fire and heard the horrible details of how life ended there.

Finally, the Federal Government began to link suspect Timothy McVeigh to certain militant groups and proclaim their danger to America. Broader control of these groups and their activities was advocated.

It was almost the straw that broke the camel's back when President Clinton tried to make political hay by linking the bombing to talk radio and made broad statements about the need for additional control by the federal government to "protect the American people."

As with any other event of this nature, the media immediately converged on the area and attempted to monopolize anything that occurred. I was heartened when officials managed to maintain a semblance of privacy for the families of those still inside the building, keeping the media at the perimeter of activities.

Of course, there was immediate pre-empting of all programming to bring viewers on-the-spot coverage of all the [gory] details. We saw the mangled bodies and bloodied injured as they were brought from the wreckage. Unfortunate relatives and friends of the victims who happened to get in the media's way were immediately interviewed. What insensitivity! The almost 24-hour-a-day coverage of every detail of the search and rescue operation continued until it became evident they would find no one else alive.

As news that many of the victims were children who were being cared for in the day care center, the focus immediately turned to the parents of those children. One picture that made the front page of almost every major newspaper in America was that of a police officer holding the bloody body of a child as he rushed from the building toward a firefighter. Another photo, taken a few minutes later, showed the firefighter cradling her in his arms. Other haunting photographs were of parents of children still inside who were having to be restrained from rushing in, and close-ups of badly injured adults.

I question whether the number of those types of photographs per page in the newspapers was really necessary. Those of us who are parents did not have to look at a photograph to feel the anguish the parents were experiencing. The public did not have to see blood dripping from people to understand the types of injuries that occur in a bombing. I have to say I think the majority of the photographs were for shock value rather than for information.

Typical headlines were, "Tears, grief in relatives' search," "Lilt of kids' laughter silenced by the bomb," "Rescuers now in cadaver mode," and "Oklahoma learns 'no place is safe'."[41]

Then as the memorial services were held in a stadium, throughout the proceedings, the cameras repeatedly focused on the relatives of the victims, especially the parents of the children who were killed. I think this intrusion into the moments of their almost unbearable grief was one of the most wanton demonstrations of the media's inability to sacrifice sensationalism for consideration or respect.

As I watched the coverage at various times during the week that followed the bombing, I developed a sense of admiration for the people of Oklahoma City who simply dropped less important things and rushed to help their fellow citizens. I also admired the way the families of the victims were protected against the tentacles of the media octopus that threatened to coil around them as they stood watch and waited for news of their loved ones. This protection, of course, was not complete, but it did help lessen the bombardment of media attention.

Why would the federal government wish to link the Oklahoma City bombing to the Waco tragedy, and why would the media try to capitalize on that information? What part did the media play in causing the tragedy?

ADVOCACY JOURNALISM

In a broader criticism, several mediamakers including Robert Novak have criticized the current trend in reporting. Novak claimed, "A free press is one of the foundations of a free society. Yet Americans increasingly distrust and resent the media. A major reason is that many journalists have crossed the line from reporting to advocacy. They have, in effect adopted a new liberal creed: 'all the news that's politically correct' to print."[63] He continued, "The news sections of most newspapers are even more ideological than when I first criticized them twenty-two years ago. Once the editorial page was the place for journalists to express their opinions, but now they do so on every page, including the front page—under the misleading banner of objective reporting."[64]

Echoing his sentiments, Lyn Nofziger also related it to our government. "The press wants absolute freedom for itself, but it often sides with the actions of the government and the proposals of presidents that take freedom away from individuals.... They are zealous defenders of their First Amendment rights, but they ignore the Tenth Amendment, which reserves to the states and to the people those powers not specifically granted to the federal government."[65]

Eleanor Clift, *Newsweek* White House

Correspondent discusses the role bias plays in reporting the news. "First, there is the media's natural preference for simple two-sided debates. It likes to reduce every issue to two extremist positions. The second...comes from its emphasis on personalities rather than concepts. It is hard to cover intangible principles and complex ideas, but it is easy to cover people and events." The third is "the media thrives on statistics. It can tell you...how many people were killed by handguns this year, but not how many lives were saved by handguns." The final one is that "fifty-five percent of all journalists identify themselves as liberal, and at least eighty percent are members of the Democratic party."

With statistics such as these, I find it hard to believe they are not reporting in a manner that will further the liberal agenda. Those of us who believe we are receiving unbiased reports are, I believe, sadly in error.

Has our media exploited the prejudices we hold and fears of the unknown we all feel? Has it, by its policy of following a private agenda, let the truth lie in unmarked graves along the way? Has it forgotten a part of its mandate–to help us remain an informed populace that will be able to make mature judgments even as the color of the face of our country's changes? I must say I think the media, in too large a part, has relinquished its position of positive leadership in guiding us to become a country in which people of all types of ethnic groups can work together in harmony and respect for one another's individuality. I believe this has happened because mediamakers are too intent on pursuing their goals of sensationalism, numbers, and private agendas rather than their true calling–informing people of the truth.

I charge the media on two counts. The first is that the irresponsible media does not live up to its original obligation as disseminator of the truth so the people of America can continue to live in freedom. The second is that not only does the media fail to live up to its original obligation, it has assumed a responsibility it was never intended to have. It has designated itself as the guide for the direction our country is to take, and that guide is far afield of the original intent of the framers of our Constitution. When it designated itself as the guide, it also set the rules by which it will abide; and those rules place achieving the agenda above reporting the truth.

Do you find the media guilty or not guilty?

WORKS CITED

1. Wickham, DeWayne. "Race war rages in USA." *USA Today* 10 May 1993.

2. "Q & A." *TV Times* 5-11 September 1993 15.

3. Stone, Andrea. "22% unconvinced Holocaust happened." *USA Today* 20 April 1993 1A.

4. Griffiths, Eldon. "The media overplayed their bit part in L.A." *The Orange County Register* 20 April 1993 Commentary 5.

5. Machan, Tibor, visiting professor. "Due process vs. desired results." *The Orange County Register* 20 April 1993 Metro 11.

6. Ferrell, David. "L.A. Awaits Verdicts With Mix of Frayed Nerves, Hopeful Calm." *The Los Angeles Times* 17 April 1993 A26.

7. Sub headline. *The Los Angeles Times* 18 April 1993 A1.

8. Headline. *The Honolulu Advertiser* 18 April 1993 A1.

9. Editorial. *The Salt Lake Tribune* 18 April 1993 A18.

10. Deutsch, Linda. "Split Verdicts: Two officers convicted; L.A. calm." *The Las Vegas Review-Journal* 18 April 1993 1A

11. "Some reactions to verdict." *The Honolulu Advertiser* 18 April 1993 A21.

12. Ibid.

13. Stewart, Sally Ann. "Koon: 'King should feel guilty'." *USA Today* 20 April 1993 5A.

14. Hamilton, William and Castenada, Roben. "Angelenos' anxiety turns to relief as verdicts free pent-up tensions." *The Las Vegas Review-Journal* 18 April 1993 1A.

15. "Looters: Many Were Not Strangers to Justice System." *The Los Angeles Times* 2 May 1993 A37.

16. Ibid.

17. Cerone, Daniel and Pristin, Terry. "Hollywood Post-Riot Aid Called Flop." *The Los Angeles Times* 4 May 1993 A24.

18. Editorial. "Still Digging Out the Lessons." *The Los Angeles Times* 16 June 1993 B12.

19. Sowell, Thomas. "Scoring Points." *Forbes* 28 February 1994 52.

20. Marvel, Bill. Book review of *There's No Such Thing as Free Speech* by Stanley Fish. *American Way* 1 March 1994 120.

21. Wills, Garry. "Rescuing the City." *The Los Angeles Times* 15 May 1992 T1.

22. Molyneux, Guy. "Bolster the 'Other' America—Rethink the Great Society." *The Los Angeles Times* 15 May 1993 T7.

23. Troutt, David Dante. "Fires Cleared South L.A.—Now Residents Can Redefine It." *The Los Angeles Times* 15 May 1993 T3.

24. Davis, Mike. "To Restore Hope to Lost Generation, Talk to the Gangs." *The Los Angeles Times* 15 May 1993 T4.

25. "The Make a Difference Day Awards." *USA Weekend* 16-18 April 1993 4.

26. Ibid.

27. Ibid.

28. Hardy, Charles C. "Challenge to black cops." *The San Francisco Examiner* 18 April 1993 A1.

29. Gamerman, Amy. "Angeleno Korean Food Scene Survives Riots." *The Wall Street Journal* 20 April 1993

30. Eaton, Tracey. "Korean-Americans roll up their sleeves, look to the future." *The Orange County Register* 19 April 1993 News 4.

31. Walters, Donna K. H. "A Blossom Rises From the Ruins." *The Los Angeles Times* 3 May 1993 D1.

32. Abcarian, Robin. "She's Dancing Again Despite Riot Scars." *The Los Angeles Times* 25 April 1993 E3.

33. Zoroya, Gregg. "Sympathy for King-Case Cops." *The Orange County Register* 13 June 1993 Metro 1.

34. DuBrow, Rick. "Some TV Stations Forget Promises of Restraint." *The Los Angeles Times* 17 April 1993 A27.

35. Duncan, Scott. "Media treat looming verdict with caution." *The Orange County Register* 17 April 1993 News 9.

36. Rosenstiel, Thomas B. "Coverage of Waco, King Trial Criticized." *Times Mirror* Survey 29 April-2 May 1993.

37. "Platform: The Danger is to Think That Everything is Wonderful." *The Los Angeles Times* 19 April 1993 B8.

38. Rauzi, Robin. "With Verdicts Imminent, Movie Plans are Changed." *The Los Angeles Times* 17 April 1993.

39. Katz, Jesse. "Participants in King Case Try to Cash In." *The Los Angeles Times* 25 April 1993 A1.

40. "King case becoming cash cow." *Arizona Republic* 25 April 1993.

41. *USA Today* April 1995.

42. Smolowe, Jill. "February 28: Sent into a Deathtrap?" *Time* 3 May 1993 33.

43. Media. "Cult leader's address dominates the ratings." *The Dallas Morning News* 4 March 1993.

44. Ibid.

45. Davidson, Joe and Harlan, Christi. "As Waco Crisis Ends,

Clinton's Leadership Comes Under Scrutiny." *The Wall Street Journal* 20 April 1993 A1.

46. Fair, Kathy. "No crueler blow than Koresh's fiery finale." *The Houston Chronicle* 25 April 1993 1F.

47. Goodman, Walter. "As TV, Drama in Waco Had a Grim Inevitability." *The New York Times* 20 April 1993 B1.

48. Kantrowitz, Barbara. et. al. "Day of Judgment." *Newsweek* 3 May 1993 22-27.

49. *The New York Times*. "Evidence indicates 2 dozen members of cult were shot." *The Orange County Register* 5 May 1993.

50. Liu, Melinda and Barrett, Todd. "Hard Lessons in the Ashes." *Newsweek* 3 May 1993 31.

51. Mayfield, Mark. "Congress delves into Texas siege." *USA Today* 28 April 1993 1A.

52. Bock, Alan W. "Trampling the First Amendment." *The Orange County Register* 8 April 1993 B11.

53. Schulman, J. Neil. "Was Waco Warranted?" *The Orange County Register* 16 May 1993 Commentary 1.

54. Torriero, E. A., Knight-Ridder Newspapers. "Young innocents pawns in Koresh's game." *The Orange County Register* 28 April 1993 News 16.

55. Cockburn, Alexander. "From Salem to Waco, by Way of the Nazis." *The Los Angeles Times* 27 April 1993 B9.

56. Religious News Service. "Groups Warn Against Using Waco tragedy to Define a Valid Religion." *The Los Angeles Times* 8 May 1993 B8.

57. Sahagun, Louis and Conner, Doug. "2 White Separatists Win Acquittal in Fatal Shootout." *The Los Angeles Times* 9 July 1993 A20.

58. Quillen, Ed. "No one asks the right question." *The Denver Post* 25 April 1993 3E.

59. "Speak Out." *Denver Post* 25 April 1993 6E. "Our Readers Write Us." *The Orange County Register* 22 April 1993 Commentary 4.

60. Review & Outlook. "Weird in Waco." *The Wall Street Journal* 20 April 1993 A18.

61. Thomas, Cal. "Koresh Case Demonstrates That Government Has Marginalized Religion." *The Salt Lake Tribune* 25 April 1993.

62. Stange, Mary Zeiss. "The 'Crazy Label Was Lethal." *The Los Angeles Times* 21 April 1993 B11.

63. Novak, Robert. "Political Correctness in the Newsroom." *Imprimis* November 1994 1.

64. Ibid. 3.

65. Ibid. 5

Chapter 13

YOUTH SPEAKS OUT

Probably the most conspicuous method of speaking out against the media was chosen by Lee Bolli of Tucson, Arizona. After viewing himself on an NBC presentation about the "lost generation," he went into the bathroom and hung himself with his shoestring. Chosen by Tom Brokaw and NBC News, he was an example of young people who despair at their failure to achieve the material success of their parents. He had agreed to participate in the show hoping that it would prove helpful to other young people who were having trouble finding their way.

Obviously, it did not help him; it only reinforced his despair. A high school drop-out and an inmate of Pichacho Correctional Work Center at Eloy, Arizona, since being convicted on burglary charges, he was quoted in the program as saying, "When the jobs aren't there, you just either lose your dream or you get mad. If you're lucky, you might get some work behind the counter, doing a sales job, working in a restaurant. They treat you like crap. If you don't like it, then you can rob a house."[1]

His partner in crime, John Garland, was also quoted in the program, "If the younger generations can't look down the road and see where they're going, or see anything they want to go after, then I think it's obvious they're going to try crime, drugs, violence, suicide."[2] After Bolli's death, Garland apologized to Bolli's mother. "I guess he didn't see anything down the road. Maybe what I said just brought it back to him."

In their prepared statement following his death,

NBC claimed they shared his hope and mourned his loss. Evidently they did not do so to the extent they offered any hope or solution to the situation, which he must have seen as hopeless. What responsibility should the media assume for reinforcing these feelings? By presenting his story with his hope to help others, did they also obligate themselves to offer help, not despair, to him?

On a more positive note, three children under the age of twelve felt a need for their neighborhood to have a weekly voice, so they published *A.D. & Co.* for the residents. Over a hundred subscribers and ten advertisers agreed.[3] Washington's Radio Zone stations air *Radio Aahs* for young listeners twenty-four hours a day. The music they play is for young ears–"Puff the Magic Dragon," "Baby Beluga," or songs by Alvin and the Chipmunks. Their world news contains information about the same countries adults hear about, but does not cover the violence that is happening there. The "Storytime Theatre" features tales young people want to hear, brain-stimulating games, and movies reviewed from a child's perspective.

In what I feel is a most responsible attitude, they have an 800 number children can dial to make a request or ask for help if they are threatened with a situation they cannot handle. The station also maintains emergency numbers at their fingertips to help when these calls come.[4]

Although choosing different methods to do so, all of these youths are saying, "Media, you aren't doing the job we think you should do."

NOT A BAD ATTITUDE

In general, how does the youth of America view the media? I'm sorry to report that I've talked to no one in that group who said they felt the media was doing a really good job of presenting unbiased news. This is an extremely sad commentary when you hear the media priding itself on being unbiased and doing a good job of "being there when it happens." What do young people in America think of the media today? To find out, I interviewed a number of students at local colleges. Let's listen to some voices.

Over and over, I heard the same comments; "I have a pretty bad attitude about the media." "I'm skeptical of what I hear." "I take it all with a grain of salt." "I filter out and try to get at the truth."[5] Personally, I think this is a very healthy attitude. Perhaps they will not be influenced to the extent the media would like to see. I sincerely hope they will be able to filter out the garbage and bias and arrive at the truth.

A The Los Angeles Times survey revealed area teenagers think, "[The media] sensationalizes instead of covering things objectively. Adults think we're rowdy and bad. The media has made it hard for the responsible teen-agers who want to do something. Adults look at you like your age group is only interested in killing and drugs when it's really not like that."[6]

In the same article, a Korean-American was quoted as saying, "I don't feel like our image in the media has been very positive. I still think the media has quite a ways to go before it understands our races. We are very under-represented and we need more opportunities in the media."

A friend of mine, who happens to be an attorney and an African-American stated, "I hate watching TV. Not all black people are gang members." He cited the television show "Cops" as being one of the worst offenders in this area. Then he asked, "Don't white people ever commit crimes?" He even included the show, "Seinfeld," which is situated in New York City, as never having even one black person on it. In New York City?

"The impression people get just from watching the evening news is that some of the most violent people on the face of the earth are teenagers. Every time a crime is committed, the suspect is 16 to 19 years old. I think it's starting to rub off negatively on elementary school-aged kids. They are starting to show up with weapons, drugs and alcohol because they want to identify with the older kids. The sad thing about this is that only a handful of kids are the bad ones. The media seems to follow around this one bad group, and they make it seem like every teenager is bad."[7]

I challenge the media with this question, Is that what you really want to do? Turn good kids into bad ones so you can have more stories of violence to air? If this is your objective, then you have prostituted the original objectives of the media. You have sullied what used to be lofty goals by dragging them in the gutter of life.

WHY NOT PAINT THE REAL SCENE?

Members of minority groups are especially hard on the media today. They resent being portrayed as rioters, thieves, looters, or carjackers. They point out they have many representatives who lead exemplary lives. They also feel members of the white community are equally responsible for the violence for which they receive the blame. Said one student at a predominantly black school, "TV shows are getting better, however. I've seen more white crooks stealing cars and stuff lately." What a tragic commentary on the news today! It is driving wedges between the ethnic groups instead of building bridges.

It is interesting to note that many singled out "Beverly Hills 90210" as a show they watched. The comments were pretty evenly divided, however. Residents of areas that are predominantly inhabited by minority groups felt it was entertaining, but not a show to which they could relate. The lives shown on television were unrealistic. They said if guns were brought to Beverly Hills schools, the news would be covered up; whereas, in their schools, it was featured in the news.

Students in predominantly white neighborhoods felt it was great–some violence, but realistic, although occasionally too goody-goody. The exception to this was one comment by a student who grew up in an affluent resort town but had come to the metropolitan area for college. She asked if you would really want pre-teenagers watching the show? She felt it presented and encouraged a too liberal lifestyle.

In a biting letter to the editor, a young black American questioned the media's representation of black America. "As the flames are fanned to sell more newspapers and the focus is narrowed to scrutinize the base and obscene, we have to strain to see a positive glimpse of a beautiful people. The high-achieving, decent role models are available but obscured...we are led to believe that our relationship can only be adversarial. The media serve to magnify the negative as they eagerly await the next juicy bit of trouble they use to sell their product. Unfortunately, subjects such as responsible parenting, church attendance, financial stability, and non-racist attitudes aren't marketable commodities. It would do a lot of good to have these attributes revealed."[8]

I ask, What purpose does the media think it is serving when only the bad side of any ethnic group is presented? It appears they have assumed the role of Captain Queeg[9] in America. They think they are the catalyst we need in order to act. Unfortunately, I believe they are inciting us to act in the wrong direction. They are driving ethnic groups in America farther apart instead of helping the healing process by bringing them closer together.

BE SURE TO BUY . . .

Lest you think they are doing this out of ignorance, the media is perfectly aware of its influence on the youth of America. Star Broadcasting signed up more than 1,000 schools for its radio service in its initial season. Luring the institutions with its promise of making an average of $20,000 a year for a school of 1,500 students (or even more if they sell additional advertising to local merchants), the students will hear music and commercials as they change classes and eat lunch.[10] It appears that being assaulted by this type of programming is not going to be restricted to after-school hours. It will now be a part of their "learning process." I trust the students will be able to differentiate between what they should learn and what they should tune out.

THE MEDIA MADE ME DO IT!

A poll sponsored by Children Now, an advocacy group, showed that children and teens today think there is far too much bed hopping by unmarried TV characters and it is prompting our youth to start sex early. Continuing with the critical evaluation of television, the majority said it implies most people are dishonest and children routinely talk back to their parents. Cited as evidence of the disrespect with which children treat their parents were "The Simpsons" and "Married With Children."

The media's influence is often so subtle we do not always recognize it. I asked one college student if he felt the media had influenced his belief system. Without hesitation, he answered, "No, I've made my decisions based on other factors." Later, as we were talking, I asked him if he felt he was more liberal or more conservative than his parents. He said he thought he was more liberal. When I asked him why that was, he said, "I think probably the media had a lot to do with it." He could not explain why he thought the media had not influenced him and why he also thought they had made him more liberal in his thinking.

Most of the students with whom I talked felt their value systems closely approximated those of their parents. However, they also admitted that generally they were somewhat more liberal than their parents because "Things are just different today." How do they know that? They replied, "By what I see in the media," and "That's just the way things are today."

Another student emphasized the fact that if the media would present the news without interpretation and present all the facts, we could form our own opinions and make better decisions. His comment was countered by another student who pointed out, "You know we have a burden ourselves, and we are very lazy. We are shifted left and right by the media because we allow it. We have to stop and think where they're coming from. That's why I read a lot–things written by people who are all part of our culture. Some of them will make me say, 'This is part of me.' Others will challenge me. You have to work it out. You have to put some effort into it. You can't just let the media do it for you."

I was impressed by the students' insights into the media's shortcomings. "We think the media have done all the research, so they must be right. I know it's not true, but people just sort of fall for it. It's in the news so it must be true. It's so convenient." I think that describes too many citizens of our country today–instant everything–anything as long as it can be labeled convenient. We do not want to have to search for the truth. We want it dropped into our laps where we can pick it up, glance at it, digest it instantly, and turn it into wisdom. Unfortunately, that's not the way it works. As another student said, "When you get the same information in the newspapers and on TV, it's really easy not to think and question what is the truth. You just kind of think it must be true–that's the way it really is."

RUSH TELLS THE TRUTH

A student named John commented, "I think one reason Rush Limbaugh is so popular is that he tells the truth. Everybody who's sick of hearing all the lies from the rest of the media is listening to him, but Rush is politically incorrect. There was a survey of late night shows. Some of the shows weren't even on the air anymore, but he wasn't even listed. Whoopi Goldberg was there, and her show was like the worst of all. He's on here in prime time because he makes money. I think right now a lot of people are looking for the truth because of what has happened in the White House. They're starting to wonder. They don't know whether Clinton is telling the truth, and we're never going to find out from the rest of the media. Now they're saying he lies."

Another student interjected, "You go *wow*! You know Rush tells the truth, brings out the truth.

Sometimes he's apathetic, sometimes he bangs off of people, but he brings out the truth about our media."

UP CLOSE AND PERSONAL

Their disillusionment with the media was even more evident as they talked of their personal experiences. The news across the country following heavy rains caused a lot of concern among families living elsewhere. "My mom was talking to Aunt Cindy, and she said, 'Are you guys all flooded out over there?' We had to tell her it wasn't even raining out right now. She had thought from her news reports all of Los Angeles was under water. The streets were flooded around here, but there weren't any cars under water."

"Yeah, it's like you can go down to Skid Row and you can make people think all of LA is like Skid Row; or you can go to Beverly Hills and do a story on it and make everyone think all of LA is like Beverly Hills. I used to think before going downtown in LA to help out that you would see people lined up against buildings, standing around and just waiting for a hand-out. It totally wasn't like that. The people are in the back alleys. There are trucks that go by once a night and once during the day to hand out blankets and food. [The media] makes it out to look like we treat these people like dogs and they don't have anywhere to go. Actually, they get treated pretty good, and they get hot food."

"Sometimes it's really worse than you think. I remember after the hurricane in Miami. They showed the damage and everything, but I was there and it was ten times worse than what they showed on TV. People came down to help, and the media showed people being given other places to stay, but there were thousands of people who were without water and didn't have anywhere to go. The media kept saying everything was totally under control. The storm people were there, but it was completely different from what the media was saying. There again, it can be either way."

The students shared their concern about our media's influence in foreign countries, especially on the youth. "When I was in Hungary, the college students over there thought everything was like "Miami Vice." Everyone's driving around in Ferraris and Lamborghinis. It's totally unreal. Then they see us, and they're magnetized toward us. They just want to talk to us because we're from this incredible land they've seen in the movies."

"I remember one guy named Stephen. He was a walking billboard for Nike. He thought this was how to be an American. He had learned to speak English from watching American movies. I suppose that was good, but every sentence contained a word we wouldn't use in polite conversation. That's something you have to keep in mind when you talk to them. You have to get past that and think about what they're trying to communicate. Then I started to think about us here in America. That's exactly how we are. We've got to have the latest fashions and the latest electronic toy we see on TV or read about. We see everything through a limited lens, and there's so much more going on outside that window. You have to remember anytime you look through a window, you lose details on the edges and you lose the context in which that window is presented."

"Over there, lots of the girls are topless at the beach. When you ask them why they do this, some of them said, 'Isn't that what you do in America?' We just fell back in our seats. Talk about foreign perception. They think this is the pinnacle of society, and they want to get just as far over in their country."

When I look at the movies being produced today, I shudder to think of the image of American life we are portraying to the rest of the world. If they think we are a bunch of minority-bashers, bent on sex with every acquaintance, and living in cities filled with vice and corruption, how long can we expect to command the respect of those citizens of other countries who still honor higher values?

Many students see the media today as having a really rampant sense of artistic freedom. They feel the media will paint things however it sees them. As long as it thinks the public will like it, the media will continue to make their statement. "You know, they've got their ears out there, and they're asking what the people like. What do they like? It's not so much their opinion. It's the opinion they think the public wants to hear."

THEY MUST KNOW

"I remember when I was back in high school, I looked at media figures and people who wrote articles as individuals who had completely researched their topics. I looked at them with a certain amount of respect. I didn't understand the media could be biased, and that they would do anything to sell their stuff. If they don't sell, they don't have a job.

"I looked up to these people as authorities. I thought they must have deductively reasoned their opinions. There must be a basis for what they were saying, and it must be the mainstream view. I didn't understand what they were often doing was sensationalizing the mainstream view to create sales.

When you're in high school, you don't know that. When you're in high school, you think the media have vowed to tell the truth, and they're in this deep search for truth. I never understood how biased they could be until I hit college and began to debate with people who challenged me."

"[High school] is probably the most important time. That and when you first enter college. By the time you get through the first year of college, you're pretty well set with what you believe. The dangerous part is that everybody, every opinion, every viewpoint is competing for your attention when you're undecided."

Another student added, "I remember how commercials influenced me when I was in high school. They presented gorgeous people who were thin and had wonderful make-up. Then they said you should try this make-up, or do this, or do that. I knew a lot of girls who were bulimic because they thought they had to look like a certain person. They had to be thin. It really has an effect on who you think you are."

TV–MY ONLY FRIEND

"Lots of times, especially when you're alone, the TV is the only friend you have. You flip it on. It keeps you company. I remember I used to ask my parents on Saturday, 'What's for breakfast?' They said, 'Later.' so I turned on the TV and watched cartoons." I asked this collegian if he would want his children to watch cartoons today. He told me "No, I don't even like them anymore. They're not for kids."

Another student interrupted, "Things have changed a lot on TV. What used to be not acceptable is now OK. I remember hearing a girl called a bitch not too long ago, and it blew my mind."

I watched the premier of "NYPD Blue" to form my own opinion regarding all the hype about sex, violence, and foul language. This show aired at 8:00 p.m., and my then-nine-year-old son went to bed at 8:30. Although I did not allow him to watch the show, he could have done so had he been unsupervised and watching television. Here is my assessment; it clearly failed the "It's OK to Watch Test." Within the first fifteen minutes, I watched a cop sleep with a prostitute, an attempted murder, and the following use of the English language: bitch, asshole, scumbag, and bastard. I was totally shocked! I can handle foul language, but this stuff was on prime-time TV!

Fortunately, the show was moved to a later time slot, but the fact that it aired at all during prime time was evidence of the disregard television producers hold for who may be watching a production.

SEX SELLS

Other students who were interviewed felt it wasn't just violence and foul language that was being used by the media to sell its wares. Sex was also being used as a come on. One young man, a member of the wrestling team, commented, "I used to buy magazines on weight lifting and hot rods, but I don't anymore 'cause there are all these chicks in G-strings." You flip through it and go, what does this have to do with weight lifting? Rad articles about cars and everything, but then there's this chick in a G-string on the cover and everywhere. I'd buy those magazines if they wouldn't just have sex all over them."

"We had this debate on advertising in one of my classes last year. Sex sells. I don't think you can equate sex with anything. Sex just sells, and people buy it. That's just the way it works."

"*Seventeen* used to be a really neat magazine, now it's all sexy. It's tame by the standards of today though. I picked up a copy of *Glamour* the other day. I started to read one of the articles, and it was about which position was the most comfortable when having sex. Excuse me! In *Glamour* magazine! You pick up anything, and it's about sex and violence and that stuff, 'cause it's popular."

"*Sassy* is supposed to be for high school kids. I ordered it when it first came out. It looked like the best magazine. It was the-e-e worst! It was all about sex and 13-year-olds who were glad they were having babies. I thought, 'This isn't anything for high schoolers.' Even when you're a freshman or sophomore in college, this teaches the wrong things."

"I think it's part of the breakdown of the family. People are looking for significance just because they don't have a reason to know their own significance. Sometimes, I think the media does it to sell their products. They want you to feel inadequate so you will buy."

NO, YOU CAN'T!

By and large, today's youths have not experienced much censoring of their TV watching. Some parents limited the amount of time the television set could be on because they wanted their children to participate in other activities or go to bed at a certain time. Most did not restrict the type of programming. Some parents did limit the movies they permitted their children to see to ones that had been rated for their age groups. The youths acknowledged this was not too successful because, "You know how kids are, they sneak out and see them anyway."

I took my son to see the movie, *The Good Son*.

When my little boy first asked me to take him to "a McCauley Caulkin movie," I quickly agreed. Fond memories of *Home Alone* danced through my head. When we arrived at the movie theater and were standing in line for tickets, I noticed the movie was rated R. I assumed that any movie with McCauley Caulkin would be rated no worse than PG. My son adores this child actor and was thrilled when, after writing to him, McCauley's agent sent my boy an autographed picture, which he hung on his bedroom wall.

After realizing the movie was rated R, I told my son we could not see it. My son protested, "Dad, you promised." The woman behind us said she had spoken to the manager of the movie theater who assured her that *The Good Son* had received the R rating only because it was scary (no sex, etc.). Since my son does not scare easily, I "caved in" and decided to keep my promise.

It turned out that we really enjoyed the movie. I do not think the movie was too scary for my son nor were there any sexual situations. However, one thing I will never, ever forget (nor forgive the makers of the movie for doing), is one sentence McCauley Caulkin uttered. "Don't fuck with me!" Why couldn't they have said, "Don't mess with me"? My son asked me why it was O.K. for McCauley to use bad language. Poor choice of words? Or, once again, was Hollywood sensationalism hoping to stir up controversy?

Another example of a poor choice of words is an expression used in the movie *Jack*, with Robin Williams. The adult-child played by Williams discusses an erection, or a "boner" as he called it. My friend Joe was floored when his nine year old daughter asked, "Dad, what's a boner?"

Some of the students I interviewed were younger children who were stuck with watching what older siblings chose. However, they did not remember watching programs that today they deem objectionable for children.

The one exception to parental censoring was a young man who remembers a period of tight restraint in his life. His dad took all the radios and the TV set and locked them in a closet because he did not like the programs–especially the music. "I think he did that because we were out of control. Then later he let us watch TV, listen to music, or whatever.

I don't think this was good for me because I got exposed to a lot of bad influences. I went through a period when I acted out all these things in my life. I didn't think too much about it at the time, but now that I have my life back together, I look back to the time when I had to pull from myself, and it was just garbage."

In contrast, the same youths say they would severely restrict their children's media exposure, especially to the television set. Things just have changed too much. There's too much violence and sex for younger children to understand or handle. They cited the early evening reruns of what used to be late night shows as being especially objectionable today. They even felt that wise parents should probably preview movies because the rating system is not that reliable an indicator of objectionable content–especially for very young children. They also said that in all probability, premium cable would be off-limits.

If I understand correctly what they are telling me with their analysis, they fully understand the influence of the media in lives even if they felt its impact on their own was minimal. They understand how easily opinions can be changed and the tragic implications of the youthful perception of adult subjects.

As support for this point of view, Milton Chen's book, *The Smart Parents' Guide to Kids' TV*, says parents should limit children's watching to no more than two hours per day. He also advocates encouraging them to watch such shows as the "Reading Rainbow," "The Magic School Bus," and "Ghost-writer," and making shows that are intended for adults and even the popular "Mighty Morphin Power Ranger," off limits.

He asks the parents of children to evaluate their own television watching as well as observing what their children watch. He then asks this probing question, "Are there periods that could be better spent in learning activities with your child?" I daresay there are not many parents who could answer this question negatively.

CHALLENGING THEIR FAITH

Those youth I interviewed who felt the media had greatly affected them were largely from homes where religion had played an important part. The next few comments show they agreed the media had challenged their value system and their beliefs. They had been taught one thing, and suddenly their beliefs were being subjected to an onslaught of counter-beliefs.

As one student put it, "It put me at odds with myself. When I was in high school, being a Christian was confusing because I believed in God, but I saw what I thought was the truth of what the media was saying. I accepted it as truth at the time because I thought they had researched everything. I felt really outcast. I believed what I had been taught, and I believed what the media was saying; and there was conflict between the two. I found myself really in the middle, really questioning and really confused as to where I stood as an individual and what I believed and why there could be so many different views. Then when I got into college and starting researching things for myself, I found myself getting more and more cynical about the media.

"When I was younger, I really assumed Christians were bigots, stuck a few centuries back, narrow-minded, unwilling to face the truth, uneducated, basing all their decisions totally on faith, and trying to block other people's civil rights because that's how it was presented in the media. You know, sometimes you can read an article and insert the word Nazi for fundamentalist Christian because of what the media is saying. It's like we're the new bogeymen of America. But then I look at myself and think, I'm a Christian, and I'm not that way. If I don't catch myself, I'm kind of dismissing my own position.

EVEN THE HOLY GRAIL

"There was this one episode of the "Young Indiana Jones Chronicles" set in India. This new Hindu teacher was a kid, and there was this one lady, incredibly smart and wise, and she ends up denying the truth just because she has this 'belief.' You can just see how they were pointing to some groups and saying 'They're reasonable to a point, and then when you give them the truth, they just say, no I believe in God.' I thought that's incredibly wrong. It's not fair at all.

"It's been said nations that fall look to their youth for advice and for counsel. Today, we're looking to the children for ultimate truth because they're unbiased, they're young, they're fresh, and uninfluenced by the world, so we look to them for wisdom. We now have the youngest president in our history. To me, we're dealing with a basic principle that is the foundation for everything in this country. You go to the wise, the elders, who have been through these things, those who have experienced them and struggled with them instead of the young, idealistic ones who have no idea what they're talking about. Our society and the media are teaching us well. We know what the problem is, but if we can just reach the young people... What are we going to learn from them? They should be the ones who are learning.

"I don't want to paint this as a broadbase conspiracy with all these people getting together and saying, 'Let's delude the American public.' I don't think it's so much that as it is the media is composed of immoral people from an immoral society–me included. They have to behave in that way to cope with our society and avoid the reality of life.

"The media is misleading people more and more. More than they understand. I don't think they mean to, but they are. The answer is not within ourselves. I don't think they see what they are doing because I think they deny the validity of a lot of things they don't believe could happen–the intangibles. Movies and commercials say you will find your best hopes and dreams within yourself. Just choose whatever you want. But the fact remains–truth is the truth."

MEDIA LIES?

Another student said, "You know, it makes me mad when they present something as fact and then turn it around and make it lies. Take the Rodney King thing. They made him some kind of a hero. They didn't show the whole tape. Then one night after the trial was all over, they showed the entire tape. And when you saw it, no wonder he was getting beat! This guy was constantly up, up, up, up!

Before the trial, they didn't show the before and after part. They just showed the beating. I think if they had shown the whole thing, there might still have been a little bit of discontent among the races, or whatever, but there wouldn't have been as big a riot with all that happened. I think just showing that little part was like saying, 'Look what's happening in LA. You people aren't doing your job.'

"It made me so mad the day after the sentence in the second trial. The media's supposed to be unbiased and everything, and the next day here's the paper and the headline was 'Sentence 2 1/2 years. LA Justice?' They couldn't just report the sentence. They had to question it. Like *2 1/2 years*? That's nothing. Instead of being unbiased, they take their opinion and try to make it yours.

"That's true in every major field, whether it's journalism, psychology, philosophy, or whatever. They look back on history with their own eyes. You now have more information, so you go through a revisionist period. You want to correct the mistakes you see and read your own opinions into the facts.

"Remember, when you first started to study history and you were told George Washington was this national hero–almost perfect–never told a lie, and you know. Every time you took that course in American History, you learned more about him, and by the time you were in college, he had really changed. Because we have more information than any other generation has had, we try to go back and find meanings between the lines–that maybe aren't even there. And remember, what used to be politically correct is not always politically correct now–like being a police officer.

"Most of the time, I don't think the news is under the control of the government. It's under the control of some very liberal people who are managing the news for their own agenda, but sometimes, I think there are times when the government does have some influence with the media, so they can both benefit. Look back at JFK. You have a synergistic media building an image. Now, you read a book about him, and he was a far cry from who people thought he was.

"I'm an education major, and I see the same things in my classes that I see in the media. It's really scary. This year I've been studying the teaching curriculums and it's making me almost scared to be a teacher or to ever have to put my own kids in school.

"The media sees what they are looking for. You can't just get the plain facts. I watch CNN and I read the newspapers. I love information. The media says 'No, we're unbiased.' But they're not. If I'm not thinking about what I'm reading, I just swallow what they are saying and don't realize this is coming from a definite point of view, and it isn't necessarily the truth. This is just what somebody saw. It's very subtle. There's only so much time. You have a job or you go to school, and that's a full-time job. It's so much easier to just flip on the TV with the remote control.

"You say, how far can things be distorted? Some of it, of course, is a journalist's opinion. I think a lot of it is the media believes they're really educated to be unbiased observers; therefore, whatever their reaction is to an event must be true. It's a cultural thing within journalism–that I am an unbiased observer.

"One thing you see in Iran is that they would rather feature a lie than admit they don't know the answer. Remember what happened in the Gulf War? In Iraq, people were sitting there and still saying, 'Oh, we're going to win the war,' because that was what they had been told. We sort of see the same thing here."

A NEAT LITTLE PACKAGE?

"That's not a whole lot different from what we all tend to do. Because of our human nature, rather than dealing with the questions, we tend to want the answers; but sometimes, the questions tell us more than the answers do. We are afraid of questions because we are afraid we won't find the answers immediately. The media wants everything answered and all tied up by the end of a half-hour newscast at 11:00 or an hour at 4:00 or 5:00. If it's not all tied up, they're uncomfortable. We like to have things tied up in neat packages, but the truth doesn't usually fit into a package.

"You know, for the longest time, I thought there was no more racism in the world–at all! It was all done with. Oh sure, once in a while you'd get a couple of people who were prejudiced. Then I saw something on TV about problems with the KKK in the south and how they still had separation in some of the restaurants. I went 'Ooops!' All along I had thought everyone loved everyone, African-Americans, Mexicans, and everyone. America was just one big melting pot. I was so shocked when I found out."

I commented that the media had served her well by pointing out a truth she had overlooked. She agreed, but added, "America's still the best place to be.

"I think the way the media affects me and the way I see it affecting society is that it separates our culture on the basis of progressivism. Within our culture, if you're progressive, you're moving along and you're improving our world. If you disagree with them, you're responsible for destruction and misery. I really see the media separating those in our culture."

It's ironic, isn't it. The one instrument in our world that could be a unifying force is perceived as being the tool of disunity–the thing that will drive people apart instead of bringing them to-gether.

After spending some time with them, peeking into their minds, and collecting their thoughts, I would say the youth of today seem not so much to be critical of the media as to be wary of it. Perhaps this is as a result of the learning processes now more in evidence than a generation ago. They have been taught to look for the truth and to explore both sides of an issue. I find I am now more confi-dent of the future. The media will continue to in-fluence them as it does all of us, but I do not be-lieve they will allow themselves to be blindly led. They are not afraid to question.

WORKS CITED

1. McCloy, Mike. "Arizona inmate hangs himself after TV news shows his plight." *The Orange County Register* 31 July 1993 News 10.

2. Ibid.

3. Santoyo, Gus. "Young news hounds keep tabs on neighborhood." *The Orange County Register* 31 July 1993 Metro 1.

4. Kelly, Katy. "Radio Aahs, where kids rule airwaves." *USA Today* 5 August 1993 1D.

5. Unless otherwise credited, quotations are from personal inter-views with students in the Los Angeles/Orange County metropolitan area, 16 September 1993 and 24 September 1993.

6. Masterson, Danielle. "The Media Make It Hard for Responsible Teen-Agers." *The Los Angeles Times* 26 April 1993 D2.

7. Ibid.

8. Kearon, Mike. "Black America gets a bad media rap." *The Orange County Register* 9 May 1993 Commentary 5.

9. Wouk, Herman. *Caine Mutiny Court Martial.* New York: Doubleday, 1954.

10. "Ads could hit school halls." *USA Today* 30 July 1993 B1.

11. Elias, Marilyn. "Teens themselves say TV is a bad influence." *USA Today* 27 February 1995 1D.

Chapter 14

GOOD NEWS ONLY

A popular Sunday cartoon shows the rug rat of the family perched in front of the television set. Dad walks in and says, "That's the fourth time you've seen this video today. Can Daddy see what happened in the real world?" As Dad flips through the channels, he tunes to, "Worst day of fighting since (Click!) Allegations of fraud (Click!) kidnapping (Click!) execution style slaying (Click!) brutal murder of a tourist (Click!) sentenced for molest.... (Click!) malnutrition." His expression goes from interest to concern to a frantic (Click!) (Click!) (Click!). The last frame of the comic strip shows Dad holding the rug rat and happily listening to the Barney song, "I love you. You love me. We're a great big fam-i-ly."[1]

How often have you felt you have been overdosed on bad news and violence and the tiny tot videos were far preferable to the channel programming? Yes, I know, I've been there too. I have watched the news and gone to bed either so upset by what was happening in the world, I almost thought there was no hope; or so angered by the constant barrage of violence, I seriously thought of bashing in the television set.

Then I remembered you must be careful not to throw out the baby with the bath water. The media offers a golden opportunity for good to be aired, the perfect sounding board for inspiring people to do better, and a perfect billboard for good works. All that needs to happen is for the trend of violence and bad news we are now experiencing to be reversed.

That brings to mind the interesting question

posed by another cartoon's daughter to her father at the breakfast table, "If everyone gets so upset about bad news, why do they publish it?"[2] Yes, why do they publish it? Why not publish only good news?

WILL IT SELL?

I asked a local student if he felt a newspaper would sell if it contained only good news. He answered, "No, and therein lies the problem. It's a matter of what sells. What sells? Violence and sex are what sells. In that sense, the media reflects the culture. Why does the media feature mostly negative stories? It's more spectacular and it's what sells. If people weren't buying it, it wouldn't sell. It's a Catch 22 situation. People complain and complain about it, so the media changes. Nobody buys, so they change it back. Then the people complain about it again. That's the way it is, whether you like it or not."[3]

Whoa! That is a really pessimistic view. Let's pursue the concept a bit further. Do I believe a newspaper would sell if it featured primarily good news? The answer, as naive or gullible as it may sound, is yes. Despite the fact we have become hooked on bad news, I think the public is hungry for good news, stories of Good Samaritans, glimpses of the occasional knight in shining armor that rides through our midst, and for confirmation that man can and does do good deeds.

Does the media tell us about the good things that people do? Yes, but you have to look for it. It won't be featured as a headline. In fact, it probably won't even make it into the first section. It will be buried back in another section that features a brief look at other items of interest. It may be labeled, "People," "Society," "Accent," or any number of other designations. If the story features a sports figure, it will probably be found in the sports section (in contrast to the bad news about sports figures that makes front page headlines).

A BREATH OF FRESH AIR

Occasionally, you do have a mediamaker who breaks with this tradition. I was delighted to see the *Honolulu Advertiser* feature the recipients of its Thomas Jefferson Award for Public Service in the first section of the newspaper. While the story did not make the front-page headlines, it was on page three; and there were in-depth looks at each of the winners in a separate section of the paper.[4] Their stories emphasized how one person can make a difference in many lives. In one case, being blind simply did not deter a determined woman from offering service to others. The areas in which they served were varied, and the recipients were from across the whole social fiber of the islands–from the native population to the military personnel stationed there to "Skid Row."

How often do we see people receiving public service awards featured by the media at all? Some channels and radio stations do have their "Person of the Week" who has done something out of the ordinary, but these honors are few and far between.

Personally, I do not believe it is because there is a shortage of worthy recipients. I think the media is simply reflecting their belief that these stories are not newsworthy because they will not sell.

I think they will sell. Wouldn't it be wonderful to pick up a paper and read about all the good things going on in our world? I think so. I think we would also receive a hidden benefit. If we believe the premise that violence in the media is promoting violence in the public, then why wouldn't the converse be true, that goodness featured in the media would foster goodness in the public?

WHAT IF...

Let's take a hypothetical situation. You are getting ready for work. You would like to be up on what is going on in the world. Your elementary school-age child is also getting ready and is tuned in any time the TV set is on. The news tells us there is continued fighting in the world's hot spots; there was a terrible accident on the freeway and three children were killed; gang fights broke out as the result of an argument over turf control; a brush fire is out of control near a neighboring city; and the trial of a child involved in a murder, all in the first fifteen minutes of the broadcast. As it continues, additional tales of violence and man's inhumanity to man surface. You and your family eat breakfast to an eyewitness report of a drive-by shooting that police believe is linked to an earlier gang fight.

Your child seems a little withdrawn and hesitant as you go out to the car. He doesn't even really act as if he wants to get in. As you drive toward his school, you notice your child grips the edge of the seat tightly as you merge into the freeway traffic. When you let him out at his school, he eyes a group of larger children huddled together in one part of the playground. He goes to the gate at the end of the grounds farthest away from them and enters–off to another happy day at school.

When you pick him up at the extended day program, there is a note from his teacher. This was not another happy day at school. His teacher reported he picked a fight with a group of older children who, according to the playground supervisor, had asked him and his friends to move over a little ways so they wouldn't be in the way of their ball game. Instead of cooperating and sharing the playground, he had chosen to shout, "It's my place. You can't have it," and start a fight. As you question him about it later, he mirrors the comments of the gang member interviewed earlier on television. Clearly, his day started out in the wrong way and his attitudes were set by what he had watched earlier.

Now, let's relive this scenario as though good news were as freely accessible as bad news. The featured story of the day is the day's most honored person. The station chooses one person every day to honor for public service, acts of selfless beauty and random kindness, honorable accomplishments (recipients of scholarships, honors, induction into special honor fraternities, etc.), or simply someone who quietly goes about the day's business with dignity, a pleasant attitude, and accomplishes the job well.

Then there are the stories of a group of people restoring their decaying neighborhood, the food fund for needy people sponsored by a local club, and a job bank established by merchants in the area. The story of a small child who wandered away from her home but, because of the neighborhood watch program, was found and returned safely to her family within a few hours tugged at your heart as a parent.

The story of two teenagers who found a billfold in the street containing several hundred dollars in cash and returned it to the grateful owner who rewarded their honesty especially caught your child's attention. You think to yourself, "He may never be in this situation, but he's learning the lesson of honesty."

Another human interest story featured as you

eat breakfast is about an organization that has been beset by intense rivalry among its leaders. The story of a new member who brought the rival factions into harmony and agreement by her peace-making efforts left you feeling there really are no problems that cannot be solved by arbitration.

Your child grabs his lunch box and hops into the seat beside you. As he fastens his seatbelt, he asks, "Hey, Dad! What kind of trucks do you think we'll see on the freeway today?" You laugh and answer, "I'm betting on a car carrier." As you pull onto the freeway, your son points excitedly, "Look Dad! There's one."

When you pick him up that evening, there is a note from the teacher. It says, "I just wanted you to know that Anthony received the Good Citizen of the Week award because of his actions on the play-ground today. An aggressive group of children wanted him and his classmates to go into the cor-ner of the playground so they could have the space for their game. Your son became a mediator and helped work out a solution whereby the older group could have plenty of room for their game and he and his friends had their spot to play in–and it wasn't in the corner. Good Work!"

We find that newsletters, which contain only information and advice on a specific subject, sell. Seminars sell without having to include bad news or sensationalism. I commend *USA Today* for of-fering to the public much more in the way of good news than other newspapers. Obviously, this ap-proach has not hurt its sales.

While, admittedly, this good news approach is simplistic, I believe the trend in behavior would be in the direction of positive action instead of vio-lence if the news were good instead of bad. Not only children, but adults would also be motivated to find solutions that do not include violence to the problems that occur in all of our lives.

LEAVE ME ALONE

I think the American public would rather have good news instead of bad news. I think they are tired of hearing about only negative happenings, and I think their bodies are tired from the constant bombardment by missiles of violence and depravity. They want the refreshment that good news brings.

I was impressed by a colleague who had been on a vacation. The rules of the vacation included no radios or television sets on the premises. The time was spent in reading and meditation uninterrupted by what was going on in the world. He told me he felt as though he had been on a mountain top. When he came back down into the valley of the real world, he could face the problems that would surely arise because he had been refreshed by the positive reinforcement of good thoughts, time alone, motivational reading, and time to simply think about things.

As a people, our nation needs this, too. We need to hear about the good things that really are happening and be refreshed and motivated by them. One college student expressed her views in this way.

"I don't like watching the news on TV because it's always so horrible. There's never anything good on it. Oh, once in a while you get something like Baby Jessica being rescued from the well. They have harrowing stories with happy endings, but they never say, 'Well, three more people got jobs today, or there's this guy who's been in the streets, had a drug problem and is finally now cleaning up his act, and has a job with a good company.' These are little things, but it makes me feel better knowing there are good things going on out there.

"There's news out there that's good stuff. It's not all bad, but it seems like 95% of the news is about murders, killings, violence and all the bad things that go on. And then the good little interesting things only get 5%. Too often the good news is about something like an animal that got rescued in bad weather or off of the freeway. Have you noticed most of those little special true stories are about animals? It seems like you hear more about animals than people. Oh, there's 'Rescue 911.' You have good stuff in there, but there has to be something bad to catch people's attention. They really take a tragedy and make something good come from it."[5]

ARE YOU OFFENDED?

Do I think the media gloom and doom offends normal, everyday people? I think it offends most of us including the man working in the gift shop at Caesar's Palace in Las Vegas who told me he deliberately wraps all his Sunday newspapers with the comics section facing out because, "The rest is all gloom and doom, and I want my customers to laugh first."

I think it offended the Arizona man who, in a letter to the editor, complained that the tragic stories printed about violence and crime in his newspaper could almost be mistaken for a police report with its detail. He closes with the thought, "The paper should contain more local, inspirational stories and less tragic ones. Reporting of inspirational stories does not limit the section only to soft news. Reporting of inspirational news is some of the best journalism there is."[6]

I think it offended the California woman who

wrote her editor and asked, "How about good news?" She wondered why we can't have some news about what people are doing and accomplishing in the community. She closed by admonishing the paper to lighten up and print something about people who aren't always screaming about their rights.[7]

Even Al Neuharth, founder of *USA Today,* lamented in a tribute to the late Governor of South Dakota, George Mickelson, that bad guys steal the headlines while the good guys get taken for granted. In a commentary on why this was true, he stated, "My head understands why bad guys like [former Governor of Alabama] Hunt get headlines. But my heart goes out to good public servants like Mickelson. There are so many more of the latter than the former. In city halls, courthouses, statehouses, the White House. Sadly, some are taken before their time. And most are taken for granted. Thank them while you can."[8]

It clearly offended my father-in-law, whose 18-year-old son was killed in an auto accident, when a local Connecticut newspaper printed an account of the boy's past misdeeds rather than relating the current events–how over 400 people came to pay their respects; people who were crying and lamenting the loss of such a great friend and good person.

I second the sentiment Al Neuharth expressed. I too would like to see more thanks given to those who serve faithfully and well. I would like to see them receive as much publicity as those who abuse their power. It is a sad day in America's medialand when bereaved parents are compelled to write to a newspaper and protest the unfair, hurtful, insensitive, and inconsiderate handling of the news of the death of their beloved child. News that was presented in a manner full of innuendo that was not supported in any way by the findings of law enforcement personnel. Personally, I find these reporters to be an abomination on the American journalistic scene.

Why should the "forces of bad" win the battle of the media? They should not. The American public is just as interested in the good people as they are in the bad people. They just have not been given the opportunity to know about them.

In all honesty, it was not until after Governor Mickelson was killed that I learned what a respected man he was; and yet, from the beginning of the investigation into ex-Governor Hunt's finances, I was aware of his misdeeds. I am truly sorry I did not know what an insightful leader Mickelson was. I missed out on an important part of American history.

I CAN DO IT!

My heart was always warmed when I watched "Life Goes On." This program was a tremendous piece of good news. Good news that people with Down's Syndrome do not need to be isolated. There is a place for them in mainstream America. They can be included in all aspects of life. While they may experience problems unique to their situation, they can be productive members of our society. I venture to say there is not a parent in America whose child has Down's Syndrome that was not encouraged by this program.

In the same vein, I am sure when the good news of Bert Shepard's playing in baseball's major leagues reached others who had lost limbs, they were encouraged immeasurably. But who shared the news of his reunion with the German doctor who had saved his life during World War II with the public? Most newspapers buried it back in the sports pages, if they mentioned it at all. My hat is off to Mel Allen, host of "This Week in Baseball," who featured the story in one of his broadcasts. Thanks for sharing the good news with us as a top story.

WHO ARE YOUR FRIENDS?

Yes, good news does sell. It encourages us. Very few of us are by nature "gloom-and-doomers." Look at your friends and those people with whom you like to spend time. How much time do you spend with someone you know who will tell you only bad news and freely share with you the worst prognosis for everything? On the other hand, how many times do you seek out those are pleasant company and delightful conversationalists who will encourage you by telling about the good things in their lives?

Take another look at the role of your radio, television set, and reading matter. You spend a lot of time with them, so they have to be regarded as friends of a sort. Are you picking the same type of friends among them as you are among your real-life friends, or do you run with a different crowd? Just like any other bad habit, it is hard to break; but I believe Americans, on the whole, want the same type of media-friends as their flesh and blood friends.

Americans will buy papers and magazines that have mostly good news. They will go to movies and watch television shows that feature uplifting stories and noble aspirations. They will respond to the good in action around them in a positive manner.

I am not saying people should not be kept informed of the bad things around them; I am simply suggesting that for every one item of unpleasant news, there should be nine reports of something good that has happened. The bad news reports that are given should not be hyped, sensationalized, or otherwise capitalized on; they should simply be re-counted.

Why am I so confident in the power of good news? Because I know the emotions that are generated when I am exposed to good stimuli as opposed to the emotions I feel when I am subjected to bad influences, and I much prefer those that result from the good stimuli. I also believe I am not unique. I believe I am part of a large group who also feels this way.

We are stuck on violence and crime not because we prefer them; but because these subjects are more readily available and we have not made the concentrated effort to seek a change. However, if we truly had a choice, and could have the good and noble just as easily as the violent and corrupt, we would choose good more often than not.

A newspaper or newscast that offers only good news? I yearn for one, and I would wholeheartedly support it.

AT LAST...

In the near future, we may have this opportunity–at least via computer. Microsoft® Windows now offers a program called "Journalist," that will allow you to design your own newspaper. You can choose both the general and specific types of subject matter you want to read and how you want it formatted. Not all news services are currently available, but a wide variety, including some foreign ones, are presently searched for stories.

Just think, no more wading through the disgusting to find the enlightening. No more editors deciding what you should read and where it should be in your newspaper. You can publish your own newspaper and fill it with the type of news you want to read.[9]

Way to go!

WORKS CITED

1. Kirkman, Rick/Scott, Jerry. "Baby Blues." *The Los Angeles Times* 10 October 1993. Sunday Comics.

2. Machlis, Gail. "Quality Time." *The Los Angeles Times* 10 May 1993 E5.

3. Personal interviews with students in the Los Angeles/Orange County metropolitan area, 16 September 1993.

4. Krauss, Bob. "12 winners get Jefferson awards." *The Honolulu Advertiser* 18 April 1993 A3.

5. Personal interviews with students in the Los Angeles/Orange County metropolitan area, 16 September 1993.

6. Mayeda, Dolan. "Readers want inspirational news, not all this violence." *Arizona Republic* 25 April 1993.

7. Boyer, Helen. "How about good news?" *The Orange County Register* 28 July 1993 M9.

8. Neuharth, Al. "Hearts at half-mast in USA's heartland. *USA Today* 30 April/2 May 1993.

9. Magin, Lawrence J. "Edited-Just-for-You News is Now Available in Your Desktop Computer Every Day." *The Los Angeles Times* 14 May 1993 D2.

Chapter 15

WHAT IF...?

We have all looked back on our experiences and wished we had done some things differently, or even wished we had chosen a different path at a crossroads in our lives. Each time we play this what-if game, we know we can never undo the past, but we like to comfort ourselves with the thought that things would have been better had we made a different choice. I'd like to propose a little exercise where we let our imaginations take charge and speculate what the outcome of several recent key issues would have been had the media responded in a different manner.

NO RIOTS?

The first issue that comes to mind is the Los Angeles Riots. If the media had acted during the first trial of the four officers who beat Rodney King as they acted during the second trial of the officers and the trial of the youths who beat Reginald Denny, what would have been the outcome? Would the riots have been avoided? I think they might very well have been. Why do I say this?

Let's compare the actions of the media during the two trials of the officers. From the time the video taken of the four officers beating Rodney King was made public, we were subjected to continued viewing often accompanied by inflammatory remarks voiced by the media. Generally, the media expressed the opinion that the book should be thrown at the officers.

Very little, if anything, was said about King's past conflicts with the law or his previous arrests.

The media very definitely tried to create an atmosphere that projected police brutality visited on a poor, downtrodden black man. The 100 mph chase preceding the arrest was ignored, along with King's attempts to resist arrest. The natural apprehension the officers must have felt while having to try to make an arrest under those circumstances was not mentioned. Once again, let me say that I do not condone what the police officers did; I just do not consider Rodney King a model citizen.

As the trial progressed, the image of an innocent Rodney King persecuted by cruel, racially prejudiced officers was presented at every turn. I also speculate that if the victim had not been of a minority group, the whole case would have been just "ho-hum" to the media. Because King was a member of a minority, the "media sharks" smelled emotion.

As the time for the verdict neared, the riot hype escalated. The Los Angeles area expected an uprising to happen because the media predicted it would be the natural result of anything but a guilty verdict for all four officers. When the verdict was announced and the violence began, the media seemed to do everything within its power to keep it going. As you remember, I discussed this in detail in the chapter on "Gross Injustice."

In marked contrast, during the second trial and the subsequent trial of the youths in the Denny case, most of the media presented a law enforcement agency that had everything under control and civic leaders who were encouraging non-violence and expressing confidence there would not be another riot. As a citizen of the metropolitan Los Angeles/Orange County area, I would have been very surprised if another riot had erupted simply because of the type of coverage that was offered not only to the public in general, but to the black community in particular.

A RIOT IS A RIOT IS A RIOT

I think had the media not begun relating the violence that began at Florence and Normandie to the verdict, but had treated it instead as street violence by irresponsible individuals, there is every possibility it would have been contained in that area. If the media had presented the Police Department as ready and able to stop the action instead of saying they were not responding and would not be able to stop the rioting, other would-be rioters would not have been encouraged to join those already in the streets.

The criminal element would not have been stimulated to join the original rioters if the media had not glamorized the coverage as a major event that was the result of a gross miscarriage of justice. If they had treated the riot as civil unrest and, therefore, subject to criminal penalties instead of an accepted normal reaction to an unwelcome verdict, the rioting would not have occurred on the scale that it did. Indeed, it might not have happened at all.

One of my professors, Dr. Daryl Freeland, stated in a graduate class two days after the riots, "My immediate reaction was that I wanted to break a plate-glass window, but since I was able to control my rage, I didn't." What about those less fortunate people who do not have the faculties or other releases to control their tempers? This thought is very interesting. Did the media hype become the straw that broke the camel's back?

If the media had presented the same arguments against rioting during the first trial that they presented during the second, I think the minorities would have been discouraged from destroying their community and would have perhaps demonstrated in a more acceptable manner. An interesting statistic to emerge from the riot is that the largest number of rioters who were arrested were not black but Hispanic. This seems to belie the media's claims the riot stemmed from white injustice to a black.

If the media were as conscientious in their efforts to present the true facts as they were in creating a false picture to further their agenda, they would have delved into the reason for this discrepancy. They would have searched for the real roots of the riot.

AND JUSTICE FOR ALL

If the media had spent as much time trying to heal the hurts among the different ethnic groups prior to the trial as they were in widening the rifts that already existed, I think the riot would not have even been a possibility, even though there would still have been just as many people who felt the verdict was a gross miscarriage of justice. They would have been already started on the road to reconciling differences, peaceful resolution, and a determination to see that our judicial system was fair to all–both defendants and plaintiffs. They would have recognized that a jury trial can have human error, and there may be times when justice is not carried out. However, they would never have condoned a method to right judicial errors that included killing, burning, and pillaging.

If the leading daily newspaper in Los Angeles had offered news of the positive actions that had taken place, work that was still in process, and plans for the future instead of inflammatory speculations on what would occur should a guilty verdict be handed down, the riot quite possibly could have been averted. Certainly, there would have been no need to publish an entire section, on the first anniversary of the riots, full of blame directed at those who had nothing to do with the riots, did not sanction them, and in many cases, were prime movers in trying to improve conditions in the inner city.

It is not only in possibly unleashing emotions previously held in check that the media must be held responsible. It is also responsible for creating a false sense of security, prosperity, or decline in areas where the truth is being suppressed for other reasons. I have wondered why the media wanted the American people to think the economy was so bad during the last quarter of the year? I think we would have seen a dramatic difference in the economic climate and confidence in the dollar had the truth been told instead of a constant barrage of...

THE WORST ECONOMY IN FIFTY YEARS

Could the media have made a difference in the outcome of the economy? As is becoming increasingly evident, the media has withheld the truth about the economy on several occasions during recent months. If the media had been honest in their reporting, what would have changed?

I think the first thing to change would have been the attitude of the American people. We are consistently subjected to a barrage of stories about the high unemployment rate, homeless people, loss of income, closure of businesses, and the poor economy in general. The gross domestic product (GDP) has grown over the past two years while small-business confidence in the economy has plummeted.[1]

However, a closer examination of the facts reveals some startling discoveries. The American public is enjoying prosperity as never before enjoyed by the average American citizen. There is currently more money available for discretionary spending than there ever has been. Despite negative media reporting, during the 1980s the job growth that occurred was spectacular.

As a result of the negative media feedback, Bill Clinton was able to claim the economy was an absolute disaster and that the only cure was to put the Democratic party in power. In truth, the economy was expanding at rates from 3.4% to over 5% during the time five out of six media analyses were negative. As a measure of the media's inflated opinion of itself, three out of four journalists surveyed then rated the coverage of the economic situation as good-to-excellent.[2]

AN UNFAIR CAMPAIGN?

If the media had been honest in its reporting, the 1992 election might have had a different outcome. However, the American public had been so brainwashed that they believed the economy was in danger of failing because of its decline during the Bush Administration. If the public had known the truth, the election could have been determined by factors other than a fictitious one. Think of the confidence the people could have had in knowing things were improving. Many businesses that failed during this time failed because either suppliers were also floundering or customers were hesitant to buy because of what they perceived as the state of the economy.

I'm not saying the economy was in a stellar state. We were still facing a huge budget and trade deficit; but give me a break–we are the most prosperous people in the world. Just visit a shopping mall in Southern California during Christmas. If the economy is so horrible, why did it take me 40 minutes to find a parking space at the Brea Mall? This mall was no different from most of the rest. I heard even worse horror stories about Main Place in Santa Ana.

American free enterprise would have been served well had the truth been known. Companies would have prospered because of the confidence the American citizens had in the future. They would not have been afraid to invest and to purchase. The economy would have continued to improve, and the outlook for the United States would have been much brighter.

WE'RE #1

We have all heard the allegations that American productivity is well below that of several other major countries including Japan, Germany, and Switzerland. Not so! America leads the world in worker productivity in every major sector. Although the press is either omitting these reports from the news or deliberately suppressing them, manufacturing has not dropped since 1960. We are making different products, and the need for certain items has diminished, but the overall rate has not changed.[3]

We lead the world in total export sales. These sales are not just in hard goods. They also include finance, education, tourism, and engineering. NEC, which once had a significant corner on the world's computer business, is now being seriously threatened by aggressive American companies such as Dell and Compaq, according to *The New York Times*.

The Kiplinger Newsletter states that America's

manufactured exports have doubled in value over the past five years, and U.S. exports as a share of GDP have nearly doubled, to a current rate of 11.5%, while Japan's share has dropped to 10.2%. Why don't we hear these reports on the news? Think how encouraging they would be to American business.

President Clinton would not be able to make totally erroneous statements like, "The U.S. is slipping behind its trading partners," without being challenged. Because the media is not making the truth known and the truth has been hidden for so long, our President is free to change our economic policies to less productive patterns. He also is free to try to institute policies other countries have seen lead to their economic fall: universal health care, family leave programs, worker training and apprenticeship programs, government job programs, price controls, infrastructure investments, and direct industry subsidies.[4] In spite of the fact other countries are finding that socialism does not work, Clinton seems determined to implement it here.

BUY AMERICAN

If only the media would tell us the truth, and nothing but the truth–no hype, no bias, no opinion, just cold hard facts! Then, not only would the economic picture continue to improve, but people would be encouraged to support American businesses, establish new ones, and the future for America would be much brighter than the one being painted for us by the media at this time. The American citizens' confidence in their country would be restored, and we would see a positive growth pattern emerge in all areas.

Instead of being afraid to invest in products, people would have the assurance their jobs were likely to continue and would purchase not only the items they need but those luxury items they want. They would not fear the future was so bleak they should not make the investment. They would not be afraid to leave a secure position that no longer challenged them to make that leap of faith in another direction. The security of their present situation would not be so important because they would know the economy was basically good and they would have every right to be confident in any change they might make.

LET'S RELAX AND ENJOY

In addition, many industries besides the primary one affected would benefit from this mindset. There would be more business lunches and dinners. This would assist the restaurant and catering industries to continue to be prosperous. The public would attend more movies, travel more, and seek more entertainment activities instead of staying at home because they were concerned there might be a lack of income in the future and they should not spend frivolously. The movie and entertainment industries are so diverse that whole cities would have a marked economical upswing just from the increased patronage.

Increased travel would help not only our country prosper but the world as a whole. With the upswing in tourism, manufacturers of foreign goods would benefit from the increased buying power of travelers. The transportation industry would not be faced with having to cut back employees, routes, and services simply because they do not have the volume to support them.

PROSPERITY AND GROWTH

Businesses would not downsize as they are currently doing because of their fear for the future–fear of what new government regulations will bring and fear of what the allegedly bad economy will do to their future. There would not be cuts in benefits for employees, decreased working hours, and eliminated perks that created jobs for employees in other industries. Companies would continue to grow and look confidently toward the future.

I'd love to see a "profit dollar per employee" look at the companies that use downsizing as a facade to placate their shareholders. Downsizing for the sake of downsizing simply does not work. In fact, I call this "corporate dumbsizing."

Not only would many types of businesses benefit from the change in attitude, but the housing industry would not have been subjected to the downswing it has experienced. People who bought homes four or five years ago would not now be walking away from them simply because they have no job, no prospects of one in the future, and find they can't meet the mortgage payments. They do not try to sell the home because they know that even if they could find a buyer, the value of the house has dropped so drastically they would still owe money after the sale.

The attitude exhibited by our parents and grandparents would still be in evidence. A home was a rock on which to anchor the future. If worse came to worst and they must sell it because of the death of the breadwinner, illness, or unemployment, then the equity that had accumulated was a financial cushion that would help them through rough times. However, selling the home was a last-ditch measure. A home offered security and was valued. This attitude was possible because people still held hope for the future. They had not abandoned it to the purveyors of economical gloom and doom that have poisoned our thinking.

Had the media reported the state of the economy honestly, we would not be in the depressed economic attitude we find ourselves in today. I think the attitude would instead be one of positive assurance that tomorrow will dawn much brighter than today. Our citizens would be confident the country as a whole will continue to prosper, and those who were unemployed would view it only as a temporary situation instead of fearing that it was permanent. I cannot help blaming the media's negative, irresponsible reporting for being the root cause of the recession/depression we see today.

AND THE NEW PRESIDENT IS...

Finally, I'd like to propose a different resolution of the Presidential Election of 1992. What if Bill Clinton had not won and Ross Perot had instead? What differences would we now be seeing in our country? Would NAFTA have passed? Would an improved economy be touted as the result of electing a president who is a member of the Democratic party? What else would we be experiencing as a result of the election that we are not now?

MEN AND WOMEN OF INTEGRITY

First of all, I think we would see men and women of a different caliber in cabinet posts. Instead of the liberal element that has consistently promoted and invoked more government control in private lives, there would be those of a more rugged, individualistic type who would have opposed this intrusion. Instead, they would have proposed other approaches for the same problems, approaches that would challenge our thinking as individuals and demand that, as a nation, we work together to solve our problems. No "magic government sugar daddy" would be ready to step in and make it all go away. Mr. Perot would also have made sure his cabinet was diverse in culture. Although he does not get the credit for this, he understands the importance of different points of view.

GOVERNMENTCARE? NO!

In the area of healthcare, the solution would not have been a government-mandated program but would have been one that stimulated the private sector to provide these much-needed benefits. Perot would not have appointed a family member–even if he felt strongly one was qualified–as the overseer of this important issue. All hearings would have been public because of his strong belief that he was the "People's Advocate."

Perot and his aides would then have worked with the insurers and healthcare providers to establish a plan whereby even those who could not afford the regular rates for insurance could receive necessary care at a rate they could afford. His "I-look-after-my own" attitude would have extended to the public as a whole. Perot would have worked faithfully to provide healthcare for everyone, but there would be one vital difference; it would be through the private sector.

DEATH IN WACO

Based on Ross Perot's handling of the Vietnamese POW situation and the brilliant rescue of his imprisoned employees in an Iranian prison, had he been President, there would not have been a bloody ending to the stand-off at the Branch Davidian Compound. I am convinced it would have ended in one of two other ways. He would have negotiated with honor, resolve, and authority, presenting a solution that would have permitted the members, including David Koresh, to surrender with dignity. Should that negotiation effort have failed, I believe Perot would have devised a way to take Koresh and the other leaders prisoner outside of the compound. Having removed the key members, he would have been able to persuade the rest of the members of the group to surrender peacefully.

Because of Ross Perot's past actions, especially in the Iranian rescue, the high value he places on human life is apparent. This high regard for life would have led him to insist the efforts to effect a surrender must be without loss of life. I believe he and his associates would have been able to accomplish that goal. He would have personally become involved and would not have left the solution to an appointee who obviously places her personal agenda above considerations for a wise, compassionate, and conservative solution to a problem.

PUNISHMENT TO FIT THE CRIME

On the issue of gun control, we would have seen a real difference. Instead of working on provisions that penalize or regulate the populace as a whole, Perot would have concentrated on the lawbreaker. We would have seen an emphasis on stiffer penalties for crimes using weapons and increased penalties for possession of illegal firearms. Dealers of illegal firearms would have been sought rather than all possessors of any type of weapon.

Ross Perot's respect for the Constitution and the Bill of Rights would not have led him to think the answer to preventing crimes carried out with guns was to prohibit all citizens from owning them. Instead, he would have concentrated on preventing the criminals from keeping them or obtaining and using them.

NAFTA

Would NAFTA have passed? That's a hard call, because Congress made that decision. However, I believe it would have failed because Perot would have worked long and hard to present an American free-enterprise alternative solution. As a result of this effort, Congress would have reconsidered and decided to postpone any such far-reaching agreement. They would have given American businesses the priority because Perot would have encouraged confidence in and support of the American Way.

The Senate and the House of Representatives are no different from the rest of us. After all, they are made up of people just like you and me. In reality, we all listen to the person doing the talking. Clinton was talking and encouraging those who supported NAFTA. He and his supporters made it seem like the answer to America's economic woes because it was on their agenda.

Had Perot been doing the talking, we would have heard just as much about the adverse affects of the agreement, should it pass. Congress would probably have thought it was not such a good idea to pass it, and it would have gone down to defeat.

If Ross Perot had been elected President, we would now begin seeing at least something of a turn in the direction of getting out of debt. Honesty in presidential reporting would have prevailed.

Instead of saying, "I'm saving $1 million in this area of the budget because I cut it from $2 million," when the truth is that the previous year the budget had called for only $1 million but Clinton's proposed budget had called for an increase, Perot would have said, "I'm saving half a million because I'm cutting the budget from last year half a million in this area."

As the people began to see the net worth of the country increase, confidence would have risen, and their positive attitudes would certainly have generated an atmosphere where debt could be reduced. Then the nation could have embarked on a journey to restore the economy to its once all-time high. Prosperity would have reigned!

TELL THE TRUTH, PLEASE!

What if the media were more truthful in its reporting, calling things by their real names, giving us just the facts instead of offering their opinions for causes yet to be determined, and not filtering what we hear through their preconceived notions and evaluations? Perhaps many of the important issues facing our country would be resolved in a completely different way. The media does the American people a definite disservice by establishing themselves as the determiners of what information should be forwarded to the public.

The media has an obligation to present all the news–whether it meets their approval or not—and let Mr. and Ms. America make their own decisions. They do not have the right to chart the path the country is to take because of their own personal agenda, personally withholding vital news so that subsequent actions will or will not take place. They must realize that trying to mold public opinion is not their prerogative. Presenting the facts and letting the public mold their own opinions should be their primary concern. If the effort that is being spent to change our opinions to match theirs was spent on telling us the whole truth, a different America would emerge.

The media has the responsibility to tell us all the news in an unbiased manner and let us make our own opinions. They are accountable to us. In this respect, had they acted and reported in a responsible manner, history would have been different.

Scary thought, huh?

WORKS CITED

1. D & B Annual Survey. Inc. February 1994 11.
2. Limbaugh, Rush. "America's Competitive Edge." *The Limbaugh Letter* January 1994 3.
3. Ibid 11.
4. Ibid 12.

Chapter 16

MORE EVIDENCE

While writing this book, a number of additional instances of biased or irresponsible actions by the media came to my attention. They all show evidence of persons who either slanted their reporting to reflect a specific point of view or chose to sensationalize the facts in order to capture a larger audience. As you read these examples, you can decide for yourself whether there was a deliberate attempt on the part of the media person to present the facts in a way that would sway public opinion.

IT'S THE LAW–OR IS IT?

That the media often predicts the impact a bill awaiting a congressional vote will have on the public in an erroneous manner leads one to wonder, Why the discrepancy? Is it because of an honest misinterpretation, or is it a deliberate effort to conceal the truth of the measure from the voters? Several such instances have come to light recently. The most striking was the so-called Imhofe bill. This bill ended a secrecy rule that had been used for 62 years to prevent bills from reaching the floor of the House of Representatives.

Although Representative Jim Imhofe (R-OK), sponsor of the bill, was interviewed on seventy-one radio talk shows, the issue was largely ignored by the broadcast news journalists. To understand the importance of the legislation, and thus to question why the media did not deem it of enough importance to cover, let's take a look at Congressional operations.

Prior to passage of the bill, the only way for blocked legislation to reach the floor for a vote was the discharge petition. However, for a discharge petition to cause a bill to come to a vote, a majority of members of the House had to sign it. Not a problem, you say? Unfortunately, it was a problem, because the only people who knew the names on the petition were sworn to keep those names secret under provisions attached to the discharge petition.

Thus, it became an easy task for the Speaker of the House to bring pressure on signers to remove their names if it appeared a vote was imminent. Worse yet, Congressional members could publicly support a bill, but withhold their names from the petition, thus insuring that it would never come to a vote.

A number of bills were defeated in this manner—a recalculation of Social Security payments, campaign finance reform, and the balanced budget amendment—all of which were important pieces of legislation that would have had a major impact on the public. It was the effort to provide the balanced budget amendment that convinced Imhofe reform must happen for the public interest to be served.

He filed a resolution that said, "Once a motion to discharge has been filed, the Clerk shall make the signatures a matter of public record." In this way, constituents could know exactly where their representatives stood on any given issue and react as their consciences led them.

When the names of those who had not signed the petition were published, interest began to build. Citizens questioned why their representatives had not signed the bill, and radio talk shows discussed the issue and tried to query members of the House on the telephone during air time.

Although several newspapers did cover the

story, including *Roll Call,* a newspaper that covers Capitol Hill, the major networks maintained a stony silence. America's leading radio talk show hosts–Rush Limbaugh, John Carlson, Stan Solomon, and Jane Chastain–knew the story was reaching into the grass roots of America because of the response they were getting from the public. People called in to ask about the bill or to ask the host to talk about it. Ross Perot urged people to contact their representatives and tell them to sign the petition.

Representatives yielded to the pressure from their constituents, and Imhofe had enough names to force a vote on the issue. As support continued to grow, the major newspapers throughout the country began giving the story minimal space. As they commented on it, most tried to indicate it was such a minor issue that not much attention should be paid to it. However, it soon became evident this was another issue that had guarded secrecy when public disclosure should be made. The public won.

Why did the major mediamakers ignore the story? There were several reasons proposed, among which was the idea that missing a major story is such an embarrassment, the media would rather continue to downplay it rather than admit they missed a scoop. It's rather like saying, "If I ignore it, it's not really there."

However, the importance of the story was soon made evident when the House issued its call to the Senate to end its secrecy rule. *The New York Times* featured this story as well as *The Wall Street Journal, Washington Post,* CNN, and network radio. The disparity of coverage also pointed out the irresponsibility of a media that simply will not admit it when they ignore a truly important story because they failed to recognize the importance of it.

This same irresponsibility tried to cover up the omission with their lame excuses and an effort to do better on the second installment; but that does not alter the grave injustice done to the public. They were deprived by the major mediamakers of information that was important to the continuation of the American legislative process.

CABLE RATES TO DROP

Maybe you believed the media when they told you your cable rates would go down. If so, you were probably very startled when you got your cable bill following the implementation of the new rate table. Most people saw their bills go up–not just a few cents, but quite substantially–for the same service. Why had the media led the public astray?

As the facts are examined, it appears many factors played a part. First of all, the reporters simply could not get through the maze of regulations included in the 1992 cable law to achieve real understanding. Then, without bothering to check the facts for accuracy, mediamakers picked up on news wire releases stating that cable rates had increased at triple the rate of inflation because it was such a catchy phrase–"Triple the inflation rate."

Upon subsequent examination of the facts, it was revealed that the rates had gone up because more services and channels were offered, not because there had been an increase in the rates for the services previously offered. As people opted to include more channels in their service, their bills naturally increased, although the basic rates stayed the same. But the media loved that catchy phrase, "Triple the inflation rate!"

As the bill passed through the legislative

process, changes in the character of the regulations began to be apparent. Although *The Wall Street Journal* alluded to the unpredictability of the results of the impending legislation and the impossibility of exercising congressional control over the industry, other newspapers and network programming ignored the warnings and continued to headline the original intent of the bill. *U.S. News & World Report* even proclaimed, "Consumer advocates say the new bill could lower the average costs of basic service by six dollars a month."

As the 1992 Presidential Election neared, the cable bill became a political issue. The media, in its effort to defeat Bush, portrayed him as being unsympathetic to the man on the street who had to closely examine the amount the he could budget for cable in order to make ends meet. In other words, "Bush just didn't get it." All of this ignored his repeated statements on national television and in the press that the cable bill would benefit special interests rather than the public.

Bush vetoed the bill after an appeal by his long-time friend, cable television magnate, Bill Daniels. The media chose to ignore the merits of the issue and why Bush had reversed his position and turned it into grist for the election-mill. Some mediamakers even chose to feature opponent Bill Clinton's remark, "Bush made a mistake." In retrospect, many lawmakers now admit that at the end, the issue became one of defeating Bush at the polls, and not one based on the merits of the legislation.[1]

Today, of course, these same mediamakers are featuring articles about the rise in rates so many subscribers are experiencing and the apparent blunder the Federal government, the FCC, and Congress foisted on the public by passing the cable bill of 1992. Unfortunately for the public, they ignore the fact that they were responsible for turning an important piece of legislation into a political issue rather than probing to the heart of it and the affect it would have on the citizenry.

Again, the American people had been misled by the reassuring murmurs of the media instead of being alerted to undesirable legislation. By its actions, the media shirked its responsibility to keep the public informed and, therefore, brought a substantial penalty upon the people as a whole.

GOTCHA!

In quite another way, the media has corrupted its first call–remaining a responsible and honorable profession–in its pursuit of "the story." Evidence of what has come to be called "gotcha journalism" can be found in reports from our nation's capitol as well as from cities throughout the country where conventions are held by lawmakers.

News cameramen hound the participants–not to gather information of importance to the constituents, but to uncover compromising situations that can be used to embarrass the participants. The media may follow a person closely, use concealed cameras, or be constantly in their face. The stories that are subsequently published as a result of this type of reporting usually present only distorted half-truths and often conceal the real issue at hand.

Frequently crews are sent exclusively to photograph people doing recreational things during conferences. Such was the case of KING-TV of Seattle, St. Paul's KTSP, and the *Las Vegas Review Journal* at a recent National Conference of State Legislatures.

That they were sent to cover hoped-for exposé stories was evident in that these crews were not seen at business meetings. Some journalists and photographers were chosen because they were unknown to the legislators. Others even lied about whom they represented when they were questioned.[2] Unfortunately for the readers and listeners of America, scandal-mongering takes precedence over the importance of the conference itself, with its opportunities for lawmakers to share with one another what works and what doesn't work on the important issues of the day. Often the public is not even made aware of these issues in the flood of juicy gossip released following such an event.

By featuring such conferences (in which the majority of the people are attending sessions and learning from them) as junkets and covering only the misbehavior of participants, the media has shortchanged its audience. The public is not learning of the problem-solving, the sharing of experiences, and the spirit of cooperation that is a result of these meetings.

They are presented with a picture of the taxpayers' money being wasted in fun and games by their elected officials. The media ignores the personal financial sacrifice most of the legislators are making to serve the public.

They also ignore whether the taxpayers are actually footing the bill. By focusing on the playtime activities available at a conference, the media negates any positive contribution made by the conference to the lawmakers' abilities to perform well in office and may actually destroy a political career without reason.

I deplore the deceptive means and this use of sensationalism to create news. I believe it simply reflects the depths to which irresponsible mediamakers have sunk in order to capture an audience.

The media's own lack of personal integrity allows them to slander others, sensationalize incidents, and in essence, lie to the public in an effort to make headlines. It also allows them to suppress important events and facts instead of presenting them to the voters of our country.

If the media were to act in a responsible manner when covering conferences such as the one mentioned previously, we would read headlines like, "Legislators Offer Creative Solutions to Crime in the Cities," or "Benefits of Discussing Mutual Problems Lauded," instead of, "So and So Caught Playing Instead of Working." These types of headlines and the resulting stories would serve the public interest better and be more representative of the actual story. They would also present a more positive image of lawmakers today; one which many observers claim is desperately needed.

Please do not misunderstand my intent. I believe if there is actual wrongdoing or malfeasance, then these should be brought to light. However, concentrating on leisure-time activities without researching the facts is not good reporting.

RACIAL BIAS?

Although we can understand and appreciate that the media does often have its favorite son in an election, that does not excuse a conscious effort to promote that son at the expense of the other candidate. Evidence of this type of double standard was shown by *The New York Times* in the New York City mayoral race between David Dinkins and Rudolph Giuliani. This newspaper that can usually be relied on to present impartial and accurate reporting chose to ignore the other factors in the campaign and focus on the racial aspect.

Color did have some impact on the results, as evidenced by the fact Dinkins received 95% of the black vote and Giuliani 77% of the white vote. However, the reasons for those votes were not totally racially motivated.

Throughout the election campaign, the *Times* insisted the election was a referendum on race. This, of course, favored Dinkins and worked against Giuliani. The paper ignored the bigger issues and focused on Giuliani's campaign as being one of borderline racism, while at the same time ignoring the overtly racial aspects of Dinkins' campaign. Evidence of this was clearly shown when Dinkins belatedly and lamely commented on pro-Fascist remarks about Giuliani that had been made on television in his presence.

Because of the decrease in white voters, Giuliani realized early on he needed black votes in order to win and so had assiduously avoided the racial issue. However, the *Times* continued to characterize him as a racist, an intemperate right-winger, and a throwback to the '60s, who was running against history.

In the process of trying to present Giuliani in a bad light, the newspaper ignored Dinkins' performance as mayor. Knowing full well that other members of the media relied on the *Times* for their analyses of issues, the paper, nevertheless, treated Dinkin's tenure with kid gloves. It ignored his inept handling of civil unrest in the Crown Heights area, inclusion of racial militants in his administration and campaign, and his relationship with WLIB (a station that broadcasts ugly racial demagoguery and death threats to journalists who are critical of the militant black agenda).

Newsweek, in its analysis of the election, ventured the opinion that the *Times* was in a descent and throwing away a century of responsible journalism in pursuit of "trendy, disingenuous correctness on matters racial." The *Daily News* charged that the *Times* had overlooked the real issue of the election, David Dinkins as just another mayor, in its effort to prove that whites could vote for someone different from themselves.[3]

Whatever the reason for the *Times'* very biased view of the issues of the election campaign, it became evident to not only the other members of the media but also to the American public that the *Times* did not act in a responsible manner when covering these issues, or other topics they perceived as issues. They attempted to maneuver public opinion, and thus the vote, to prove a position they were pursuing.

This subterfuge is bad when found in any mediamaker, but to find it in a major newspaper that is highly regarded within the profession and used as a benchmark is inexcusable.

HOW DO YOU VOTE?

The foregoing reports of media distortion, sensationalism, and efforts to mold public opinion serve as a warning for the future. As you read the accounts, what was your opinion? Did you think the reporting was accurate and without bias; or do you believe that the media exhibited irresponsibility in their presentation?

How did you vote?

WORKS CITED

1. Carl M. Cannon. "To the Editor: Did Your Cable Rates Go Up?" *MediaCritic* Volume 1, Number 2 1994 36-41.

2. Peter A. Brown. "Gotcha in San Diego." *MediaCritic* Volume 1, Number 2 1994 66-73.

3. William McGowan. "Race, Double Standards & *The New York Times*." *MediaCritic* Volume 1, Number 2 1994 59-65.

Chapter 17

PORTRAITS

As we analyze the integrity of the media, we see a number of portraits emerging. There are those who deserve a place in the **Media Hall of Fame** for their perseverance in offering to the American public an unbiased view of world and national events. They present an unadulterated report of events and continue to offer people hope. Hope that tomorrow will indeed be better because there are solutions to the problems we face today.

On the other hand, there are other portraits that are certainly less flattering. In fact, if these were family portraits hanging in the halls of an ancestral home, the men and women would be regarded as *Bouc Èmissaire* of the family. These prodigal mediamakers have consistently altered news reports to match their agendas, withheld vital information, and saturated their programming with sensationalism, violence, and sex. They have painted a picture of gloom and doom ahead and promoted the philosophy of increased governmental control as the only course of action that can alter our nation's situation. Traditional American free enterprise and rugged individualism are dirty terms. Anyone who is less liberal than they is subject to ridicule and often becomes the victim of distorted reporting.

In my analysis of the media today, there are certain individuals or groups of individuals who stand out as either members of a **Media Hall of Fame** or a **Media Hall of Shame**. As mentioned in Chapter 14, Good News Only, let's concentrate on only the positive—The **Media Hall of Fame**.

MEDIA HALL OF FAME

Let's wash our hands of those who defile the name of mediamaker by their irresponsible, biased presentation of the news or other programming to the American public and turn to those who restore our faith in the concept of Freedom of the Press. These are the people who not only report the news in an unbiased fashion but also keep the flame of hope burning in our hearts that there will be a restoration of our traditional way of life and a better America. The following people stand out as bright lights in medialand. They point the way toward what the media should represent in the future.

Rush Limbaugh

At the risk of being labeled an extremist, I place Rush Limbaugh at the top of my list. This EIB Network talk show megastar has over 14 million listeners! His voice of conservatism and traditional values has astounded the liberal world—a world that does not listen to the deeper "words behind the words" when he speaks. They do not seem to be able to forgive his sometimes entertaining and controversial candor in order to hear his real message.

In the midst of the claims by those representing this liberal viewpoint that a new way of thinking has taken over the United States, Rush is saying, "No. The American people still prize traditional values and private enterprise," and the public has responded to him overwhelmingly. They are saying, "Thank you, Rush, for speaking out for us."

I also say, "Thank you, Rush." Even though he is far to the right, he always speaks his mind and bases his conclusions on facts and research. His candor and insight into what is happening politically are much needed and appreciated today. His courage and willingness to explore current situations that seem to have something awry about them is admirable. In Rush's eyes, there are no people so immune or so powerful he has to suppress information he believes the American public should have. In the words of Siskel and Ebert, he rates two thumbs up!

Jimmy Breslin

Richard Vigilante, writing in *MediaCritic*, tells how the press botched one of the biggest stories of the year. Because they failed to adequately research the facts regarding exposure to asbestos, the media unleashed a near-panic on the city of New York. Thousands of schoolchildren had their education disrupted as the city launched a multi-million dollar clean-up campaign. The deteriorating state of many schools in NYC was headlined and stories of corruption within the school system and how the district had broken federal laws were featured. The real hazard presented by asbestos was ignored in the flurry surrounding the alleged danger to the children.

Ignoring the real issue–were the schoolchildren ever really in danger?–most journalists blindly accepted the press releases from the School Board and wrote their stories based on the hand-outs. The journalists presented a picture of children in great danger and asbestos as a major killer. The occasional quiet denials of danger to the children made by the School Board were largely ignored in the media's efforts to "expose this scandal."

Reporters failed to ask important questions and thus often wrote exaggerated reports about a subject they did not fully understand. They described certain conditions as threatening to the children that were not, in fact, actually dangerous, and set standards for contamination that were not based on scientific findings. In fact, the reporters apparently did not even understand what the building inspectors meant by the term, "asbestos contamination."

Although his newspaper had followed the early trend of sensationalizing the danger to the children from the asbestos used when constructing their schools, Jimmy Breslin of *Newsday* chose to do some detective work on his own. He went to Sloan-Kettering Memorial Hospital (the leader in cancer treatment) and the Rockefeller Research Laboratories for statistics on the actual danger presented by the asbestos.

As the city's parents were gripped with hysterical fears for their children's safety, he began to present the real story. Originally, when the schools were tested for asbestos contamination, the tests proved the schools were clean. Asbestos poisoning is not a common occurrence. It usually occurs only among workers who have worked unprotected in high levels of asbestos dust for extended periods. The Rockefeller Lab even showed him a 1990 *Science* article that stated the asbestos panic in the United States must be curtailed because unwarranted and poorly controlled asbestos abatement programs resulted in unnecessary risks to the workers who in later life could develop cancers related to their exposure to asbestos.

When Vigilante interviewed other reporters to see if they thought the sensationalized reporting had contributed to the public's panic, they said they did not think so. They claimed that reporters lack the training to settle scientific issues. They contended that even though the laws regarding asbestos had been passed for political, not scientific, reasons, the schools must abide by them. They stated the real issue was that the schools had allegedly fouled up the required inspections.

Breslin, on the other hand, called these excuses baloney. He is quoted as saying, "The only point of being a journalist is to tell the truth, to find out things that will help people." It was evident the majority of the media simply reacted to press releases rather than researching the real story as Breslin had done. They had not looked for the essential truth around which the story revolved. In other words, they did not have a nose for news.[1]

Arthur Sulzberger, Jr.

Although Arthur Sulzberger, the publisher of *The New York Times*, is an avowed liberal, I believe in his inherent honesty. When I met Arthur, his candidness and zeal for life impressed me as he spoke passionately and fervently about his craft. The viewpoints he publishes are those to which he adheres; he really believes what he prints. In publishing a more liberal viewpoint, he is exercising the right to voice his opinions: the right we call Freedom of the Press. In general, the news reporting found in *The New York Times* is perhaps the best in America today. More facts are presented to the public than in most other newspapers. These facts usually are not presented in a sensational or biased manner. They are simply presented, and the reader is left to draw his or her own conclusions. The editorials and other commentaries are usually well thought out and presented in a nonsensational and non-inflammatory manner.

Bernard Shaw

At the top of my list of news persons is CNN anchor, Bernard Shaw. Not only has he covered some of the most important events of recent times, he has been covering the news responsibly for over thirty years. I admired the dignity he maintained during the bombing of Baghdad. Most of us would have been basket cases.

As evidence of the high regard in which Shaw is held, he has been singled out as the one newsperson chosen to cover an important event on several occasions. At other times, he has been one of two mediamakers chosen. These exclusive reports included being asked by Martin Luther King's family to accompany King's body to Atlanta.

His sense of professionalism and discipline caused him to respond positively to his network when it called him from this assignment to cover the civil unrest that had broken out in the wake of King's death.[2] He was infuriated because he was personally devastated by King's death. The qualities in a person that permit him or her to put aside personal preferences for professional principles cause us to admire them.

His integrity has never been questioned by listeners or other news personnel. As evidence of the high regard in which he is held by those in his field, he has received the Golden Award for Cable Excellence, the George Foster Peabody Broadcasting Award, and the ACE for Best Newscaster of the Year. Because of his excellent achievements in journalism and his unsurpassed professionalism, he has earned a place in the Media Hall of Fame.

Thomas Sowell

Another journalist I have come to admire is Thomas Sowell, whose commentaries appear regularly in *Forbes* magazine and major newspapers using the Scripps-Howard News Service throughout the nation. He is not only a conservative economist, which our country desperately needs, but also a philosopher. Currently, he is a senior fellow at the Hoover Institution in Stanford, California.

When one reads his editorials or longer dissertations, he helps you sort out the important from the trivial. His strong pro-family and pro-human rights stands are in stark contrast to many other writers. After reading one of his columns, I couldn't help feeling, "Thank you, Thomas, for sharing your viewpoint with all of us."

A case in point is the denunciation of an essay that appeared in a book review section. This essay was discussed in detail when we examined the issue of racial injustice. Although the article was not focused on an irresponsible media, he also voiced an insight that is part of the message of this book. Sowell stated, "Perhaps it is too much to expect realism from an essay in the "Book Review" section...but it is gross irresponsibility to review books about youth crime in the ghetto by making all of America responsible." This willingness to view his own profession honestly as well as his ability to go to the heart of an issue places him in an enviable position within the media.

Cal Thomas

Cal Thomas, writer for *The Los Angeles Times* Syndicate, pens a column that appears from time to time in major newspapers. He shows great insight in his analysis of an issue and then thoughtfully carries this analysis through to its resolution as he explores a subject. This type of journalism has great merit even if we do not agree with the writer's findings, simply because of the care that is shown in reaching the final determination. It is not a different opinion that is to be feared but a hastily drawn one that has not been carefully deliberated. These opinions without thought threaten rational decision making because the evidence is not weighed against a preconceived idea.

George Will

Much needed today is George Will's assessment of the political scene. This journalist for *Newsweek* and The Washington Post Writers Group, while favoring no one political party over another, looks at an issue or event and evaluates it. He has a gift for going right to the heart and dissecting it from the core out. This approach gives the rest of us who are not so close to the problem insights we would not otherwise have. To be commended is his honest and non-partisan approach to the issues we face today as a nation.

P. J. O'Rourke

Although I've laughed until I cried over some of his analyses, P. J. O'Rourke ruthlessly cuts to the heart of the problem at hand. An author of several books who also writes for *The American Spectator* and *Rolling Stone* magazine, this political satirist's caustic wit amuses, but the message under each jibe is clear: what the liberals are saying is pure hogwash. I loved his comment in *Rolling Stone* magazine following an interview with President Clinton. "Bill Clinton should remember that America wasn't founded so we could all be better. America was founded so we could all be anything we damn well pleased."[3] In the style of many other political analysts, he varnishes the truth with a coating of humor.

William F. Buckley, Jr.

One of the pioneers among those in the media who are willing to be held accountable for their viewpoints is William F. Buckley, Jr., who is publisher of the *National Review* as well as writing for the Universal Press Syndicate. A veteran of network ideological wars, Buckley has been around the scene longer than some of us have been on earth. We tend to almost forget him in the chorus of newer voices. However, his *National Review* and network talk programs, such as "Firing Line," have long been a forum where the conservative voice can be heard. His dignified demeanor in spite of often combative participants is something I've always admired. That he has influenced other reflective conservatives cannot be denied. This patriarch of the modern responsible media deserves a place of honor in the Media Hall of Fame.

Larry King

I salute Larry King for opening his program, CNN's "Larry King Live," to the candidates during the last presidential election, letting the public see and hear them in unedited appearances. It is to be hoped his pioneering of this aspect of political broadcasting will continue so the public will have an unfiltered basis on which to form their own opinions about the candidates.

HONORABLE MENTION

Radio and Television

Other radio and television media makers who are doing a good job of responsible reporting or interviewing are *Jerry Williams*, host of the Boston Talk Show, *Mike Siegal* of Seattle, and C-Span's *Brian Lamb*. In a field in which the sport is often not only executed badly, but also reported in extremely biased terms, *Shaun O'Grady* and *Al Bernstein* stand out as commentators who are able to bring integrity and honest reporting into the boxing arena. Honorable mention goes to *Bryan Burwell*, the sports writer for USA Today. He is always willing to present both sides of an issue.

Also to be commended are programs like the *ABC Afterschool Specials* that explore issues affecting teenagers today. *The Children's Television Workshop* and the *Learning Channel* are to be applauded for their efforts to provide education in an entertaining atmosphere.

Magazines and Newspapers

Scientific American has long been in the forefront of honest journalism, although admittedly in a limited field. Their candid reporting is an example of the type of unvarnished truth the American people need and want to hear.

Finally, there are the newspapers like *USA Today*, *The San Francisco Examiner*, *The Los Angeles Times*, *The Dallas Morning News*, *The New Jersey Record*, and *The Orange County Register* that regularly publish retractions of incorrect information appearing in previous editions. Some detractors point out these retractions contain only minor information, they never include any major stories that were in error. While that may be true for the most part, a willingness to admit any error in publication is a step in the right direction. When we applaud the smaller efforts, often the bigger ones will come in time.

Perhaps the suggestion by Harvard Law Professor, Alan Dershowitz, has merit. He believes newspaper executives should set up a court of corrections to handle reader grievances.[4] He stresses that people seeking corrections don't want money; they want vindication. I find this to be true.

THE BOTTOM LINE

In singling out individuals for the Media Hall of Fame, it should be clear that the choice was not made because of their style of delivery, lively wit, or other particular trait that has become their trademark. They also have not gained this position because of their personal beliefs. It has come as a result of seeing what fruit their words have borne. Can their words be relied on to be accurate, unbiased, and free of sensationalism? Are they to be trusted? Or by their words have they been condemned as failing to research an issue, presenting only their own point of view, and tainting reports with sensationalism? Have they shown they have integrity, or do they lack it?

WORKS CITED

1. Richard Vigilante. "The Great NYC Asbestos Panic." *MediaCritic* Vol. 1, No. 2 1994 22-35.

2. Jane Ammeson. "No more Mr. Nice Guy." *Northwest Airlines In-Flight Magazine* January 1994 30

3. P. J. O'Rourke. "Pulling the Donkey Lever." *Rolling Stone* 17 July 1994.

4. Pat Guy. "Dershowitz: Let readers have say." *USA Today* May 1994.

Chapter 18

AND IN CONCLUSION...

"Cm'on Captain. You know as well as I do that [legal] cases are no longer tried in courts, they are tried in the media." So stated the journalist to the defendant in the popular Naval legal series, "Jag."[1] Is this what our forefathers intended when they established freedom of the press?

As I stated in the Introduction, the intent of this book is to show how a certain few media makers abuse freedom of the press. As we explored a number of issues, the pattern of distortion of facts, sensationalism, and the use of violence became evident. The primary reason for this appears to be the desire of the media to attract listeners and make sales, regardless of what they use to accomplish their goal. That they have a responsibility to the public as a whole to present the unvarnished facts and let them speak for themselves apparently is not a major consideration of the media today.

This same media, with its disregard for truth in reporting, has also consistently incorporated its own liberal viewpoint into reports. They have given the conservative viewpoint very little consideration, so this viewpoint has almost become a silent majority.

In addition to voicing its liberal viewpoint, the media often acts in an exceedingly careless manner when collecting data, which often results in erroneous stories. At times, these stories have even given rise to needless panic.

THE FUTURE

The foregoing reports of media distortion, sensationalism, and efforts to mold public opinion serve as a warning for the future. The media must be examined for its political stance, its value-system, its allegiance to special-interest groups, and its honesty in presentation. Does it substitute a sensational side issue for the real issue at hand? In other words, is it trustworthy? We owe it to ourselves and to future generations to insist on objective, honest reporting of the issues and events.

The media often wonders what it needs to sell newspapers or capture an audience and hold them. I believe the answer is news–real news. Not this sensationalized bedroom-scene, scandal ridden, violent stuff they are currently trying to cram down our throats, but fact-filled, information-laden news about what is really happening in America, in our Legislatures, on Capitol Hill, and in the lives of our citizens.

When the media chooses to express an opinion, it should be clearly stated as such and carefully separated from the news presentations. This is particularly important since our opinions often reflect the last thing we have seen or read. If they are speaking for a special-interest group, that fact should be included in the editorial. They should eliminate completely the subterfuge of presenting an agenda as a news item. Newspapers should also make a concentrated effort to offer editorials of substance to the public. If the writer of the editorial cannot sign his or her name to the piece, it should not be printed. In the same spirit, if the piece does not have real merit, he or she should substitute something of value rather than fill the space with empty words.

A LABOR OF LOVE

This analysis of the media and its ability to make or break not only people but issues, ideologies, and government policy has been a labor of love. It is a statement that must be made. The irresponsible liberal arm of the media cannot be permitted to continue its dominance unchallenged. Those of us who believe in the American Way of Life must stand up and be counted. We must ask why the conservative viewpoint is often not even represented in so-called unbiased discussions. We must evaluate the news that we hear and the opinions routinely presented as facts. We must then reject them if they do not meet the criteria established for a responsible media.

Just what is the criteria that determines what is responsible? I believe it is best summed up by Bernard Shaw. He states, "I feel very strongly about old-fashioned journalism. I don't think I, as a reporter, have any place in a news story. I have very strong feelings and personal beliefs, but they have no place in my reporting, have no place in my writing. None whatsoever. Viewers of CNN should not have to contend with how I feel personally about an issue. Viewers should know without any question that what I am reporting is balanced, accurate, fair and dispassionate."[2]

I agree.

WHAT CAN WE DO?

First of all, we can remember that enough ones make a majority. If we each do the same thing, it is bound to make an impact on our country. Secondly, we can disregard the rampant "attitude journalism" that exists within the media. We have always assumed honesty and fairness in reporting.

Instead, we get biased opinions of the news. It would appear that certain members of the media believe they are better qualified to provide news interpretation, context, and analysis. This leads me to believe that the media itself may have created the axiom, "Freedom of Speech (Press) is the backbone of our country."

We need to take certain steps to fix our media-hyped society. These steps will help to ensure that freedom of speech is enforced the way our forefathers intended it. I suggest these specific actions to improve the media's presentations to our citizenry.

1. Install the V-chip on our television sets to monitor what our children watch. Encourage support for the recently passed "three educational programs per channel" mandate originally submitted under the Children's TV Act of 1990.

2. Insist on a standardized, more realistic rating system for television shows.

3. Implement an Internet rating system. The Platform for Internet Content Selection (PICS), a world-wide-web consortium at Massachusetts Institute of Technology would be a good start. As outlined in the September 1996 issue of *Scientific American*, PICS would "resolve the moral contradiction that lies at the heart of existing schemes to regulate the Internet." I do not believe we want the courts to decide what we feel is or is not offensive. The PICS program encourages a variety of rating systems, including the use of self-rating, advisory council ratings, and a requested rating mechanism.

4. Support tape delay broadcasts of events that could incite civil unrest until the authorities have the situation under control.

5. Establish consumer focus groups to improve television and radio program quality.

6. Increase support for publicly supported television programs.

7. Insist on training for journalists that would educate them how to report fairly and responsibly.

8. Monitor the content and subjects allowed on television and radio talk shows via a media review board.

9. Support publications and stations that eliminate offensive reporting and programming.

10. Support family-oriented programming with letters of support to the programs, their sponsors, and the stations that carry them.

We can make a difference if we just pull together and start taking action.

Won't you join me?

WORKS CITED

1. "Jag." CBS Television. 13 March 1996.

2. Jane Ammeson. "No more Mr. Nice Guy." *Northwest Airlines In-Flight Magazine* January 1994 25.

Index

About The Author

Tony Vercillo has 20 years of experience as a management consultant, public speaker and seminar leader. He has consulted with hundreds of companies, ranging from small businesses to Fortune 500 companies. His consulting experience includes work in the public and private sectors, governmental agencies, and numerous trade associations. His speaking engagements are in great demand due to his industry proclaimed "infectious enthusiasm." Vercillo currently resides in southern California.

WATCH FOR THESE NEW COMMONWEALTH BOOKS

WATCH FOR THESE NEW COMMONWEALTH BOOKS

WATCH FOR THESE NEW COMMONWEALTH BOOKS

	ISBN #	U.S.	Can
❏ **DOUBLE INHERITANCE**, Winnie Bennett 1-55197-026-0		$4.99	$6.99
❏ **A CANADIAN TRAGEDY**, Joel Fletcher 1-55197-022-8		$4.99	$6.99
❏ **THE TEAKWOOD CROSS**, Harry Mileaf 1-55197-028-7		$4.99	$6.99
❏ **THE TWO GREAT PROPHETS**, E.V, Kemp 1-55197-030-9		$4.99	$6.99
❏ **THE CHRISTIAN'S CUSS BOOK**, M.S. Aue 1-55197-036-8		$4.99	$6.99
❏ **PRESCRIPTION: MURDER**, J.L. Evans 1-55197-001-5		$4.99	$6.99
❏ **PAIN GROWS A PLATINUM ROSE**, G. Martorano 1-55197-009-0		$4.99	$6.99
❏ **FALSE APOSTLE**, Michael E. Miller 1-55197-011-2		$4.99	$6.99
❏ **LIGHT ALL NIGHT**, Richard Robinson 1-55197-015-5		$4.99	$6.99
❏ **THE PROMISE**, Andrew R. Gault 1-55197-007-4		$4.99	$6.99
❏ **PLAYING AS ONE**, O'Neil/Saltonstall 1-55197-013-9		$4.99	$6.99
❏ **PIMPINELLA**, Ilse Kramer 1-55197-003-1		$4.99	$6.99
❏ **MADNESS IN THE STREETS**, Dana Landers 1-55197-005-8		$4.99	$6.99
❏ **A LITTLE GIRL LOST**, Isabel Sinclair 1-55197-040-6		$4.99	$6.99
❏ **THE RIVER RAN BETWEEN THEM**, James Allen Welch 1-55197-032-5		$4.99	$6.99
❏ **WESTERN THUNDER**, Freeda Brown 1-55197-027-9		$6.99	$8.99
❏ **ALONE WITHIN**, Dianna DeBlieux 1-55197-044-9		$4.99	$6.99
❏ **MEMORIES FOREVER**, Jody Lebroke 1-55197-017-1		$4.99	$6.99

Available at your local bookstore or use this page to order.

Send to: COMMONWEALTH PUBLICATIONS INC.
9764 - 45th Avenue
Edmonton, Alberta, CANADA T6E 5C5

Please send me the items I have checked above. I am enclosing $_____ (please add $2.50 per book to cover postage and handling). Send check or money order, no cash or C.O.D.'s, please.

Mr./Mrs./Ms._____

Address_____

City/State_____ Zip_____

Please allow four to six weeks for delivery.
Prices and availability subject to change without notice.

Freedom of the Press—our forefather's dream or todays nightmare? What Madison, Jefferson, and Franklin saw as a right to be protected is today being abused by those who seek to further their own selfish interests. What we hear, read, and see is being distorted for a variety of reasons.

In *Death By Media*, Tony Vercillo explores these reasons as well as the questions the public now wants answered. However, he not only presents the problem, he offers a solution—one that can involve every citizen today.

Death By Media

by

Tony Vercillo
